I0033998

Law Out of Context

ALAN WATSON

LAW OUT OF CONTEXT

THE UNIVERSITY OF GEORGIA PRESS
Athens & London

Paperback edition, 2012

© 2000 by the University of Georgia Press

Athens, Georgia 30602

www.ugapress.org

All rights reserved

Designed by Walton Harris

Set in 11/14 Centaur by G&S Typesetters

Printed digitally in the United States of America

The Library of Congress has cataloged the hardcover edition of

this book as follows:

Watson, Alan, 1933–

Law out of context / Alan Watson.

xviii, 213 p. ; 24 cm.

Includes bibliographical references p. [173]–197 and index.

ISBN 0-8203-2161-3 (alk. paper)

I. Sociological jurisprudence. 2. Roman law. 3. Law in literature. I. Title.

K370 .W367   2000

340'.115—dc21   99-32393

Paperback ISBN-13: 978-0-8203-4116-3

ISBN-10: 0-8203-4116-9

British Library Cataloging-in-Publication Data available

For Emma

CONTENTS

PREFACE

My subject is the complexity of the relationship between law and society. I am unhappily aware that parts of the book may appear to have an unusual configuration, but this cannot be avoided and is in the nature of the subject. Equally in the nature of the subject is that some chapters make difficult reading, especially chapters 1 and 5. The former must satisfy specialists in Roman law; the latter, students of South African law, especially of South African legal history. No abstract theory is possible or desirable for the theme but only concrete examples, and these concrete examples must be not only of important subjects but also at times detailed and foreign. It would be a mistake to be more superficial or general than I can help. Furthermore, I must emphasize that the examples are precisely that: I have chosen them to illuminate law and society also at other times and in other places. My basic thesis is simple. Often the perspective presented in law is skewed; the balance is not where it should be. Somehow the legislator or subordinate lawmaker or law teacher presents the law as rather different from what it is. I am uneasily aware that some readers may regard my book as indicting the sociology of law as it is often practiced.

In a book of this kind I must inevitably rely in some places on earlier work. Thus part of chapter 1 is very much my article "The Law of Citations and Classical Texts in the Post-Classical Period," in 34 *Tijdschrift voor Rechtsgeschiedenis* (1966), and part of the same chapter greatly derives from my "Prolegomena to Establishing Pre-Justinianic Texts," in the same journal 62 (1994). Part of chapter 3 is based on chapter 5 of my book *Ancient Law and Modern Understanding: At the Edges* (Athens, Ga., 1998). And chapter 6 contains a very much rearranged version of my "Introduction to Law for Second-Year Law Students?" in 48 *Journal of Legal Education* (1996). My original aim in these works was description; in this one it is explanation.

Some readers may prefer to begin with the final chapter, chapter 7, which may be regarded as setting out my conclusions and in which the complexities of exposition are avoided.

I must express my gratitude to my friends Paul Finkelman and Vernon Palmer, who read the entire typescript with sharp critical eyes, and also to Gracie Waldrup, who, with continual charm, typed draft after draft.

INTRODUCTION

The theme of this book is the complexity of the relationship between law and the society in which it operates.[1]

Law is out of context much of the time, perhaps even most of the time. The fact is unremarkable and usually unremarked. A society makes law; the society changes, politically or economically, but the law remains the same or little changed. Or the center of gravity of the society's geography changes dramatically and/or so does its religion. Or one independent state accepts much of the law and legal structure of another despite different circumstances. Or a conquering nation imposes its law on the conquered. And having regained freedom, the conquered state retains the conqueror's law or much of it. Or law is represented in literature with an unusual configuration. Or literary devices cast law in an unnatural form. Or legal scholars ignore whole tracts of the law under which they live, such as administrative law or bureaucratic regulation. Or faults in legal education skew the appearance of law for student and professor alike.

The fact that law is out of context is unremarkable, but often it has astonishing consequences. In this book I have no intention of setting out a general theory of law out of context. Rather, I want to take a number of striking examples that have been generally unremarked or underemphasized and use them to indicate some of the dimensions of law and society. The relationship of law and society is much more complex than is usually admitted, and it demands exploration. Those involved with the sociology of law must rethink their approach. It must take account of comparative legal history, a subject in its infancy and consistently ignored.

The first six chapters of the book are independent, but to indicate the richness of the material for study, I have chosen topics that can be interwoven. The relationship between religion and law is prominent in chapters 1–4, as is natural law. The Roman *lex Aquilia*, the statute that dealt with damage to property, is, as an example, the subject of chapter 4, and, in a new guise, of chapter 5. Different aspects of law and literature are the subject of chapters 2–4, but the topic occurs again in chapter 6. Rhetoric and law are the focus of much of chapters 2–4 and surface once more in chapter 6. Natural law also reemerges in chapter 6. Legal education is an issue in chapter 1 and is the focus of chapter 6. Chapter 1 indicates that when a society is ostensibly the same but circumstances have greatly changed, the official statement of the law may represent reality very poorly, and chapter 5 shows that law may be greatly transformed in transplanting and yet be relatively well fitted for new conditions while still referring back to the old law treated as relevant. My main intention in chapter 6 is to hint that educational approaches to law may be so flawed that—a subject on which I touch in chapter 1—even when the society does not change, even when law is not borrowed, the law may be so skewed as to be out of context from the outset.

In chapter 1 I deal with a massive transplant but of a very particular kind. An empire, specifically the Roman, moves its center of government to a very different environment: from pagan Rome to (soon to be) Christian Constantinople, from the Latin West to the Greek-speaking East. Greek becomes the language of government (in the dominant East), but Latin remains the language setting out the law. Latin legal culture continues to prevail, and it inhibits change.

Yet even before the move to Constantinople, changes in the sources of law were to have a great impact, changes that are not recorded in the early Byzantine texts and are not emotionally recognized. To a very great extent legislation as a source of law disappeared from Rome after the emperor Claudius (who died in 54). The praetors, the elected officials who inter alia had control of the courts, were great innovators in the law. At the beginning of their year of office they issued an Edict setting out the types and forms of action they would allow. But in the reign of Hadrian (117–138) the Edict was stabilized, and no further changes were made. The jurists by their interpretations played a decisive role in lawmaking, but around 235 they stopped writing their books. Thereafter, the sole important source of new law was the rulings of the emperors. Yet in the early Byzantine texts the obsolete sources appear as if they were still operative.

The writings of the old Roman jurists continued to be much respected, and it is important for me to show that before the Byzantine emperor Justinian (527–565) their expressed views had not been much tampered with. Justinian himself when he produced the massive compilation known as the *Digest* from the writings of the jurists—all pagans—did not give his team authority to change the law. And they did not do so, I believe, though there was a very small group of specific types of exceptions. So the Byzantine *Digest* of 533 contains almost exclusively Roman law existing before 235. When Justinian decided to issue the *Institutes*—simultaneously a textbook for first-year students and law—he modeled it on the *Institutes* of the pagan Gaius, which was written around 160. The *Digest* and *Institutes* present a very lopsided view of law in early Byzantium, which was fanatically Christian, implacably at war with various heresies, and awash with theological debate. In the body of these works Jesus does not appear, nor do the apostles or saints. No arguments are drawn from the opinions of the church fathers. God, a nebulous figure neither pagan nor Christian, scarcely rates a mention. From the *Digest* and *Institutes* one would not know that Byzantium was Christian. It would even appear that the ruling elite was supremely indifferent to any religion.

Christianity was reserved to the *Code*, Justinian's collection of still relevant imperial rulings. But even here there are twists. Legal education occupied five years. The first year was devoted to the *Institutes*, moving on to the beginning of the study of the *Digest*. Years 2, 3, and 4 were dedicated to the *Digest*. Only in their fifth year, when their attitudes to the law had long been fixed, did students come to Christianity in their law, when the *Code* was the object of study. Law was very much out of context.

There is, of course, very much more to this issue. If Christianity is omitted from the *Digest*, then so would be other areas of the law, including postclassical developments that were not treated by the jurists. One example is enough at this stage. The jurists were rigorously positivist in their approach to law, almost totally uninterested in natural law. But there were in their day vibrant philosophical traditions of natural law to be supplemented by Christian theorists such as St. Augustine. But of such traditions there is no trace, not in the *Digest* or *Institutes* and not even in the *Code*. This absence would have an impact on the future. Another example that the book does not treat may be emphasized even if only in passing. For historical reasons the Roman jurists were almost exclusively interested in private law. Consequently, neither the *Digest* nor the *Institutes* reveals much of bureaucratic law. Moreover, what there is in the *Digest* is almost only that of classical Rome, and much of it was obsolete. Byzantine bureaucracy does not appear.

The *Institutes* had a vital role in legal education in Justinian's time and has had

right up to the present day. The drafting team had only elementary writings before them as they worked, and when they dealt with a point of law not treated
by Gaius or one of the others in their textbooks, the draftsmen seem not to have
consulted other legal sources. They relied on their memory, which sometimes
failed them, and they got their law wrong. On some important issues students
were misled from day one.

Chapters 2–4 consider a very different aspect of law out of context: law and
literature. I devote three very different chapters to the subject. The first concerns
law in literature, and I choose to look at the Gospels. These, most notably Mark
and John, are remarkably full of law in action. Though they focus on the behavior of the same person, Jesus, the accounts in Mark and John are quite different.
Yet both books show great literary awareness of the legal episodes, which are
certainly manipulated in John and also, in a different way, in Mark. Mark shows
an escalation of hostility, step by step, by Jesus toward law as understood by the
Pharisees. They respond first by curiosity, then by determined hostility. In John,
Jesus opens with enmity, and there can be no escalation. Again, the response of
the Pharisees at the beginning is very muted. The sources by their nature dictate
the different approaches to legal issues, but the art is that of the final redactors.

The stress in the chapter, however, must be on the behavior of the leading
Pharisees and Sadducees after Jesus is arrested. The accounts in Mark and John
cannot be reconciled, yet both are internally consistent. Each presents a heart-
wrenching legal problem for the leading Jews—how to deal finally with a dev-
astating troublemaker whose behavior does not legally warrant the death sentence but may bring disaster on the nation and Temple. Both accounts show the
members of the Sanhedrin behaving outside of the law and with impropriety yet
not without justification and also with real concern for moral issues. In Mark,
the Sanhedrin tries Jesus at night. A night trial on a capital charge is illegal, but
the Jewish leaders felt they had to act after Jesus had disrupted the Passover
sacrifices and payment of the Temple tax, and they were afraid to arrest Jesus
during the day "because of the crowd." Still, the members of the court insisted
on observing the very strict rules of evidence until they were overcome by the
bullying of the chief priest, Caiaphas. At the second necessary session in the
morning, they refused to uphold their verdict of guilty but delivered Jesus to Pilate on many charges. In John the precipitating event for the Jewish leaders was
Jesus' raising Lazarus from the dead. The leaders arrested Jesus and questioned
him at night, but there was no trial. This time the real horror for the leaders was

that, if Jesus could raise one man, the Romans might fear that he could raise an army, and the Romans would destroy the Temple and the nation. Many were in favor of doing nothing to Jesus but were overcome by Caiaphas's argument about a Roman attack and improperly handed Jesus over to Pilate. Still, even then they did not lay specific charges against Jesus.

Thus in Mark and John we have two very different accounts of what must have been one event. The common elements are a legal, political, moral dilemma. In both the leaders act illegally, yet at the same time they very much want to observe the legal niceties that would favor Jesus. In both, Caiaphas is the villain. No doubt, his behavior was self-serving. But in both accounts he wanted to avoid a religious disaster: in Mark from the crowd if they regarded Jesus as the Messiah, in John from the Romans. In this chapter I consider legal events shaped and recounted by nonlawyers for nonlegal purposes. The redactors' purpose was not literary but religious, yet the message is given literary form reformulating the legal events. Moreover, the accounts in both Mark and John betray a degree of artificiality, yet both are internally consistent, a fact that must trouble those interested in uncovering historical reality.

Law was out of context, or context was out of law. Here are four accounts of legal maneuvering, all from the same partisan side but all different. Yet the trial or trials have enormous significance.

Chapter 3, law as literature, examines a legal text by the southern lawyer Thomas R. R. Cobb that is not what it appears to be. Ostensibly the book, even by its very title, is an account of slave law in the United States. In fact, it is a justification of slavery in the South.

Cobb builds his case slowly, with organizational skill. He emphasizes that his search is for Truth, but he admits the possibility of bias. While philosophy is the handmaid of law, he insists that history is the only sure basis of philosophy. On history he will rely. And the great lesson of history is that slavery has existed everywhere. (To be understood: slavery in the South is no anomaly.) When finally, halfway through the book—a fact that is rather disguised—he comes to the law, he draws a distinction between Absolute Slavery (where the slave has no rights, which no longer exists) and Slavery (where the slave has rights, which has been found everywhere). (To be understood: southern slavery is essentially moderate.) He turns to slavery and natural law and derives much comfort from Justinian's *Institutes*, which, as I mentioned above, shows little interest in natural law. He correctly observes, as had leading scholars, that when

Justinian says slavery is "contrary to nature," he means "contrary to the original state of affairs" and not "contrary to the law of nature." Besides, the meaning of the law of nature is by no means clear, nor are the rules that can be derived from it. Still, whatever the law of nature is, it owes much, he says, to the nature of man. When humans differ, whatever the cause, then the law of nature as applicable to them also varies. Natural law cannot be one and the same for all. (Expressed: Africans from certain regions are intellectually and morally inferior but have the physique for physical labor.) Negro slavery is consistent with natural law. Slavery is beneficial to blacks in the South, but it may not be for the free population. He continues by showing that Negro slavery is consistent with Divine Revelation in the Old Testament and New Testament alike.

When at long last—at long last, but Cobb is never boring—he actually reaches slave law in the United States, he has a skillfully unbalanced perspective. Fully a third of the chapters here are devoted to conflict of laws in America, a subject of enormous importance that allowed the South to present itself as a victim of northern states that did not observe the "Comity of Nations" and thus made civilized dealings between states impossible.

Finally it is to be noticed that—a matter of great significance—Cobb does not treat the whole of U.S. slave law. He ignores the vital topic of slaves as property. He promises a further volume on the subject, never to be forthcoming.

Law, in Cobb's book, is out of context. The book purports to be a work by a lawyer on a branch of substantive law, but in reality it is primarily a political tract and is shaped to this end.

In chapter 4 I deal first with law as literature without reality. The specific subject matter is the Roman jurists' discussion of legal issues. It is also almost law without literature, except that striking examples, usually imaginary, are chosen to provide spice. It is standard, and to be expected, that legal discussions ignore many human facts that are vitally important. This omission is most obvious in statute law, which has to be general, remote from a particular occurrence. But it is a marked feature of Roman juristic writing, where the jurists commonly posit a factual situation, often with intriguing details, then discuss the law ignoring human involvement, the rhetoric of the courtroom, issues of procedure, the difficulties of proof, the foibles of the parties. Despite the intriguing facts, the jurists deal with unreal, bloodless persons. In an important way, this treatment made the subsequent reception easier. The medieval and later scholar could approach the legal issues without being bothered with social facts. Still, the law as presented by the Roman jurists is very much out of the context of living reality.

In the second part of the chapter I look at literature in the shape of Roman legal rhetoric from which the law has almost disappeared. The Roman rhetoricians present legal situations for debate. In some the law is entirely fictitious. In others, the law may be Greek with no relevance to Roman conditions. Or the law may be Roman. But even when the law is Roman, the law scarcely appears in the debates. It is merely a peg on which to hang the colors of life and argument.

In this chapter we have, therefore, extreme examples of legal interpretation without human realities and of legal rhetoric with human experience but with no law.

Chapter 5 returns to the theme of legal transplants. But this time my first concern is with a much more usual case, the borrowing of the law of one people by another. I have chosen a complicated example: from Rome to early Byzantium, then to seventeenth-century Holland, from there to the Dutch in South Africa, then from them to South Africa under British rule until independence as a republic in 1961. I have chosen to look at Aquilian liability, the main branch of torts law, partly because I treated aspects of it in Roman juristic writing in chapter 4 but primarily because of the great transformation that the law underwent. Indeed, it was argued in the past by distinguished jurists that the lex Aquilia had not been received in Western Europe. And for this there is a good, but not total, case. Furthermore, in general it must be said, as it cannot for many transplants, that Aquilian liability in 1961 was basically satisfactory for modern, very different circumstances. Yet nonetheless in South Africa there are frequent references to the old law and to obsolete social conditions. These mentions obtrude to the extent of making the understanding of law more difficult and even at times hinder a satisfactory solution. There is also the intrusion of English law. The complexities of the relationship between law and society appear in the gerrymandering, successful or not, of the old authorities.

In chapter 6 I reach my own setting in life, legal education in the contemporary United States. The casebook method, regarded as fundamental especially for first-year students, does not present law as it is. Law students are misled from the start. A few cases on a particular point are chosen for study, but the relevant law is likely to be based on hundreds of cases. Little attention is paid to understanding law—the relation of one branch of law to another, the factors in legal development, the importance and weight of authorities. In the second year the top students, skilled in this skewed approach, become editors of the law review, which is regarded as the most important, or even the sole, vehicle for academic scholarship. The students choose the articles for publication. But they lack the experience to judge the originality, accuracy, or importance of the articles submitted to them. Since professors' tenure and promotion depend primarily on the publication of two law review articles, these must be long: an article with one important idea that could be fully developed in ten pages will have to stretch to sixty. Their main purpose is not to be read; they are seldom read and play virtually no role in legal education. Professors choose students to act as their research assistants. Typically, the assistants collect and select the materials, mainly cases and law review articles, from which the professors will work for their articles. How far professors rely on student research varies, but the students usually play a role greater than simply fetching cases, and so forth, from the library. The aspiring new graduates become law clerks to judges, mainly thanks to recommendations from professors, including those for whom they were research assistants. They do the fundamental legal research for their judges, may help to shape decisions, and may even write opinions. After a year of clerkship, and a few years in a law office, the aspiring lawyers who wish to teach become law professors. They have published nothing and have done no organized research under the guidance of a scholarly mentor. Their capacity for creative legal thinking is not an issue in their appointment. They teach from casebooks and write law review articles. The circle is completed. From the start, law professors present law students with a false picture of law, "law out of context." They know no better.

   I wish to emphasize that I am working with examples of what has happened and is happening in law. Any approach to law in society must emphasize what does occur rather than rely on abstract theory. I believe my examples are true examples. They all concern major issues of law in society. Every one of them can be matched by countless other instances from another time, another place, another context.

CHAPTER ONE

THE FIRST RECEPTION OF ROMAN LAW

Early Byzantium and Justinian

In most states, at most times, law mostly develops by taking from elsewhere. Legal transplants come in all shapes and sizes. An independent state may accept one rule or institution from another or may take many or even all. It may or may not make changes in what it borrowed. A conquered state may have the victor's law thrust upon it. Members of a society may, in a dominant role, migrate to a very different geographical area and may take their law with them.

Transplanted law is likely to appear, or to be, somewhat different in its new home. Swiss law received in Turkey will not operate to the same effect as Swiss law in Switzerland. A topic of particular importance for understanding law in society is what one might call "law out of context." The former life of the law retains an impact that causes the law in this new home to be, or to appear, skewed: it does not altogether fit the realities of life. The law as stated may not even represent the law as it exists in actuality. A prime example relates to the first reception of Roman law. Modern Western private law rests on the foundation of the great compilation, now known as the *Corpus iuris civilis* of the Byzantine emperor Justinian. In large measure it does not reflect Byzantine reality of the sixth century. If the compilation had done so, it could never have been so successful.

ROME BEFORE BYZANTIUM

Ernst Levy made famous the concept of a first reception of Roman law, namely when it played an important role in the formation of the Germanic codes from the fifth century on.[1] I suggest that there was an earlier reception, into the emerging Byzantium, with the founding of Constantinople in 324. There was no sharp break in the law. The Romans in Constantinople took their law with them. Since the geographical area had long been within the empire, Roman law was already there. But within a century or so, and certainly before Justinian, the ruling elite in Constantinople ceased to be obviously Roman. In this chapter I will focus on Roman law out of context in Justinian's compilation. But I must first set the scene.

There was no sudden change from late classical Roman law to early Byzantine law, but the milieu changed. The most dramatic events occurred through the emperor Constantine. When he defeated Maxentius in A.D. 312 at the battle of the Milvian Bridge at Rome, a celestial sign led him to believe that he triumphed by the favor of the Christian God. In Milan the following year he arranged with his brother emperor Licinius for toleration of Christians throughout the empire. Licinius recognized him as senior Augustus. When Constantine founded Constantinople in 324, that city, and not Rome, became the focus of the empire. From the start the city was Greek speaking, not Latin (though imperial pronouncements continued to be issued in Latin). Almost from the start, too, Constantinople must be regarded as a Christian city; Constantine forbade the construction there of pagan temples. His attitude to Christianity may have been unclear—he accepted baptism only when he was near death—but his lawmaking shows considerable Christian influence.

Justinian's *Corpus iuris civilis*—excluding in general the *Novellae*, which were written in Greek and hence were not generally accessible to educated lawyers in the West until after the fall of Constantinople in 1453—of the 530s is one of the great foundations of modern Western law. I would regard it even as the most important. In any event its existence, with its form and content, must be regarded as a fundamental factor in Western legal development. In the shape that it had, in its structure and substance, it was simply a given. And the impact was enormous.

But the *Corpus iuris* had a prehistory. It presents the law as it was neither in Roman times nor in Justinian's Byzantium. This prehistory, as well as the history of the codification, has to be addressed if we wish to understand the *Corpus iuris* and its role in subsequent legal development.

Important changes in the making of Roman law had occurred before 324 and therefore also before Justinian. In the reign of Augustus (died A.D. 18), the basic sources were statutes, the Edict of the praetor, the writings of the jurists, and the official rulings of the emperor.[2] Justinian sets out the sources of law in his *Institutes* at 1.2.3: "Written law is statute, *plebiscita*, decrees of the senate, pronouncements of the emperors, edicts of the magistrates, the answers of jurists." Nothing in the texts indicates that Justinian is not setting out living sources of law. But the picture is entirely false for his time. It much better represents the situation in the time of Augustus.

Legislation, lawmaking by statute, was never very common, though it was rather prominent in the time of Augustus. But it more or less disappeared after Claudius (died 54), and no statute is recorded later than the second century.[3] By the time of Augustus there was no substantive distinction between the forms of legislation including plebiscita.[4] Decrees of the senate seem to have lost any independent value from an early date and are last mentioned for the reign of Probus (276–282).[5]

The praetors, especially the urban praetors, were the second-highest elected officers of state, and they controlled the courts. At the beginning of their year of office, they set out in their Edict a model formula for each type of action they would allow in their court and often also a separate description of its scope (called an edict with a small *e*). Though technically they had no power to change law, in fact through their control of the court system they did so to a very considerable extent.[6] But the Edict was consolidated by the great jurist Julian in the reign of Hadrian (117–138), and thereafter no further changes were possible.[7] There is still more to the issue. The Edict had been deliberately finalized under Hadrian because he and/or his advisers had decided that the Edict was no longer a fruitful source of law. And indeed the Edict had long ceased to be much used for making innovations. Furthermore, no later emperor reversed Hadrian's decision and had legal changes made by the Edict. This development tells us various things but especially that there was no strongly held belief that interpretational disputes could be settled, and the law improved, by modifying the wording of an edict or by adding a clause. The grand lines had long been drawn.

The emperors made official rulings on law. They were of various types, but for simplicity in what follows I will normally simply term them "rescripts." The majority of these, as far as we can tell, were issued to private individuals seeking information, and for the most part they did not innovate.

The jurists were the major factor in legal development through their interpretations in their writings. They wrote an enormous number of law books of varying types on statute and subsequent interpretation, on the interpretation of the Edict, commentaries on particular topics or on particular statutes, and collections of replies on individual problems. But they stopped writing books around 235, the year in which the emperor Alexander Severus was murdered, and that date is traditionally regarded as marking the end of classical law. It is sometimes suggested that after 235 there was a marked decline in legal standards. Such a decline before early Byzantium I would not accept. The jurists stopped writing books primarily because they had written them all.[8] The high quality of Diocletian's rescripts is widely accepted,[9] and the rescripts of the immediately preceding emperors, Probus, Carus, and his sons Carinus and Numerianus, provide little evidence for the decay of legal talent in the later third century.[10]

Thus after 235 the only source of law was the rulings of the emperors. This despite the listing of the sources of law in Justinian's *Institutes*.

BYZANTIUM BEFORE JUSTINIAN

Before Justinian, in the reign of Theodosius II, there occurred two events that are extremely important for this chapter. The first was the so-called Valentinian *Law of Citations* of 426.

> *C.Th.* 1.4.3. *Emperors Theodosius and Valentinian Augustuses to the Senate of the City of Rome.* (After other matters.) We confirm all the writings of Papinian, Paulus, Gaius, Ulpian and Modestinus, so that the same authority shall attend Gaius as Paulus, Ulpian and the others, and passages from the whole body of his writings may be cited. 1. We also decree to be valid the learning of those persons whose treatises and opinions all the aforesaid jurisconsults have incorporated in their own works, such as Scaevola, Sabinus, Julianus, and Marcellus, and all others whom they cite, provided that, on account of the uncertainty of antiquity, their books shall be confirmed by a collation of the codices. 2. Moreover, when conflicting opinions are cited, the greater number of the authors shall prevail, or if the numbers should be equal, the authority of that group shall take precedence in which the man of superior genius, Papinian, shall tower above the rest, and as he defeats a single opponent, so he yields to two. 3. As was

formerly decreed, We also order to be invalidated the notes which Paulus and Ulpian made upon the collected writings of Papinian. 4. Furthermore, when their opinions as cited are equally divided and their authority is rated as equal, the regulation of the judge shall choose whose opinion he shall follow. 5. We order that the Sentences of Paulus also shall be valid. (Etc.) *Given on the eighth day before the ides of November at Ravenna in the year of the twelfth consulship of Our Lord Theodosius Augustus and the second consulship of Our Lord Valentinian Augustus.—November 6 (7) 426.*[11]

Whether we have the constitution as it was issued in 426 A.D. or whether, as is widely believed, it was subjected to a revision in 438 A.D. does not, I think, affect us greatly, and the question may be left aside for the moment.

This constitution, inter alia, made the works of the five jurists Papinian, Paul, Gaius, Ulpian, and Modestinus primary authorities.[12] The works of jurists cited by the five could also be produced, provided in this case that, because of the age of the works, what these jurists said was confirmed by collation of manuscripts. In the case of the five primary authorities, no collation of manuscripts was demanded. Why was there this difference? There are, I submit, two possible explanations.

First, there were many good manuscripts of Papinian, Paul, Ulpian, and Modestinus, who were the last classical jurists, and of Gaius, whose work for beginning students had become very popular. The works of the earlier classical jurists were not as widely read because their substance was further removed from contemporary law, and hence the manuscripts of these jurists were uncommon and tended to be suspect. Any argument based on relative popularity and abundance of manuscripts must be concerned mainly with the age of the original works. The quality of the original writings is of secondary importance, since otherwise one would have expected the great Julian, for instance, to have been given authority and Modestinus to have occupied a less prominent place. Gaius, who is earlier than the other four primary authorities, is a special case. His importance is mainly due to his *Institutes;* and elementary books, concerned with the broad outline of the law, do not go out of date as quickly as detailed commentaries. Broad principles change much more slowly than do details. It is perhaps significant that, outside the *Corpus iuris civilis,* no fragments of the works of Gaius, apart from his *Institutes,* have come down to us and that he is not cited by

the imperial constitutions.[13] Second, the writings of the earlier classical jurists
had been corrupted or altered to bring them up to date, hence their manuscripts
were less reliable.

These two possible explanations are, of course, to some degree related. But
whichever is correct, the same conclusion follows, namely that there had been
no large-scale revision of the works of the five primary authorities despite the
intervention of about two centuries between their composition and the *Law of
Citations*. What the emperors want is the original opinions of the classical jurists;
this point is made abundantly plain by the requirement of comparison of manuscripts even if it extends only to the lesser authorities. Moreover, otherwise there
could hardly be a reason for designating five of the jurists as primary authorities. And yet it is only the manuscripts of the earlier classical jurists that are
suspect. If the first explanation suggested for the difference in treatment of the
manuscripts of the primary and lesser authorities is correct, then the popularity
of the five jurists before 426 (which accounts for the abundance of their manuscripts) must be because their works did not need substantial alteration. If the
second suggestion is right, then deliberate corruption on a large scale in the texts
extended only to the manuscripts of the earlier jurists.

It might be objected to the foregoing that in fact the popularity of the five
primary authorities resulted in "standard editions" of their works, so that collation would not be needed for them, and hence the *Law of Citations* would not
provide evidence against reediting. But, first, as noted above, their popularity
could be based only on the fact that they, unlike earlier classical jurists, very
largely gave contemporary law and did not require large-scale alteration. It
is putting the cart before the horse to derive the standardization of the manuscripts from the jurists' popularity. Second, there could be no such thing here
as a "standard edition" unless the emperors designated certain manuscripts as
having preeminent authority. There is no sign of such imperial intervention, and
it can be ruled out. One can, at least in the case of the huge commentaries *ad edictum* and *ad Sabinum*, completely exclude the idea that an unofficial revised edition could drive earlier editions from circulation. The cost of a copy of Ulpian's
eighty-three books ad edictum would be so enormous that few jurists would
throw away their existing copies and rush to buy a new edition for the sake of
what would mainly be non-Ulpianic additions. The earlier manuscripts would
continue to be used and relied on. Moreover, the smallness of the market and

the enormous size of the undertaking go very much against the idea of planned multiple copying here. Rather one would expect either that a single copy would be made when the need arose or that a very few—and only a very few—would be produced from time to time. No parallels can really usefully be drawn from the republishing of, say, literary works, where the economics could be vastly different either because of the smaller size of the work to be edited or because the purchasing public could be larger. Again, it is surely significant that all the writings of the five primary authorities are accepted free from the requirement of collation. If the works of these jurists had been subject to extensive alteration in postclassical times, then it would seem absolutely impossible that a standard edition of all of them (or even of those at all likely to be produced in court) could have emerged.

According to Otto Gradenwitz, the original constitution of 426 A.D. referred only to the five primary authorities, and the constitution was revised in 438 A.D., and only then was the part inserted that is concerned with the secondary authorities.[14] This possibility does not affect us, and we need not decide whether Gradenwitz is right or not. If he is right, it is just as significant that collation of the manuscripts of the secondary authorities was felt to be necessary in 438 but not collation of the manuscripts of the five primary authorities. It would still be difficult to attribute the difference in treatment as regards collation to oversight.

Thus the Valentinian *Law of Citations* presents very strong evidence that the works of Papinian, Paul, Gaius, Ulpian, and Modestinus had not, to any large extent, been altered in the preceding two centuries. One can probably go further. If these five had not been tampered with in that time, then it is unlikely that in the same period the works of other jurists had undergone substantial revision. So any revision of the secondary authorities must already have occurred in the classical period. It is a priori improbable that there was such revision as early as the classical period, so it is reasonable to assume that the works of these jurists, too, did not undergo any large-scale alteration at all before the *Law of Citations*. That is to say, collation of their manuscripts was demanded because such manuscripts were scarce (because of their lack of popularity, since they were out of date), old, and generally neglected and hence were suspect.

If the above arguments are correct, then the juristic writings that lay before Justinian when in 530 he decided to give them a new form and a new life were, almost without exception, 300 years or more old and had not been subjected to subsequent deliberate manipulation. The *Valentinian Law* continued to be in force, as it could not have been if there had subsequently been much tampering with the "Big Five."

The second enormously significant legal event in early Byzantium was the promulgation of the *Theodosian Code*, an official collection of imperial rescripts. From 235 onward, such imperial rulings were the only source of new law. Naturally the law changed, especially when Christianity was recognized and later became the state religion. But how was this new law to be found?

Imperial edicts were put up on a board at the emperor's residence for a short time, and he might direct an edict to be displayed for a limited period in a province or provinces.[15] *Decreta*, statements of the law issued to an individual with a problem, would become known at once to the parties to the lawsuit and would be registered in the court records. Other persons could obtain copies. *Epistulae*, replies to officials or public bodies who had asked for advice, were sent to them but were not otherwise published unless the emperor so requested. It is assumed that the chancellery department *ab epistulis* retained a copy or the original. *Subscriptiones*, the emperor's replies written at the bottom of petitions, were put up in public at Rome for a few days only.[16] Such was the extent of the official interest in publication of rescripts. No other official attempt was made to bring their contents to the attention of lawyers or other interested persons.[17] The law, therefore, would often be very difficult to find and not infrequently impossible.

The problem of access to the rescripts was exacerbated when jurists stopped writing books that might quote or explain them. This problem led to two unofficial collections of rescripts.[18] Then came the official code of Theodosius. Any inquiry into what Justinian intended to do with the sources of law and law reform in the work now known as the *Corpus iuris civilis*, and into his success, should begin with notice of the plan of the Emperor Theodosius II for codification of law in the fifth century. The starting point is in the *Theodosian Code* 1.1.5:

> *Emperors Theodosius and Valentinian Augustuses to the Senate.* We decree that, after the pattern of the Gregorian and Hermogenian Codes, a collection shall be made of all the rescripts that were issued by the renowned Constantine, by the sainted Emperors after him, and by Us and which rest upon the force of edicts or sacred imperial law of general force.
>
> First, the titles, which are the definite designations of the matters therein shall be so divided that, when the various headings have been ex-

pressed, if one rescript should pertain to several titles, the materials shall be assembled wherever each is fitting. Second, if any diversity should cause anything to be stated in two ways, it shall be tested by the order of the readings, and not only shall the year of the consulship be considered and the time of the reign be investigated, but also the arrangement of the work itself shall show that the laws which are later are more valid. Furthermore, the very words themselves of the rescripts, in so far as they pertain to the essential matter, shall be preserved, but those words which were added not from the very necessity of sanctioning the law shall be omitted.

Although it would be simpler and more in accordance with law to omit those rescripts which were invalidated by later rescripts and to set forth only those which must be valid, let us recognize that this code and the previous ones were composed for more diligent men, to whose scholarly efforts it is granted to know those laws also which have been consigned to silence and have passed into desuetude, since they were destined to be valid for the cases of their own time only.

Moreover, from these three codes and from the treatises and responses of the jurists which are attached to each of the titles, through the services of the same men who shall arrange the third code, there shall be produced another code of Ours. This code shall permit no error, no ambiguities; it shall be called by Our name and shall show what must be followed and what must be avoided by all.

For the consummation of so great a work and for the composition of the codes—the first of which shall collect all the diversity of general rescripts, shall omit none outside itself which are now permitted to be cited in court, and shall reject only an empty copiousness of words, the other shall exclude every contradiction of the law and shall undertake the guidance of life—men must be chosen of singular trustworthiness, of the most brilliant genius. When they have presented the first code to Our Wisdom and to the public authority, they shall undertake the other, which must be worked over until it is worthy of publication. Let Your Magnificence acknowledge the men who have been selected; We have selected the Illustrious Antiochus, Ex-Quaestor and Ex-Prefect, the Illustrious Antiochus, Quaestor of the sacred imperial palace, the Respectable Theodorus, Count and Master of the Bureau of Memorials, the Respectable Eudicius and Eusebius, Masters of the Bureaus, the Respectable Jo-

hannes, Ex-Count of Our sacred imperial sanctuary, the Respectable Co-
mazon and Eubulus, Ex-Masters of the Bureaus, and Apelles, most eloquent jurist.

We are confident that these men who have been selected by Our Eternity will employ every exceptionally learned man, in order that by their
common study a reasonable plan of life may be apprehended and falla-
cious laws may be excluded.

Furthermore, if in the future it should be Our pleasure to promulgate
any law in one part of this very closely united Empire, it shall be valid in
the other part on condition that it does not rest upon doubtful trustworthiness or upon a private assertion; but from that part of the Empire in
which it will be established, it shall be transmitted with the sacred imperial letters, it shall be received in the bureaus of the other part of the
Empire also, and it shall be published with the due formality of edicts.
For a law that has been sent must be accepted and must undoubtedly be
valid, and the power to emend and to revoke shall be reserved to Our
Clemency. Moreover, the laws must be mutually announced, and they
must not be admitted otherwise. (Etc.) *Given on the seventh day before the kalends
of April at Constantinople in the year of the consulship of Florentius and Dionysius.—
March 26, 429.*[19]

The decree is dated 26 March 429, and we know from the minutes of the Senate of Rome for 25 December 438 that it was the work of Theodosius. These
minutes record the completion of the first of the two planned codifications.

The first codification was to be, and was, of the rescripts of the first Christian emperor, Constantine, and of his successors.[20] It was to be modeled on the
two unofficial compilations, the *Codex Gregorianus* and the *Codex Hermogenianus*,
which have not survived. Nonetheless, we know that the *Codex Gregorianus*, the
larger work, contained imperial rescripts from 196 to the reign of Diocletian,
while the *Codex Hermogenianus* concentrated on 293–294. Many of these rescripts
appear in Justinian's *Code*.

Theodosius's *Code* was not to repeat these earlier rescripts of pagan emperors, but they were not invalidated. More to the point, Theodosius's instructions
to his compilers were not to cut out from the rescripts of Constantine and his
successors those that were overruled by later rescripts but to give them all: "Although it would be simpler and more in accordance with law to omit these re-

scripts which were invalidated by later rescripts and to set forth and to set out only those that are fittingly valid, let us recognize that this Code and the prior ones were composed for more diligent persons to whose scholarly efforts it is granted to know even those which consigned to silence have passed into desuetude, to be valid for the affairs of this time only." Theodosius is here rather disingenuous. It is obviously simpler for the compilers to repeat all of the rescripts (with appropriate permitted changes) than to decide which rescripts or which parts of them had been superseded. It does, however, make the task of interpreters much more difficult. The only guidance that exists is the basic rule that later law invalidates those parts of earlier law that are inconsistent with it. This is expressly laid down in §4. The rescripts, significantly, are arranged in chronological order.

The compilers were further instructed that when their work was completed, they were to proceed to prepare a further code, from the *Codices Gregorianus, Hermogenianus,* and *Theodosianus* and from the treatises and responses attached to or closely connected with each of the titles. The Latin, "et per singulos titulos cohaerentibus prudentium tractatibus et responsis," is ambiguous. We cannot tell whether the opinions of the jurists were to be attached to each title of the code, presumably after the rescripts, or were to be interwoven. This code was to present no more error or ambiguity. Hence this time, everything that was obsolete even in the rescripts in the first code of Theodosius was to be excised. We need at this stage take Theodosius's instructions no further, except to state that this second proposed Theodosian code was never compiled.

After the reign of Theodosius, emperors continued to issue rescripts. For a time, up to 468, some minor collections of constitutions appeared. But thereafter, there was no easy access to imperial rulings. Such were the sources of law when Justinian became emperor.

JUSTINIAN'S COMPILATION

On 10 July 518, Justin, the Thracian peasant turned soldier, now *comes excubitorum* (i.e., commander of one of the palace regiments), was pronounced emperor in the hippodrome at Constantinople. He was then probably about sixty-eight years old. He immediately made his nephew Justinian a patrician and *comes domesticorum,* commander of the imperial bodyguard. From that time Justinian was obviously a man of great political influence at the palace. On 1 April 527, the mortally ill Justin proclaimed Justinian coemperor, and Justinian became sole emperor on 1 August of that year, on Justin's death. On 13 February 528, Justinian sent to the senate his order to compose a new codex. The word "codex" has the ordinary sense of "book" but in this context has a specific meaning, a collection of imperial rescripts. There were, as we have just seen, three earlier codices, the unofficial *Codices Gregorianus* and *Hermogenianus*, both from around the end of the third century, and the official *Codex Theodosianus* of the emperor Theodosius II, published in 438. It is because of them that Justinian speaks of the composition of a "new Code." The order begins:

> These things which necessarily were seen by many earlier emperors to require correction, but none of them between times dared to bring to effect, we have determined at the present time to complete for the common good, with the aid of all powerful God, and to cut out the prolixity of litigation; cutting back on the multitude of constitutions which were contained in the three Codes, *Gregorianus, Hermogenianus* and *Theodosianus,* as well as on those constitutions that after these Codes were issued by Theodosius, of holy memory, and other later emperors, and also by Our Grace; composing one Code under Our Auspicious Name in which constitutions ought to be collected not only from the three aforementioned *Codes,* but also from new constitutions after them.

At the very beginning of his reign, Justinian was tackling the major problem facing the lawyers of the day, that of knowing the law contained in imperial rescripts.

In the following section, §1, Justinian lists the team he had selected to compile the *Code.* Then §2 reads:

> We specifically permit to them the cutting out of prefaces that are unnecessary to the substance of the law as well as repetitions and contradictions unless they are helped by the old division of the law; of those, too, which have become obsolete; to compose from the same three *Codes* and new rescripts certain laws written in a brief form, to bring them under fitting titles, adding indeed and subtracting, even, further, changing their wording when the usefulness of the matter demanded that, even collecting in one law matters scattered in various rescripts, making their mean-

ing clearer; provided, however, that the chronological order of these same rescripts appears not only by including dates and consuls but also by their arrangement, with the first being put in the first place, those subsequent in the second place, and, if any are found without the date and consul in the old *Codes* or in these collections of new rescripts, to place them in such way that no doubt can arise as to their general binding force, just as it is plain that those receive the force of a general rescript which were addressed to individuals or originally to a community but which are included in the new *Code* because of their usefulness.[21]

The instructions are clear and precise—witness the repetition of references to "the three old *Codes* and later rescripts." What really matters to us in the present context is precisely the power that is not given, namely to innovate and change the law found in existing rescripts. Wording may be altered, repetitions and contradictions are to be erased, obsolete law is to be deleted, several rescripts may be made into one, but nothing allows the introduction of new law.[22] Even when several rescripts are turned into one, some parts may seem to say something other than was in the original, but this will be because of deletion and because of the incorporation of materials from other rescripts.

The obvious conclusion is that Justinian's first *Code* was not meant to reform the substantive law. This conclusion is made certain by four other considerations. First, it is not the job of compilers, as such, to change the substantive law. Second, no such reform had been envisaged for the *Theodosian Code* or for Theodosius's other, more ambitious plan that failed. Third, the preface to the completed code, *De Justiniano codice confirmando*, which was published on 7 April 529, repeats in detail the instructions to the compilers, and once again there is no sign of any power to introduce new substantive law in the constitutions. Fourth, and above all, there is the existence of the *Quinquaginta decisiones*, the *Fifty Decisions*, intended by Justinian to resolve outstanding disputes among the classical lawyers. The plan for them was conceived as a separate enterprise and, indeed, only later. Yet the existence of the disputes was obvious, and compilers of a code whose purpose was law reform ought in it to have resolved these disputes. By doing so, indeed, they would have obviated the need for Justinian's second *Code*, the *Codex repetitae praelectionis*. The *Fifty Decisions* is, in fact, the vehicle chosen for Justinian's reform of the substantive law.

From the discussion so far, it follows that this first *Code* contained all the

changes in private law from the end of the classical period that were still relevant. (I use "private law" in a sense customary among civilians to indicate all
topics dealt with in Justinian's *Institutes* with the exception of actions and criminal law, that is, the contents of about three and a half books out of four.) When
the classical jurists stopped writing books, the only changes in law were those
made by imperial rescripts (in the widest sense). Since, as is well known and as
we shall now see, the compilation of the *Digest* was not contemplated for a considerable time after the promulgation of the *Code*, the *Code* would also contain
those numerous rescripts that gave a reply but did not innovate. Thus, much
classical law would be set out in the *Code*.

There is ample evidence that when the first *Code* was promulgated, there was
no plan for a collection of approved juristic texts. To begin with, a papyrus from
Oxyrhynchus contains an extract from the title rubrics of the first *Code* and also
the inscriptions of the rescripts, and it shows that the Valentinian *Law of Citations* of 426 or 438 was still in force.[23] This, as we have seen, gave authoritative
ranking to five classical jurists: Ulpian, Paul, Papinian, Modestinus, and Gaius.
The *Law of Citations* is omitted from the second *Code*, naturally enough, since it
would be superseded by the publication of the *Digest*. But the *Law of Citations*
could not have been contained in the first *Code* as a transitional provision, because §3 of *De Justiniano codice confirmando* insists that its provisions are to be in
force forever: "Therefore we have seen to it that this code which will be valid
for eternity comes to your high knowledge." Again, this same §3 forbids the citation of the rescripts from the writings of jurists in a form other than that of
the *Code*: "We permit no one to quote from the books of the interpreters of the
old law these rescripts in a different form." The old jurists were thus still authoritative, though when they quoted an imperial rescript the only valid and
official form was that in the *Code*. Finally, here, the strongest evidence is in
C.1.14.12.5: "After exploding these ridiculous doubts, the emperor alone will
properly be judged as much the interpreter of the law as he is the founder. This
law derogates in no way from the interpreters of the old law because the imperial majesty permitted this to them also." C.1.14.12 of 27 October 529, declared
that the judgment of the emperor in a particular case settled the law for the future (though earlier the force of the emperor's decision had been disputed by the
jurists). Then at the end comes our passage. The opinions of the classical jurists
are still to carry weight because emperors allowed this. That is to say, the authority of jurists as founders of the law is based on the emperors' earlier consent

to this effect and not on Justinian's excerpting and publication of their writings as law. Thus, six months after the promulgation of the first *Code*, the collection of juristic opinions was not contemplated.[24]

Still, though the *Code* solved the most immediately pressing problem—how lawyers were to find imperial rescripts and how they were to determine which were authoritative—its very existence would highlight two other problems: the multiplicity of relevant juristic writings despite the Valentinian *Law of Citations* and the classical disputes that had never been settled by subsequent rescripts.

These two problems would in time be resolved, that of the multiplicity of juristic writings by the *Digest* and that of the surviving classical disputes by the *Fifty Decisions* and subsequent rescripts. There is a difficulty about the relationship between the *Fifty Decisions* and the *Digest*, a difficulty that I believe cannot be resolved. There are two real possibilities. One is that the *Fifty Decisions* was issued as a preliminary to the *Digest*, to establish which classical view was to be accepted. This view I previously favored. The other is that the rescripts forming the collection were issued simply to clarify the law, without being linked with any plan to codify the juristic writings. This now seems to me possibly more likely. Though not all of the *Decisions* can now be recognized, they or many of them were incorporated into the second *Code*. They were, accordingly, not treated simply as telling the compilers of the *Digest* which classical juristic view to accept. Fortunately, in the present context there is no need to resolve the difficulty. What matters for us is that on either possibility the purpose of the *Fifty Decisions* was the same: to reform the substantive law. The *Fifty Decisions* was Justinian's vehicle for the reform of substantive law (plus, of course, his earlier and later constitutions).

We have little direct textual evidence for the *Fifty Decisions*, but §1 of the preface to the second *Code*, *De emendatione codicis Justiniani et secunda eius editione*, tells us what we need to know. In the *principium* Justinian speaks of the making of the first *Code*, then adds in §1: "But afterwards, when we had undertaken to take into account the old law, we issued *Fifty Decisions* and also promulgated very many relevant constitutions for the benefit of the proposed work, by which the majority of previous rules were amended and shortened, and we delivered up all the old law, free from unnecessary prolixity and also condensed, in our *Institutes* and *Digest*."

"For the benefit of the proposed work" does suggest that he did have a proposed *Digest* in mind when the *Fifty Decisions* was made, but of course this passage was written after the promulgation of the *Digest*. In any case, two matters should attract our attention. The first is Justinian's pride in his reform of the substantive law. As with his other achievements, he is not hiding his light under a bushel. This attitude makes even more apparent the fact that he did not give the compilers of the first *Code* powers to introduce new law. The second matter to note is at the very end of the text: the reforms in the *Fifty Decisions* and in the later rescripts enabled him to deliver the *Digest* and *Institutes* in a form shorter than would otherwise have been the case. More important, what the *Digest* and *Institutes* contained was "all the old law": nothing is said about their containing any new law.

The sources of law, therefore, were very much reduced in Justinian's time from their number in early classical law. Only imperial rescripts remained. Statutes, praetorian Edicts, and juristic writings had all gone. The law in statutes and Edicts was found in the juristic texts, and as separate entities they could be ignored. The juristic texts had aged, but this obsolescence was not recognized emotionally even in the age of Justinian, a fact that had important consequences.

GOD IN JUSTINIAN'S *DIGEST*

Justinian issued the order *De conceptione Digestorum* on the composition of the *Digest*, which is usually known as *Deo auctore*, on 15 December 530. He ordered the collection and publication of juristic writings but again nowhere gave the compilers authority to change the substance. When he came to detailed instructions, he said at §6:

> Out of a large number of authors, you must not make a judgment that the work of one is better and more equitable, since it may happen that the opinion of one writer, perhaps of inferior merit, is better at some point than those of many other authors, even superior ones. You ought not to reject out of hand, therefore, opinions recorded in the notes to Aemilius Papinian taken from Ulpian, Paul, and Marcian, which once had no weight on account of the honor given to the most renowned Papinian; but if you perceive that anything taken from them is necessary to supplement or interpret the works of Papinian, that man of supreme ability, you must not hesitate to set this down too as having the force of law, so that all the

most gifted authors whose work is contained in this book may have as much authority as if their studies were derived from imperial constitutions and had been uttered by our own inspired mouth; for we ascribe everything to ourselves, since it is from us that all their authority is derived; and one who emends something that is not done accurately deserves more praise than the original author.

The passages excerpted from the jurists were to have force as if they were imperial constitutions. Justinian ascribed them to himself because they derived their authority from him. Closely tied to this proposition are the final clauses of the last sentence: "and one who emends something that is not done accurately deserves more praise than the original author." This statement relates above all to selecting the best passages from each author rather than choosing one jurist to be supreme. There is no permission here to insert new law. Section 7 begins:

There is something else of which we wish you to take special account: If you find anything in the old books that is not well expressed, or anything superfluous or wanting in finish, you should get rid of unnecessary prolixity, make up what is deficient, and present the whole in proportion and in the most elegant form possible. What is more, if you find anything not correctly expressed in the old laws or constitutions which the ancient writers quoted in their books, you should also take care to rectify it and put it into proper form, so that what is chosen by you and set down there may be deemed genuine and the best version, and be treated as if it were what was originally written; and let no one dare to assert that your version is faulty by comparison with the old text.

This provision did grant a power that might include changing the substance of particular juristic texts but only in a very special case. When a jurist quoted a law or constitution, and the wording of it was inaccurate, the correct wording of the law or rescript was to be restored. "Correct" here means, of course, the wording preferred by the compilers.[25] Section 9 has:

Repetition, too, as already said, we wish to exclude from a composition such as this. Seeing that the sanction of imperial rescripts is enough to give them their own authority, we do not wish those things which have been provided by the most sacred rescripts inserted in our *Codex* to be set out again from the old law unless perhaps this should happen by way of logi-

cal distinction or supplementation or in an effort toward greater com-
pleteness; but even then this must be done very rarely, lest, by extension
of this sort of failing, some thorny growth may arise in such meadow.

Not only was there to be no repetition in the body of the work, but the *Digest*
was not to repeat what was already in the *Code* (with rare exceptions that are
specified). But the only postclassical law that would exist would derive from imperial rescripts that were set out in the *Code*.[26] Hence the compilers of the *Digest* were not only not given the power to alter the substance of classical law, they
were indirectly forbidden to do so. Indeed, as I claimed earlier in this chapter,
classical law as set out in rescripts that did not innovate would be in the *Code*
and would hence be excluded from the *Digest*. To that extent the *Digest* does not
give classical law. Moreover, *C. Tanta*, confirming the *Digest*, §14, expressly claims
that Justinian did not allow rules laid down by imperial rescripts to appear in
the *Digest*.

The Roman jurists, as I keep insisting, stopped writing books around 235.
Thereafter their texts remained fundamentally unchanged. Juristic talents remained high. Yet when Justinian wished to codify the law and to make use of
juristic writings he was confined to works at least three centuries old. And Justinian's world was very different from that of the jurists. The *Digest*, as a result,
presents a very odd picture of early Byzantium.

To start with a very minor point. The Roman jurists were little interested in
theory or history. Exceptions for history are Gaius, whose commentary on the
Twelve Tables is historical at least in part, and Pomponius's *Enchiridion*, "Manual," which is wholly historical. The *Digest* title 1.2, "The Origin of the Law and
of all the Magistracies and the Succession of the Jurists," is taken from one relatively short text of Gaius and one very long text of Pomponius. The title is basically a condensed history of Roman law. But a consequence of the working
method of Justinian's compilers is that the history ends where Pomponius did,
in the middle of the second century.[27] A more striking example of Justinian's reluctance to interpolate, to change the substance of texts or create new texts, can
scarcely be imagined.[28] Justinian in the sixth century, in Constantinople, wanted
to provide a history of Roman law. The only account available to him stopped
in the middle of the second century. So be it: Roman legal history stopped in
the middle of the second century.

A cynic might say, "So what? Does it matter that Justinian stops legal history in the middle of the second century?" Perhaps not. But what is crucial is the mind-set. Law in the *Digest* goes no further than 235. Changes thereafter can have no place. But what about earlier texts and law? Anything that is inappropriate in the changed circumstances will be cut out. What is left may remain with a very different voice. The result may well be statements or nonstatements of law that are remote from social reality.

Moreover, the jurists were selective in their interests. They were a self-selecting group of gentlemen for whom interpretation was a hobby with important social and political implications.[29] Even with regard to interpretation they were selective in their interests. They had little concern for most of public law, so they did not much write on important practical issues such as the control of the market[30] or police activities, including control over slaves.[31] And if the jurists were not interested in a subject, then it would not surface in the *Digest*.[32]

Justinian's empire was a hotbed of debate on Christian theology.[33] But the Roman jurists were all pagans. Justinian did not add to their texts. The result is that in the body of the *Digest* there is not a single reference to Jesus or to his apostles or saints. No legal arguments are drawn from the Bible or from fathers of the church.

Just as significant, there are only eight texts that contain the word *deus*, "god." The texts are survivors. They once referred to "a god," some pagan deity, now to "the God" of the Christians. The texts reveal nothing of the characteristics of pagan religion or of Christianity. They exist only because they are so antiseptic.

Prime examples can be chosen from judicial oaths, which were a device to shorten lawsuits. At any point one party to a dispute could tender an oath to the other on a disputed matter. If that party swore the oath, the issue was regarded as settled in his favor. If he refused, the issue was settled against him. The oath would state by whom or through whom or by what it was sworn. Normally the oath would be sworn by a god, though this is not often expressed in the texts in the relevant *Digest* title, 12.2.[34] One text, however, does mention swearing on the spirit of the emperor (*per genium principis*),[35] and two mention swearing by a god (or God). One of these, *D.12.2.33*, may thus be translated: "One who swears by his own personal safety [*per salutem suam*], although he is regarded as swearing by a god (for he thus swears with regard to a divine spirit) is nonetheless not regarded as having sworn if the oath was not tendered to him in these express terms. Hence it is necessary to swear from the beginning in solemn form." I have translated the text as would be appropriate for its original author, the pagan jurist Ulpian. The notion *Salus* was personified as the deity of public safety, or the safety of the emperor, and every individual would have his or her own protective spirit of "safety." The legal issue in the text is that if the person to whom the oath is put swears "per salutem suam," and if that wording does not correspond to the form in which the oath was put to him, then even though he was swearing by a divinity, the oath was void. The judicial oath must be sworn in the form in which it is proffered.[36] The text is retained precisely because in the Christian world it would have a new meaning, demanding a different translation: "One who swears by his own salvation, although he is regarded as swearing by God (for he thus swears with regard to the divine spirit)."

Other texts more clearly betray their pagan origin but can be understood in a Christian way. Thus *D.24.1.5.12*: "So even if a husband gives to his wife as an offering to a god [*ad oblationem dei*] or land on which she had promised to erect a public building or dedicate a public temple [*aedem publicam*] the land will become sacred. But even if he gives something to her that the gift be given to a god or be consecrated, there is no doubt that it ought to be valid. Therefore if he placed oil on her behalf in a sacred temple, the gift is valid." The background of this text of Ulpian is that gifts between husband and wife were in general void. Ulpian allows gifts by a husband to be valid as exceptions where the purpose is for the wife to use them as a religious offering.

Only one more text of Ulpian, *D.48.13.7(6)*, need be quoted in this connection: "The proconsul ought to impose the penalty for sacrilege more severely or more mildly depending on the quality of the person, on the nature of the property and the time, and on the age or sex. I know indeed that many have been condemned to the wild beasts for sacrilege, some even burned alive, others hanged on the cross. But the penalty should be tempered to restrict condemnation to the beasts to those who formed a gang and broke into a temple and took away by night offerings to a god."[37]

It is very obvious that texts treated in this way, wrenched out of their context, assigned a different meaning, can give us little indication of the importance of Christianity in early Byzantium, of the status of leading clerics, and of the violence of schisms. But the present text itself could be of enormous importance— not obvious on its face and perhaps not intended—because of the hatred of heretics. The behavior of heretics, even of leading ecclesiastics, could readily be construed as sacrilege.

In the *Digest* early Byzantium comes across as a secular society. It is in this connection that I stressed above that jurists stopped writing books around 235, but there is little sign of a decline in juristic quality. The law was little altered by imperial rulings until the empire became Christian. But the situation was changed under Constantine and his successors. There was an outpouring of rescripts on religious matters, as appears from the *Theodosian Code*. I will treat this subject later in this chapter. What matters here is that once the jurists stopped writing books, they did not begin again, yet they continued to have great technical skill. If top imperial civil servants had written law books after 324, the *Digest* would have been a very different work.

But if God scarcely appears in the *Digest*, and if Jesus, the apostles, saints, and fathers of the Church appear in neither the *Institutes* nor the *Digest*, then we can be sure that these works will give a false picture of individual social institutions. Nowhere is this more clear than in divorce.

In classical Roman law the general rule was that both husband and wife could initiate a divorce for any reason without penalty except that a party who divorced without sufficient justification or gave cause for divorce might suffer with respect to the dowry.[38]

Divorce is not dealt with in Justinian's *Institutes*,[39] but its impropriety was surely a major social issue. In the *Digest* it is the subject of the rather short title, 24.2, which gives only classical law, with no sign of a moral repugnance to divorce. The surprisingly lowly place attributed to the subject is emphasized by the much greater length of the immediately preceding title, on gifts between husband and wife. But in 542 Justinian forbade divorce altogether unless made because of a "longing for chastity."[40] The Christian influence is obvious.[41]

But much earlier, Christian hostility to divorce was obvious in the rescripts of the Christian emperors. The very first Christian emperor, Constantine, declared that a wife was not justified in divorcing a husband for a "petty reason" (*exquisita causa*) such as being a drunkard, gambler, or "addicted to women" (*muliercularius*) but only for murder or preparation of poison or violation of tombs. Such a divorce is nonetheless valid, but the wife will lose her dowry, gifts before marriage, and will be deported to an island. A husband is not to divorce for less than adultery, preparation of poison, or procuring; if he does, he will forfeit the dowry and may not marry again. Still, if he does remarry, the marriage is valid, but the divorced wife is given the right to seize the second wife's dowry.[42] Subsequent Christian emperors made further changes.[43] So, indeed, did Justinian himself. Thus in 528—so before the *Digest*—he added impotence by the husband for two years from the date of marriage to the list of justified causes for divorce.[44] Subsequently he increased the period for impotence to three years.[45] In December 533—contemporaneously with the *Digest*—Justinian added to the justifications for divorcing a wife that she has an abortion, that "she dares on account of lust to frequent a bath common to men," or that she attempts bigamy.[46] To repeat myself, none of this Byzantine attitude to divorce appears in any shape or form in Justinian's *Digest* or *Institutes*.[47]

Instances where the *Digest* gives a false picture of law in Justinian's time can be multiplied. Thus the concept of ownership is presented in the *Digest* and *Institutes* as individualistic, in the *Code* as subject to authoritarian restrictions.[48] Similarly, security interests in land may be created by simple agreement in the *Digest*, but the Byzantine empire required official documentation.[49]

DRAFTING THE *INSTITUTES*

One of the most momentous events in legal history was the publication of Justinian's *Institutes* on 30 December 533, the same day as the publication of Justinian's *Digest*. The *Institutes* is a marvelous invention, a combination of statute law and elementary textbook for first-year students. Without the *Institutes* the great reception of Roman law would have been very different, if it had occurred at all. The *Digest* and *Code* are huge works, badly organized, almost impenetrable without aid. The *Institutes* gives a succinct treatment of private law, well organized. Most modern civil codes are in structure and content clear linear descendants of the *Institutes*.[50]

The *Institutes* represents another aspect of this first reception of Roman law. But how had this work come about? We have little direct information, but much can be reconstructed. We do not have instructions from Justinian to the redactors of the *Institutes*, but we first have information in §11 of *De conceptione Digestorum*, "On the Composition of the *Digest*": "We therefore command that all matters be governed by these two volumes, one of constitutions [i.e., the *Code*], the other of the law clarified and arranged in the book that is to be [i.e., the *Digest*]. Or if anything else will be promulgated by us, having the place of *Institutes*, so that the immature mind of the student, nourished by simple things, may more easily be brought to knowledge of higher learning."

This preface to the *Digest*, commissioning the work, is dated 15 December 530 but was not published until the completion of the task in 533. The question has therefore surfaced whether the reference to a work of *Institutes* was in the original or is a later addition. Did Justinian contemplate as early as 530 the *possibility* of an elementary textbook? My answer is very much in the affirmative, because the whole tenor of *De conceptione Digestorum* of 530 is redolent of a plan that existed before the completion of the *Digest* in 533. The strongest evidence for this is that in *De conceptione Digestorum* there is not the slightest sign of a planned role for the *Digest* in legal education. Section 11, just quoted, indicates that the *Digest*, like the *Code*, was meant for practice. In sharp contrast, the other two prefaces to the *Digest*, dating from 533, focus on its value in education. This focus may be to be expected in *Omnem rei*, dated 16 December 533, because it was addressed to law professors. But it is astonishing in *De confirmatione Digestorum*, "On the Confirmation of the *Digest*," dated 30 December 533, addressed "to the Senate and all peoples." The opening of this document makes it plain that the *Digest* was meant for practical use, but §§2 through 10 show that its role was strongly educative. Section 11 of *De confirmatione Digestorum* brings us back to the making of the *Institutes*:

But when we saw that men of little education and who are standing in the forecourt of the law, eager to enter into its secrets, are not fit to bear the weight of such learning, we decided that another compilation of moderate length ought to be prepared. So that they, receiving a new coloration from it and, so to speak, imbued with the first fruits of the whole subject, might be able to proceed to the innermost parts of it and absorb with eyes undazzled the exquisite beauty of the law, we therefore summoned the eminent man Tribonian, who was chosen to direct the whole work, with Theophilus and Dorotheus, *viri illustres* and most eloquent professors, and commissioned them to collect one by one the books that were composed by ancient authors containing the first principles of the law and known as *Institutes*. Whatever they found in these that is useful and most appropriate and perfect from every point of view and in accordance with the practice of the present day, this they were to be careful to take and to put into four books and make it into the very foundation and first principles of education, and thus enable young men, with its support, to grasp the weightier and more finished provisions of the law. We also instructed them to be mindful at the same time of our own *rescripts*,[51] which we have issued for the improvement of the law, and, in composing the *Institutes*, not to omit inserting the same improvements, so that it may be clear both where uncertainty had existed previously and what has since become secure. When the work had been finished by these men it was produced to us and scrutinized; and we received it favorably and judged it to be not unworthy of our intentions. And we gave orders that the aforesaid books should have the force of *rescripts*; this is set out in more detail in our own discourse which we have inserted as a preface to the same books.

I have tried to translate §11 of *De conceptione Digestorum* and the beginning of §11 of *De confirmatione Digestorum* as literally and as precisely as possible because they show the development of the idea of an elementary textbook with the force of law.

By late 530 Justinian had decided that a collection of extracts from the classical jurists should be made for the clarification of the law. This was to be the *Digest*. He did not envisage a role for this volume in legal education. But at this stage of his (or his advisers') thinking he was aware that his existing collection of imperial rulings and his planned collection of juristic texts would not make knowledge of the law easy. He contemplated the possibility, no more than the possibility, of an introductory text for students. Nothing in *De conceptione Digestorum* suggests that such a textbook, if it were ever produced, would also be legislation. As work on the *Digest* continued, Justinian's compilers recognized the connection of their work with legal education as it existed in their time. As the two prefaces of 533 show, the compilers saw the *Digest* also very much as a teaching tool. But legal education before and in Justinian's time began through an elementary text. If the difficult *Digest* was to be the backbone of legal education, it would need to be introduced by an elementary textbook. And this textbook would have to be authoritative. Hence in its turn it had to be written by leading professors and then enacted as law.

Almost inevitably, then, as soon as the future *Digest* was seen also as an important teaching tool, the preliminary introductory text would seem to be necessary. And since it is in the nature of things for humans to be swayed by what they know, the elementary books used for teaching beginners at Beyrouth and Constantinople, especially the *Institutes* of Gaius, became the model.

One might think that the draftsmen would have more freedom here than

with the *Digest:* after all, they were not attributing each passage in the *Institutes* to
a particular jurist. But such freedom they could not psychologically give themselves. The resulting textbook is as strictly Roman, not Byzantine, not Christian, as the *Digest.* It is bound by the Roman past. As already noticed, Justinian
enumerates the sources of law in *J.*1.2.3: "Written law is statute, *plebiscita,* decrees
of the senate, pronouncements of the emperors, edicts of the magistrates, the answers of jurists." Alas no! Law, out of context, was misleading the student from
the very start.[52] The only source of law then existing was the pronouncements
of the emperors!

But I have no desire to emphasize here, as I did in the beginning of this chapter, the impact of the old Roman outlook. Rather, I want to consider the impact on the three draftsmen—however they divided their task—of their meth-
odology. They seem to have had in front of them when they worked only the
writings of the old writers of elementary works.[53] This focus even appears from
§11 of *De conceptione Digestorum.* When these works were insufficient, the draftsmen relied upon their memories, with disastrous results. Even new law may be
out of context in Justinian's beginners' handbook. Three glaring misstatements
of law in this "Nutshell as Statute" will suffice. The instances are not usually
considered together. Various explanations are offered for the differences between them and the law set out in the *Digest* or *Code.* When they are looked at
together, a clear picture emerges: the compilers of the *Institutes* were working out
of context whenever they needed more than was set out in the elementary works.
I will give three examples.

> *Example 1. J.*4.6.7: Likewise the *actio Serviana* and the *actio quasi Serviana* which
> is also called the *actio hypothecaria* take their being from the jurisdiction of
> the praetor. But one uses the *actio Serviana* with respect to the goods of a
> tenant-farmer which are bound to him by the law of pledge for the rent
> of the farm. Creditors, however, pursue pledges [*pignora*], or hypothecs,
> [*hypothecae*], by the *actio quasi Serviana.* There is no difference between a *pignus*
> or a *hypotheca* with regard to the *actio hypothecaria.*

Pignus and hypotheca were a form of pledge. The terms may be used in-
distinguishably, but when they are not, then *pignus* indicates a pledge with delivery and *hypotheca* one without. The jurist Marcian tells us that the distinction
is purely verbal.[54] The actio Serviana and the actio hypothecaria were actions
available to the creditor to take over the object pledged when the creditor was

in default. The precise relationship between the two actions is not clear. My preferred solution is that the actio Serviana lay against the debtor and the actio hypothecaria against any other person who had control of the thing.[55] What matters here is that, in the law of Justinian as otherwise described,[56] the actio Serviana was not the remedy of a landowner for a claim for rent against the goods of a tenant farmer. The interdictum Salvianum fulfilled that function.[57] Significantly, a source for J.4.6.7 cannot be found in the institutional writings of classical jurists.[58] The redactors of the *Institutes*, not having a source in front of them, relied—wrongly—on memory.

> *Example 2. J.4.9pr.:* In respect of animals that lack reason, if they cause damage through wantonness, passion or wildness a noxal action was provided by the Twelve Tables (if such animals are surrendered noxally, that frees the defendant from liability because that is the provision of the Twelve Tables): for instance, if a horse that kicks struck someone with a hoof, or a bull given to goring, gores. This action lies in respect of those animals that act contrary to nature [*contra naturam*]. But if the fierceness is congenital, the action does not lie. Accordingly [*Denique*] if a bear escapes from its owner and thus does harm, at one time the owner could not be sued because he ceased to be owner when the beast escaped.

This text concerns the famous *actio de pauperie*, the action for damage caused by animals. Not only, as we shall see, does it conflict with the law set out in the *Digest*, but it is illogical on its face. The text tells us that if an animal acting contra naturam causes harm, the owner is liable, but not if the wildness is congenital. The illustration of this point concerns a bear that escapes. But the reason then given for the owner's lack of liability is not the bear's natural wildness but the fact that by the escape he is no longer owner.

I have translated *contra naturam* literally as "contrary to nature," but the usual understanding, as indeed would appear to be correct in this context, is "contrary to the nature of the species."[59] But this sense is then contradicted by *Digest* texts. Thus Ulpian in D.9.1.1.9 allows the action when an ox crushes someone with a cart or overturns something on him. Moreover, Quintus Mucius, according to D.9.1.1.11, gave an action against the owner of the aggressor animal when two rams or two bulls fought and the aggressor killed the other. For a ram or a bull to fight another of the same species can scarcely be regarded as contrary to the nature of the species.

Still, such is the power of the *Institutes'* passage that it seems to be usually believed that the *Digest* text, 9.1.1.7, also shows that the action lay only when the animal acted contrary to the nature of its species.[60] In fact, the meaning of this *Digest* text seems to me to be other, especially in light of its context: after all, D.9.1.1.7, 9.1.1.9, and 9.1.1.11 are all part of the same text of Ulpian book 18 on the Edict: "Et generaliter haec actio locum habet, quotiens contra naturam fera mota pauperiem dedit" ("And speaking generally, this action is available whenever a beast, moved contrary to nature, caused damage").

Here, too, I would accept the usual view that *contra naturam* means "contrary to the nature of the species."[61] But the text is not saying that the actio de pauperie lies *only* when an animal acts contrary to the nature of the species. Rather, its claim is that generally speaking when an animal does so act contra naturam, the action will lie. The purpose of the text is not to exclude the action in other cases, such as where bulls or rams fight. The issue of liability is a tricky one. Clearly, causation is one issue. It has to be shown that in some sense the animal caused the harm. But causation is not enough. For the liability for human behavior there had also to be negligence or malice. For animals there would be liability if the animal caused the harm plus, in the general case, when the animal acted contra naturam. Thus there would be no liability if a horse kicked out because of pain, but there would be liability if it kicked when being petted. There would be none when the animal was provoked by another.[62] But there would be liability when one aggressor animal, acting as its species does, kills one of its own kind. The line will not be easy to draw.[63]

In this instance, too, there is a difference in the law as set out in the *Digest* and in the *Institutes*. I would not try to reconcile the law in the two versions. Rather, the *Digest* gives the intentions of Justinian's compilers. The draftsmen of the *Institutes* did not consult it, with unfortunate results. The redactors of the *Institutes* dealt with law out of context.

We do not have the account of the actio de pauperie that existed in Gaius's *Institutes* because the relevant page of the manuscript, 219 of the Verona Codex, is illegible.[64] But the verbal congruence of the version known as the *Autun Gaius* §81, and *J.4.9pr.*, indicate that liability would ensue if the animal acted "lascivia aut fervore aut feritate," "from sexual wantonness, or by passion or by wildness." All of these three nouns, or any of them, would cover the case of a bull attacking another and killing it. None of them would indicate that the bull was acting contrary to the nature of bulls.

The subsequent history of the understanding of the owner's liability for damage caused by an animal is complex and will not be discussed here. It is enough to notice that because of the fundamental role of the *Institutes* in legal education, the emphasis has continually been on it and not on the *Digest*. The actio de pauperie still exists in the republic of South Africa, where the basic view is that for liability the animal must have acted "contra naturam sui generis."[65]

Example 3. J.3.23pr.: Sale is contracted as soon as there is agreement on the price, even though it be not paid nor earnest [*arra*] given in respect of it; for what is given by way of earnest is but evidence that the sale is concluded. This, however, applies to sales which are made without writing; for we have made no innovation in respect of such sales. But, for sales effected in writing, we ordain that the sale shall not be complete unless the document of sale be completed in the very hand of the contracting parties or drafted by another but signed by the parties; and, if it be prepared by a scribe, only when it be completed and executed by the parties. So long as any of these requirements be lacking, there is room for reconsideration and either vendor or purchaser may resile from the contract with impunity. However, we allow them to withdraw with impunity only if no earnest has been given: for in that event, whether the sale be in or without writing, the party who refuses to implement the contract loses what he has given, if it be the purchaser and, if it be the vendor, he must restore two-fold: and this, although nothing be expressed about the earnest.

Emptio et venditio contrahitur, simulatque de pretio convenerit, quamvis nondum pretium numeratum sit ac ne arra quidem data fuerit. nam quod arrae nomine datur, argumentum est emptionis et venditionis contractae. sed haec quidem de emptionibus et venditionibus, quae sine scriptura consistunt, optinere oportet: nam nihil a nobis in huiusmodi venditionibus innovatum est. in his autem quae scriptura conficiuntur non aliter perfectam esse emptionem et venditionem constituimus, nisi et instrumenta emptionis fuerint conscripta vel manu propria contrahentium, vel ab alio quidem scripta, a contrahente autem subscripta et, si per tabellionem fiunt, nisi et completiones acceperint et fuerint partibus absoluta. donec enim aliquid ex his deest, et paenitentiae locus est et potest emptor vel vendi-

tor sine poena recedere ab emptione. ita tamen impune recedere eis con-
cedimus, nisi iam arrarum nomine aliquid fuerit datum : hoc etenim subsecuto, sive in scriptis sive sine scriptis venditio celebrata est, is qui recusat
adimplere contractum, si quidem emptor est, perdit quod dedit, si vero
venditor, duplum restituere compellitur, licet nihil super arris expres-
sum est.

Again in the compilation of Justinian, the text on *arra,* "earnest money," and
sales in writing does not stand alone. But this time the counterpart of the *Institutes'* text stems not from the *Digest* but from the *Code,* even in fact from a constitution of Justinian himself, *C.4.21.17,* dated to 528. Once again, the problem
is the reconciliation of the two texts, and the number of solutions proffered is
enormous.[66]

The *Code* text is generally—but not universally—admitted to be the earlier
(with which *communis opinio* I agree)[67] and gives rise to no great problem. The
Latin need not be quoted. The rescript enacts in its principium with regard to
certain specific contracts, including sale and *arrarum datio,* the giving of earnest
money, that if the parties have agreed to put the contract in writing, then the
contract will be of no effect until the writing has been properly completed, that
is, reduced to its final form and confirmed by the subscription of the parties[68]
and, where it is being drawn up by a notary, completed by him and finally released to the parties. A draft in the handwriting of one or both of the parties,
we are told, will not be enough. Section 2 enacts that where arra is given, whether
with writing or without, with respect to the making of a sale, then if the person
who promised to sell repudiates the sale, he will be compelled to pay double the
value of the arra, and if the person who promised to buy withdraws from the
purchase, then he will forfeit the arra he has given. In this part of the constitution, "sive in scriptis sive sine scriptis" refers to the giving of arra.[69] The difficulty lies in the interpretation of *J.3.23pr.*

From the beginning of the *Institutes'* text to *innovatum est,* the text deals with
unwritten sales, and Justinian categorically states that he has made no change in
the law relating to them. From there to *fuerit datum,* he is concerned with sales
which are to be put into writing. He declares, first, that such a sale is not perfect until the agreement has been put into writing and the formalities demanded
by *C.4.21.17* completed; second, that as long as anything in the formalities is

lacking, either party may withdraw without penalty; third, that he can only so withdraw without penalty where no arra has been given. At this stage one could expect Justinian to explain what happens in cases of sale to be put into writing where arra is given and one party withdraws before the formalities are completed. And this, I suggest, is what he does do. My view is supported by the words "hoc etenim subsecuto," which clearly link the sentence in which they occur with what precedes. The words which cause all the difficulty, "sive in scriptis sive sine scriptis venditio celebrata est," should be translated: "Whether the sale [scil. which has to be put into writing with other attendant formalities] was agreed upon in writing [i.e., but which lacks the other formalities] or without writing." In other words, the parties have agreed on the terms of the sale but have declared it should be put into writing, and at the time of the withdrawal either there is no writing or there is writing that does not meet all the requirements laid down in C.4.21.17 and repeated in this *lex*. On this interpretation, the *Institutes'* passage would be in complete harmony with the *Code* and would also be entirely self-consistent. It is most unlikely that, in this passage, the compilers, after declaring that they had not altered the classical law of unwritten sale, would have surreptitiously introduced a new rule (not mentioned at all in the *Digest*) or could have allowed what is, on any other interpretation, so blatant a mistake, even if it did give the de facto position.[70] A view that involves holding (1) that we have suddenly moved to a general discussion of arra in sale, (2) that Justinian is altering, deliberately or accidentally, the law of unwritten sale, and (3) that carelessly he has left out *celebranda*, "to be reduced," after *in scriptis* needs too many conjectures to be readily acceptable.

Justinian was not innovating on arra in the *Institutes*; he retains the classical law for unwritten sales and follows his own constitution in the *Code* for sales to be put into writing. Confusion has arisen as a result of his careless use of words, but his choice is not unreasonable or indeed unprecedented, and the meaning was probably clear to his contemporaries.[71] The compilers did not have the *Code* in front of them. They did not check the wording. They expressed accurately the substance of the constitution but in imprecise language. They were operating out of context.

We have now looked at three instances in Justinian's *Institutes* where law is out of context. None of them directly involves a transplant (except from Rome to early Byzantium). The oddity—and it is considerable—has had important consequences. The legislative draftsmen who intended no reform but to repeat existing law in simple form did not have the existing law in front of them, and they got it wrong.

But law, as I keep insisting, often does not progress in a rational, well-rounded fashion. The example of contracts of sale to be reduced to writing is instructive also in quite a different way. Before Justinian, sale was one of the four consensual contracts, formed when the parties agreed on the terms. But Justinian declared in C.4.21.17 that if the parties agreed that a sale was to be put into writing, there was no contract until it was formalized in writing. The same applied to barter, gifts, and *transactiones*. But what about the other consensual contacts, especially lease (*locatio conductio*)? As an ongoing contract, with issues like a deposit, failure to pay rent on time, reparation for damage, removing on the due date, continuation of the contract, and so on, locatio conductio was particularly likely to be reduced to writing. But no reform akin to that for sale occurred.

I will end this section with a final example of a very different character. It again derives from reliance on classical elementary textbooks, especially on Gaius's *Institutes*, and from the compilers' not having in front of them up-to-date works of a different type. But this time we have not so much a mistake of law or even a clumsy account of contemporary law as a curious blend of obsolete law and insufficient modern law. Yet the subject matter is vital: procedure, or the law of actions. From the treatment of actions in Justinian's *Institutes*, book 4, one cannot get a picture, even an elementary one, of procedure in Justinian's time. Nor is the law of actions set out systematically anywhere in the *Digest* or the *Code*. Only with the aid of the *Codex Theodosianus* and with enormous difficulty can modern scholars piece together even an outline of how the legal process worked in theory.

The main account of procedure in the *Institutes* is in book 4, title 6. We will get some impression of how unsatisfactory it is when we notice that in W. W. Buckland's classic account of the main form of procedure, the *cognitio extraordinaria*, the title is mentioned just once.[72]

I will discuss only some fragments of title 6, and I will, for purposes of demonstration, emphasize the writings of the three greatest English exponents of Roman law of this century, J. B. Moyle,[73] W. W. Buckland,[74] and J. A. C. Thomas.[75] Of these, the first and the last not only produced a translation but

wrote a commentary. They are all conscious of the woeful inadequacy of Justinian's treatment but do not spell it out. They are all aware of the dependence on
Gaius but do not seem to comment on its consequences.

"J.4.6.1. The principal division of all actions, in which an issue between parties is aired before judges or arbiters, is into two kinds: for actions are either *in
rem* or in *personam*."

Moyle says:

§ I. The distinction of actions into real and personal is based in origin
on difference of formula, to which there is an obvious reference in Justinian's words 'intendit . . . dare facere oportere,' '(rem) suam esse inten-
dat,' which, however, have no technical meaning in the text, but merely
describe in general terms the plaintiff's contention, as expressed in the li-
bellus conventionis, or writ of summons by which the action was com-
menced. Other differences, e.g. in procedure, and in the nature of the
security to be given by the parties, have now disappeared, and a real differs from a personal action only in the nature of the right for whose protection it is brought: the opposition is material only, not formal. It will
be found that in § 20 inf. Justinian interposes a third class—actiones
mixtae—between actions which are real and those which are personal.[76]

Thomas:

§ 1 introduces the fundamental distinction of actions. Though in § 20 the
Emperor speaks of mixed actions, the basic division of actions was into
those *in rem*, the assertion of a right in a thing, and those *in personam*, the
assertion of a right against an individual. In the formulary system, this had
been reflected in the wording of the *formula:* in an action *in rem*, the statement of claim (*intentio*) mentioned only the plaintiff—'If it appears that
the thing belongs to the plaintiff by Quiritary title'—while that of an action *in personam* mentioned both parties—e.g. 'If it appears that the defendant ought to give to the plaintiff the slave Stichus'. In the time of Justinian, the distinction was one purely of substance and not of form.[77]

"J.4.6.3. Now these actions that we have mentioned and others like them derive from civil causes existing at law. But there are others which the praetor, by
virtue of his jurisdiction, introduced, both *in rem* and *in personam*, which also must
be illustrated by examples." How the actions were introduced at civil law was

irrelevant. There was even in classical law only one important civil court for citizens, that of the urban praetor. With the disappearance of the formulary system, centuries before, any distinction between civil actions and praetorian had long gone.[78]

"J.4.6.14. Actions having thus been distinguished, it is certain that a plaintiff cannot claim his own thing from another in the form, 'If it appear that he ought to give the thing': for what belongs to the plaintiff ought not to be given to him." The words "si paret eum dare oportet," "If it appear that he ought to give the thing," are taken straight from G.4.4.

Moyle says: "§ 14. Of course the expression 'si paret,' etc. has no formal or processual signification in Justinian: all that is meant is that a plaintiff cannot by a real action demand conveyance (datio) but merely recognition of his ownership or other ius in rem."[79]

"J.4.6.17. Naturally, if a deposit action be brought in respect of what was deposited because of riot, fire, a house falling down or shipwreck, the praetor gives an action for twofold damages but only against the depositee himself or his heir where the depositee deliberately does wrong: and in this case the action is mixed." The long obsolete lawmaking powers of the praetor keep coming up as contemporary law.

"J.4.6.21. Now all actions are framed [*conceptae*] for single, twofold, threefold or fourfold damages: no action lies for more than fourfold."

Moyle: "The expression in simplum, in duplum etc. concepta, which refers to the condemnatio [a vital clause of a *formula*], is another trace of the survival of the formula in the later procedure."[80]

Thomas: "Mention of actions as conceived for single, twofold, etc. damages reflects the language of the old *formula*."[81]

"J.4.6.28. Now some actions are of good faith, others of strict law."

Thomas: "The distinction between actions of strict law which appears in § 28 is again a relic of the formulary process under which it arose."[82]

Examples of a failure to modernize the account of actions abound and can even be found outside Justinian's *Institutes*. I will leave the last word to Buckland:

Much of the old terminology remained. We still hear of *exceptio, replicatio, litis contestatio*, interdict, but the terms have changed significance. When Justinian said that an *exceptio doli* was available he meant that *dolus* might be pleaded and would (in general) bar the claim; he did not mean that it was pleaded in the old way. A possessory interdict was, for him, a possessory action: the actual issue of an interdict was a thing of the past. But some *exceptiones* were now disposed of before *litis contestatio*, e.g. those dealing with capacity of parties, representatives, or the court, and also, perhaps, *exc. praeiudicialis*, and those alleging previous judgement or *transactio*, or bar by lapse of time. Others were dealt with in the old way with two modifications. *Exceptiones peremptoriae* not claimed could be brought in at a later stage, without *restitutio in integrum*, and, as an indirect result of express legislation, some *exceptiones* no longer destroyed the action.[83]

It was not just in the *Institutes* that the obsolete past dominated the present. Still, only there was a coherent attempt made to set out the law of procedure systematically. But any attempt to give the law as it was failed.

JUSTINIAN'S NATURAL LAW

Natural law theories have a distinguished ancient history whether in a Platonic,[84] Aristotelian, or Stoic mold, the last being exemplified at Rome by Cicero. Christian acceptance of the notion is seen as early as Paul, Romans 2.12ff.

All who have sinned apart from the law will also perish apart from the law, and all who have sinned under the law will be judged by the law. 13. For it is not the hearers of the law who are righteous in God's sight, but the doers of the law who will be justified. 14. When Gentiles, who do not possess the law, do instinctively what the law requires, these, though not having the law, are a law to themselves. 15. They show that what the law requires is written on their hearts, to which their own conscience also bears witness; and their conflicting thoughts will accuse or perhaps excuse them on 16. the day when, according to my gospel, God, through Jesus Christ, will judge the secret thoughts of all.[85]

Most interesting for us are verses 14 and 15, especially the beginning of the former, which I would translate: "for when nations not having the law do by nature [φύσει] the things of the law . . ." Thus, Gentiles, to whom the Law was not given, may instinctively, by nature, follow the Law. For them the Law may exist without promulgation. The law they follow by nature is God's positive commandment. This statement, I believe, incorporates a new approach. A rather different Christian approach is taken by Lactantius (circa 240–320):

> Therefore the law of God must be undertaken, which may direct us to this path; that sacred, that heavenly law, which Marcus Tullius, in his third book respecting the Republic, has described almost with a divine voice; whose words I have subjoined, that I might not speak at greater length: "True law is right reason in agreement with nature. It extends to all, unchanging, everlasting. It summons to duty by commanding, and it averts from wrongdoing by prohibiting. It does not order or prohibit upright persons in vain, nor does it influence the wicked by command or prohibition. It is a sin to alter this law, nor is it permitted to derogate any part of it, nor abrogate it altogether. Nor indeed can we be released from this law either by the senate or by the people, nor is any other expounder or interpreter of it to be looked for. Nor will there be one law at Rome another at Athens, one law now, another later, but one law, eternal and unchangeable, will contain all people and for all time. There will be one master and ruler, one god over all, the inventor, author and promulgator of this law. And he who shall not obey this will flee from himself, and, despising the nature of man, will suffer the greatest punishments through this very thing, even though he shall have escaped the other punishments which are supposed to exist." Who that is acquainted with the mystery of God [i.e., a Christian] could so significantly relate the law of God, as a man [i.e., Cicero] far removed from the knowledge of the truth has set forth that law? But I consider that they who speak true things unconsciously are to be so regarded as though they prophesied under the influence of some spirit. But if he had known or explained this also, in what precepts the law itself consisted, as he clearly saw the force and purport of the divine law, he would not have discharged the office of a philosopher, but of a prophet. And because he was unable to do this, it must be done by us, to whom the law itself has been delivered by the one great Master and Ruler of all, God.

The quotation from Cicero *De re publica* 3.22.33 embodies the Stoic notion that natural law, true law, is right reason in agreement with nature. It is of divine origin; it is independent of human promulgation and cannot be changed by human action. Elsewhere, significantly for us, as it will turn out, Cicero adds that nat-

ural law is common to god and man, since it is based on reasoning, and therefore other animals do not participate in it.[86] Lactantius fully endorses Cicero's
opinion, though he takes the author of this true law to be the Christian God. In
what follows in book 6 Lactantius develops a Christian notion of divine or natural law, with many references to Cicero.

For the developing early Christian concept, no one is more important than
Augustine of Hippo (354–430). A few illustrations from book 1 of his *De libero
arbitrio* will set the scene:

> 3.15. A. So tell me first why you think it bad to commit adultery. Is it be-
> cause the law forbids it?
>
> E. It is not bad on that account, because it is forbidden by law; but it
> is forbidden by law on that account; because it is bad.

In a different context: "5.33. Surely we will dare to declare these laws to be unjust or void? For it does not seem to me to be a law that is not just."

Further on in the dialogue, at 6.47, he argues that in a state there may be
passed two contradictory statutes, in which case the earlier is void, but this does
not entail that one of them is unjust. Then:

> 6.48. A. Therefore let us call that law, if you please, temporary that, how-
> ever just it may be, nonetheless through time may justly be changed.
>
> E. Let us so call it.
>
> A. What then? That law that is called supreme reason to which obe-
> dience is always owed, and by which the good earn a happy life, the evil
> a miserable life, by which finally that law that we call temporary is rightly
> made and rightly changed, may it not to any intelligent person seem un-
> changeable and eternal? 49. Or can it sometimes be unjust that the wicked
> are wretched, but the good are happy? Or that a modest and serious
> people create state officers for itself, but that a wicked and evil people
> lacks that freedom?
>
> E. I see this to be an eternal and unchangeable law.

Thus for Augustine, it is not law that makes an act bad but the wickedness of
an act that causes it to be condemned by law. An unjust law is not law. Human
law is temporary and changeable but need not on that account be unjust. The
law to which obedience is always owed is called supreme reason: it is eternal and
unchangeable and is always just.

Elsewhere he explains this eternal law. "The eternal law is divine reason or the will of God commanding that the natural order be kept, forbidding it to be overturned."[87] The eternal, always just law, always to be obeyed, is the will of God. Referring to Psalm 1.2, which talks of the happiness of those who delight in God's law and meditate on it day and night, Augustine adds on his own account, "because the will of God is the very law of God."[88]

But none of this learning on natural law, pagan or Christian, had any impact on the Roman jurists. Though, given the education of the time, they would be versed in philosophy, natural law plays little role in their discussion of law. They saw law purely as positive law even though jurists were not practitioners. In the empire a large proportion of the best-known jurists were imperial bureaucrats, and they too saw law purely as positive law. The notion of natural law, airy fairy stuff that the courts would ignore, an immanent omnipresence floating in the sky with no visible means of support, was not something they would deal with. But the notion was around them, and they had to say something about it. This fact accounts for Ulpian's definition, recorded in D.1.1.1.3: "*Ius naturale* is that which nature has taught to all animals; for it is not a law specific to mankind but is common to all animals — land animals, sea animals, and the birds as well. Out of this comes the union of man and woman which we call marriage, and the procreation of children, and their rearing. So we can see that the other animals, wild beasts included, are rightly understood to be acquainted with this law."

As later scholars pointed out, especially in the seventeenth century (but also much earlier),[89] this was a definition of instinct, not of law.[90] Natural law so defined was meaningless and hence could be ignored. It was so defined, I believe, in order to be meaningless precisely so that it could be ignored. The contrast with Cicero's claim that natural law was based on reason, hence was not shared with other animals, could scarcely be greater. For Ulpian, reason does not come into it. Nor does morality.[91]

T. Honoré has a different interpretation and believes Ulpian had a philosophical position: he was a Neoplatonic and believed animals had a rational character.[92] As frequently, Honoré is remarkably indifferent to what the texts actually say. He paraphrases Ulpian as asserting "that animals are thought to know about marriage, the procreation of children and their education by experience (*peritia*), and hence not merely by instinct." *Peritia*, "experience" or "skill," does not imply rationality. Actually, "skill" is a better translation than "experience," which need not be implied. But Ulpian actually says "hence comes the union of male and female *that we call marriage."* Honoré then claims that Ulpian made liability in the actio de pauperie depend on the animal acting contra naturam and says: "His examples show that, here too, he is attributing rational behavior to animals." But even if Ulpian did make liability depend on animals acting contra naturam, this would not indicate that he attributed rational conduct to them. And Ulpian's standard for liability was not restricted to an animal acting contra naturam: Honoré ignores D.9.1.1.11.

Gaius's *Institutes* is perhaps less absurd than Ulpian on the topic but no more uplifting. It contains no definition of natural law but tells us that the law that natural reason makes for all mankind is applied in the same way everywhere and is called the *ius gentium,* "law of all peoples," because it is common to all nations.[93] There is scope for confusion between ius naturale and ius gentium.

Justinian's *Institutes,* being meant for beginners, is by far the most instructive text for us on Justinian's compilers' attitude toward natural law: "*J.1.2pr.:* Natural law is that which nature instils in all animals. For this law is not peculiar to humankind but is shared by all animals which are born on land or in the air or sea. From it derives that association of man and woman that we call marriage; so also the procreation and rearing of issue: for we see that the other animals also are imbued with skill in this law." Again ius naturale appears as nothing more than instinct.[94] But it is the construction of the whole of *J.1.2* that needs to be examined.

> *J.1.2.1:* Civil law and the law of nations, however, are distinguished in this way. All peoples who are governed by laws and customs use law which is in part particular to themselves, in part common to all men: the law which each people has established for itself is particular to that state and is styled civil law as being peculiarly of that state: but what natural reason has established among all men is observed equally by all nations and is designated *ius gentium* or the law of nations, being that which all nations obey. Hence the Roman people observe partly their own particular law, partly that which is common to all peoples. Which is which, we shall explain whenever it is desirable to do so.

The law that applies to all people everywhere and thus is part of Roman law is called ius gentium and is made by natural reason. This view is starting to sound like Cicero's notion of natural law and seems to exist in the real world of men, but it has no practical or spiritual significance.[95] In §2 Justinian discusses the law of a particular state and continues: "The law of nations, on the other hand, is common to all humankind. For, through force of circumstances and human needs, peoples have developed certain measures for themselves: wars have arisen with subsequent captivity and slavery—which is contrary to natural law (for, by natural law, originally, all men were born free). From the law of nations also come virtually all the contracts, such as sale, hire, partnership, deposit, loan and countless others."

A contrast is drawn between ius naturale and ius gentium. The latter arises from the human condition. Slavery is contrary to ius naturale but is part of the ius gentium. Nothing, it must be emphasized, indicates a moral dimension here to ius naturale.[96] Slavery is contrary to natural law. This statement means not that it is an evil but only that it was not the original state of affairs. Likewise the freeing of slaves could not be part of the original state of affairs and hence is not part of ius naturale. Unsurprisingly, at *D.1.1.4pr.* Ulpian declares that manumission of slaves belongs to the ius gentium.

At *J.1.2.3*, Justinian turns to a different categorization of types of law: written and unwritten. Titles *J.1.2.4* to *J.1.2.10* deal with the sources of positive law. Ius naturale and ius gentium are ignored. But they finally surface again at *J.1.2.11*: "Now, natural laws which are followed by all nations alike, deriving from divine providence, remain always constant and immutable: but those which each state establishes for itself are liable to frequent change whether by the tacit consent of the people or by subsequent legislation." *Iura naturalia* is redefined. It is no longer the ius naturale of *J.1.2pr.* but the ius gentium. On this confusion I will not pause here. What interests us is that this law of nature is declared to be eternal and established by divine providence. No juristic source for the text has been found.[97] A divine source for natural law is predicated but is not nearer defined. The formulation is remarkably similar to that of Cicero in *De re publica*. There is no indication of Christianity. And this is my whole point. In Justinian's codification the treatment of natural law is very much out of context.

To conclude this section. Long before Justinian's Byzantium there was a philosophical tradition of natural law. Christian natural law doctrines had emerged and would continue to emerge. There were many able Christian lawyers. But these features of the legal landscape are all absent from Justinian's legal compilation.

Christian natural law had a great future with figures like Aquinas and Suárez. But the *Corpus iuris civilis* could play no important mainstream role.[98]

RELIGION IN THE SECOND *CODE*

It might be suggested that the significance of law out of context has been greatly exaggerated in the preceding three sections. I have, it might be urged, ignored the importance of Justinian's *Code* in this regard: after all, the *Code* of 530 was the earliest part of the codification, and the *Digest* and *Institutes* were thus dependent on it. The *Code* was the earliest, and no doubt its contents had some impact on the *Digest* and the *Institutes*. Perhaps it was not so necessary to insert Christianity into the *Digest* and *Institutes?* But I should emphasize at the outset of this section two points. First, the treatment of natural law in the *Digest* and *Institutes* was not influenced by the *Code*, which does not treat the subject. Second, the priority of the *Code* is not in issue with regard to the materials in front of the draftsmen of the *Institutes:* they simply failed to consult anything other than elementary works. The crux of the issue must relate to Christianity.

But for the impact of the *Code* on legal consciousness, two factors are of the deepest significance. The first concerns the role of the *Code* in legal education. No such role appears from any of the three prefaces to the *Code*. Presumably none was envisaged when the first *Code* was compiled. But then we have in §5 of *Omnem rei* for the *Digest* (533): "If they imbue themselves well with these and strive to read and thoroughly understand the *Codex* of *constitutiones* (enactments) during the course of their fifth year, during which they are called *prolytai*, they will lack for nothing in legal knowledge, but will embrace the whole of it from beginning to end in their minds; and this single branch of knowledge, issuing from us at the present time, will achieve an admirable perfection, a thing which has happened in almost none of the other branches of learning, the number of which is infinite, however worthless some may be."

And in the preface to the *Institutes* §3, which is addressed to beginners in the law, we have:

> When this had been achieved with the support of God, we summoned and gave a special charge to Tribonian, the distinguished master and ex-quaestor of our sacred palace, and to Theophilus and Dorotheus, eminent professors; three men of whose acumen, legal learning and fidelity to our commands we had abundant proof. They were, by our authority and with our encouragement, to compose Institutes so that you might acquire your first rudiments of law not from ancient stories but through the splendour

of the Emperor and that both your ears and your minds might receive the truth in these matters without that which is unnecessary or erroneous. And whereas previously at least four years would elapse before you came to read imperial rescripts, begin now at the outset with this work, meriting such honour and rejoicing in the fact that now both the commencement and the completion of your legal education proceed from the mouth of the Emperor.

Thus students would be introduced to the *Code* and, with it, to any intimation of Christianity and law only in their fifth, and final, year of study.

That the *Code* should be thought of for legal education only belatedly and then only for fifth year students should be no surprise, astonishing though this might appear at first sight. As far as all our evidence goes, which is only for the law school at Beirut, imperial rulings were not taught before Justinian until the fifth year of law study, which was then an optional year.[99] Justinian was making these rulings an integral but final part of law school. It is worth emphasizing that in the preface to his *Institutes*, which has just been quoted, Justinian prides himself on introducing law students to imperial law right from the beginning of their studies, but the imperial law in question is that in his *Institutes*, which bears no trace of Christianity. In the nature of things it is certain that law students would have their mind-set fixed long before they began their fifth year. No doubt they would be imbued with Christianity but not through exposure to legal studies or to the official statutory law. Early Byzantine law, as students would experience it from their studies, would be far from their daily reality.

The second factor that concerns us is the very limited scope of Christian impact on law even in the *Code* itself. We have, of course, only the second *Code* that dates from 534. This work is in twelve books, divided into titles (or chapters). Religious law specifically is dealt with only in the first thirteen titles out of fifty-six in book 1, a minuscule amount.

Christianity seems to be relegated to the background even in the *Code*. This point becomes still clearer when we make a direct comparison between the *Theodosian Code* and Justinian's *Code*. It is possible to take soundings for specific issues. By my calculations, which must be approximate only, an undifferentiated heading of "Christians" would result in 110 texts in the *Theodosian Code*,[100] 23 in that of Justinian;[101] a heading of "Jews" would find 15 for the *Codex Theodosianus*[102] and 6 for that of Justinian.[103] Sacrilege would give us 11 for Theodosius [104] and 6 for Justinian.[105] The relevance of this difference becomes even more obvious when we look at the rescripts on private law. The proportions are then often reversed. Thus for the contract of sale, I find 9 rescripts in the *Theodosian Code* [106] and 11 in Justinian's; [107] for possession, 5 in the former [108] and 16 in the latter.[109]

Christianity is muted in the *Codex Justiniani* in a way that it is not in the *Codex Theodosianus*. This statement holds despite the fact that Justinian's *Code* was part of a larger scheme that otherwise totally ignored Christianity. How can this be? What follows is conjectural, but it does accord with the little evidence that we have.

We do not have the first Justinianic *Code* but only the second. Did the two have the same structure? I think not. The second *Code* has basically the structure of the *Digest* except for the early titles of book 1 of the *Code*, which are concerned with religion. The structure of the *Digest* is basically that of the old praetorian Edict, which is inharmonious in the extreme.

How could such a structure for the *Code* have occurred to the compilers? It could not, I believe, have occurred to the compilers of the first *Code*, working before the *Digest* was thought of. Their natural course would have been to follow the rather different scheme of the *Theodosian Code*. This afforded a model, and it is human nature to follow a model. As we have seen, no plan existed for using the first *Code* in legal education.

Thus Justinian's first *Code* probably followed the arrangement of the *Theodosian Code* except perhaps that the titles specifically on Christianity appeared at the beginning. Christianity and public law generally were relatively prominent. When the compilation of the *Digest* was in progress, and a fundamental role was seen for it in education, it became obvious that imperial rulings also had to be studied in school, especially because so many of them are dated after the time when the jurists stopped writing. To fulfill an educational role it was important that the rulings appear in a known order, which could only be that of the *Digest*. This rearrangement was one of the reasons for the preparation of a second *Code*. The rescripts on the organization of the Church and related topics, which had no counterpart in the *Digest*, had to be put someplace, and they were very reasonably placed at the beginning. Thereafter, rescripts excerpted from the *Code* were generally to follow the arrangement of the *Digest*. This layout would involve some rearrangement of the order of titles, rather less of the order of rescripts within a title. Still, the dependence of the order in the second *Code* on that of the *Digest* had further consequences. Rescripts on subjects not treated in the *Digest*, such as matters relating to Christianity and, indeed, public law generally, were downplayed. Accordingly, emphasis on the Church and on public law in Justinian's second *Code* is very different from that in the *Theodosian Code*.

To conclude this chapter. In the treatment of Christianity and natural law, the law set out in Justinian's *Institutes*, *Digest*, and *Code* is very much out of context and gives a false impression. If this is the case with Christianity as a result of reliance on much older sources, then it will equally be the case in other situations. One example may suffice. In classical law the scope of actions was strictly prescribed by the form of process, the *formula*. If the legal facts of the claim did not fit within a particular formula, then there could be no action unless the praetor allowed on equitable grounds an ad hoc remedy called either an *actio utilis* or an *actio in factum*. For instance, the main remedy for damage to property was the "actio legis Aquiliae," "action on the Aquilian law," but this was granted only to the owner. The praetor granted the ad hoc remedies to others when it was equitable to do so: for instance to a possessor in good faith or to one who had a life rent in the property. The actions of Justinian's time no longer had such formulaic procedure. The formulae had been replaced by the procedure known as the "cognitio extra ordinem," which did not hold to the strict division between one action and another.[110] Nevertheless, the *Digest* texts on the lex Aquilia and other matters still discuss whether the direct action or an actio utilis or in factum will lie.

Finally, there is an irony in law out of context in that, at times, precisely by being out of context, law may subsequently become beneficial elsewhere as a result of being still more out of context. In point of language, the *Institutes*, the *Digest*, and (to a lesser extent) the *Code* were out of context, being in Latin in a Greek-speaking environment. In language, Justinian's *Novels* were in context, being mainly in Greek. The most noteworthy event in European legal history from the twelfth to the late eighteenth century was the so-called reception of Roman law. What was received was material in the *Institutes*, the *Digest*, and the *Code* but not what was in the *Novels*. The reason was that Latin was understood in Europe at the formative period, but Greek was not. If in language the *Institutes*, the *Digest*, and the *Code* had been in context in Justinian's Byzantium, modern European law would be vastly different.[111]

CHAPTER TWO

LAW IN LITERATURE
The Gospels

Law and literature have long been known to have interconnections. If the starting point is law, then the main literary connection is with rhetoric. The attorney must sway the judge or jury. Recitation of facts and law is not enough. They
must be presented so as to persuade. Much of modern U.S. law teaching, perhaps especially in first-year classes, seems geared to stressing rhetoric. Learning
the rules of law, indeed, understanding law, is relegated to the background.[1]
Judges' opinions are often written not just to give a particular decision but to
persuade an intended audience. In a superlative article, "A Corrupt Judge Sets
the Pace," David Daube argued that some famous judgments are based on corruption: the judge had to present his decision with extraordinary skill to conceal what was really going on.[2] The most respected legal scholars are those who
persuade their readership.

But whether law is presented in a literary form or literature presents law, the
law in question is not entirely straight; it is out of the context of legal exposition.

When the starting point is in literature, then perhaps the prime issue is
morality or justice and the relationship of these to law. Rhetoric is again ever
fascinating. Law is prominent in literature though perhaps not usually as the
main focus.[3]

For me, whichever the starting point of an inquiry, the main attention must
be on the speaker or writer and his or her immediate audience. For law in Homer,
my stress would be on how the author presented the law to his hearers; did he
get the law right, and what impact would he have had? The historical context is
all important. Of little interest (to me) would be the impact on a modern audience of Homer's treatment of law. From this perspective, law in the Gospels is
of extreme relevance. The Gospels were not written by lawyers or for lawyers.

For Christians and non-Christians alike, the Gospels are regarded as having outstanding importance. All four, especially Mark and John, are permeated with law. Still, law is not the focus. The trial(s) and execution of Jesus are not the climax but an anticlimax. The climax is Jesus' resurrection. Indeed, the point of the evangelists' writing is to persuade their readers that Jesus is the Messiah or the Son of God. The Gospels must be regarded as literature, though their purpose is religious.

My concern in this chapter is the presentation of Jesus' involvement with the law. How did those interested in the law respond to him, and how did he react to them? I start with the assumption, with which few would disagree, that there existed various traditions about Jesus before the evangelists wrote. The evangelists could be selective. Indeed, they had to be, because some traditions conflicted with others. The issues for us then with regard to law are: (1) which episodes did the evangelists choose not to address? (2) which episodes did they choose to address? (3) how did they select the way in which they would present an episode? (4) how were they using law to present their real interests to their readers?

The evangelists could be selective but not just as they liked. They could shape existing traditions, but they could not easily invent a "tradition" out of nothing. They had to be sensitive to the information available to their readership. They could not always avoid a tradition with which they might be uncomfortable.

The Gospels are even more exciting for law in action because we have here four versions of Jesus' life, and they all differ: John, especially, is in sharp contrast to the Synoptics. But the Synoptics also differ greatly in their treatment of law, and we know that to some extent they used different sources. I accept the standard view that Matthew and Luke both used Mark. This point is important because in their treatment of legal matters, both Matthew and Luke have a different perspective from Mark. We must bear in mind, though, that we cannot just assume that they both had Mark as we have it. Still, the difference between their approach to law and that of Mark must be significant. We can compare techniques.

MARK

I accept the widely held view that Mark is the earliest Gospel. After all, I do accept the general view that Matthew and Luke made use of Mark,[4] and John will be later. So a dating in the later half of the first century seems plausible. The evangelist writes at times as if his audience will be unfamiliar with Aramaic (5.41), with Jewish customs (7.3f.), and even with Palestinian geography (7.31), so perhaps the provenance could be outside Palestine.[5] But there is no strong evidence for any more positive conclusions. The general arguments for holding that it was written at Rome, namely that the text contains Latinisms and Roman customs, have no weight. The use of the Roman term "legion" for the military unit (5.9) would be common throughout the empire, likewise law that allowed a woman to divorce her husband (10.12). No more persuasive is the verse on the widow's mite (12.42): "And a poor widow came and threw in two *lepta* worth one *quadrans*." The *lepta* was a Jewish coin; the *quadrans* was the smallest Roman bronze coin. The text indicates only that Mark's readers might not know the meaning of *lepta* but would understand the more general *quadrans*. Nor does emphasis on tribulations to come (4.17; 10.30, 33f.; 13.9–13) indicate that the Gospel was written *after* Nero's persecution, just as a prediction of the Temple's destruction does not suggest that the Gospel was written *before* the destruction of the Temple in 70.[6] Nothing more can usefully be said about the specific intended audience.

Of much greater potential significant for us is the reference in Eusebius, *Historia Ecclesiae* 3.39, to the evidence of Papias who was bishop of Hierapolis around 130:

> The Elder used to say this also: Mark became the interpreter of Peter and he wrote down accurately, but not in order, as much as he [Peter] related of the sayings and doings of Christ. For he was not a hearer or a follower of the Lord, but afterwards, as I said, of Peter, who adapted his teachings to the needs of the moment and did not make an ordered exposition of the sayings of the Lord. And so Mark made no mistake when he thus wrote down some things as he related them; for he made it his special care to omit nothing of what he heard, and to make no false statement therein. . . . So then Matthew recorded the sayings in the Hebrew tongue, and each interpreted them to the best of his ability.

According to this passage, the evangelist Mark was the follower and interpreter of the apostle Peter. The simplest interpretation of the Greek is that Mark wrote down accurately the facts that Peter related of Jesus but that he changed the order. Peter, I believe we are told, in adapting his teaching to the needs of the moment, did not record Jesus' sayings in an orderly fashion. Thus Mark rearranged the order of episodes about Jesus' life, and was justified in so doing, because his (main) source, Peter, did not provide proper guidance. I believe the text should not be understood as saying that Peter recorded the facts of Jesus' life in a disorganized fashion and that Mark simply followed the order of Peter.

If the above argument is correct, then we have valuable information. Mark has imposed his order on the episodes and presumably did so with purpose. The significance for law in literature is precisely that Mark consistently, with powerful rhetoric, portrays Jesus as becoming ever more confrontational and hostile to the Pharisees' view of the law and eventually physically violent, offensively to Pharisees, Sadducees, and ordinary believing Jews.[7]

Mark begins with a flourish: right at the start of the action with John's baptism of Jesus and the voice from heaven, "You are my Son, the Beloved" (1.6ff.). The role of John the Baptist, and the baptism of Jesus, are told much more simply than in Matthew or Luke, to dramatic effect. Mark is rhetorical from the outset.

More important for us, Mark says nothing about Jesus before his ministry, nothing about a virgin birth, nothing about Jesus as a descendant of David, nothing about Jesus' childhood. Why not? It is inconceivable that the evangelist had not heard traditions that were surely current when he was writing. There are, I believe, three possibilities. First, the traditions about Jesus' birth conflicted, and the evangelist was unwilling to make a choice. Second, he was not interested. Third, he was recounting what he had heard from Peter, and Peter had said nothing apropos. All three possibilities lead to the same conclusion: the evangelist had made a deliberate choice. The Gospel of Mark is about what Jesus said and did that showed he was the Messiah or the Son of God, not about other traditions concerning him.[8]

Mark is literature, with a fixed objective. The Gospel is shaped with a purpose. In this fact lies the escalation of Jesus' hostility to the Pharisees (above all) as evinced by legal episodes.

The legal episodes in Mark tend to occur in groups, with the group introducing a new stage. In Mark, chapter 1, as it now is,[9] there are four distinct episodes concerned with law, and they have interconnections. On the Sabbath Jesus cured a man possessed of an unclean spirit (1.21ff.). This he did in public. He did it by words alone, thus without breaching the prohibition against working on the Sabbath. Immediately thereafter, so still on the Sabbath, he cured Simon's mother-in-law by a laying on of hands (1.29ff.). Thus he breached the prohibition on Sabbath working.[10] But he did so in private, inside a house in the presence only of his disciples. "When evening came, after sunset" people brought their sick to be cured (1.32). The repetition only in Mark—evening had come and the sun had set—emphasizes that the Sabbath had ended. So although the people had seen him cure without working, the idea of respect for the Sabbath is depicted as so strong that people waited until it ended before they approached him. Later in the chapter Jesus cured the leper by a laying on of hands (1.40ff.). Thus he made himself unclean (Leviticus 13.45f.): unnecessarily, because we have already been shown that his words were sufficient. This laying on of hands was in private; otherwise he would not have commanded the leper to tell no one. Still, he also told the leper to show himself to the priest and make the offerings commanded by Moses.

The episodes contrast public and private healings: in fact the order is public, private, public, private. In the private healings Mark shows Jesus as regarding himself as beyond the law: he worked on the Sabbath; he made himself unclean. But Mark also shows Jesus as far from confrontational. In the first public healing, on a Sabbath Jesus cured without working: in the second it is emphasized that the Sabbath was over. Again, though Jesus made himself unnecessarily unclean in the private healing, he ordered the cured leper to follow the law.

These four legal episodes all concern a miracle, specifically of healing. They recur in Matthew to some extent (8.14ff., 8.2ff.) and in Luke (4.33ff., 4.38ff., 5.12ff.), but the structure is lost. For instance, in Matthew 8.15 the curing of Peter's mother-in-law is not apparently on the Sabbath. In Luke 4.39 the same healing is on the Sabbath but without a laying on of hands.

With what now appears as chapter 2, Mark takes us to a new stage. There are again four episodes—four is not significant—involving law, and they are treated as a unit. They have a fivefold common structure. (1) Jesus or his disciples behave in a surprising way. (2) This behavior prompts a question from Pharisees or scribes. (3) Jesus replies in a way that silences the questioners. (4) The Pharisees or scribes are not represented as being obviously hostile. (5) Each episode concerns a specific event.

In one respect the first episode in chapter 2 is transitional. Like all four episodes in chapter 1, it involves a miracle, whereas none of the other three in chapter 2 does.

Still, it differs in a most significant way from those in chapter 1. Jesus is shown as confrontational. This is Jesus' first brush with authorities, and he, not they, brought it on (2.1ff.). Jesus said to the paralytic, "Your sins are forgiven," words that had to be offensive as implying that the speaker knew God's mind. Scribes who were present thought but—significantly for Mark—did not say that Jesus was "blaspheming." Jesus rounded on them. The scribes were not seeking to trap him. And Jesus used an argument that would not satisfy them. He asked rhetorically whether it was easier to say "Your sins are forgiven" or "Take up your mat and go home." But that was not the issue. The issue was the offensiveness of Jesus' first verbal formulation. The episode appears again in Matthew 9.2ff. And in Luke 5.1ff., but with a vital difference: the confrontation comes from the scribes.

The other three episodes in chapter 2 have further elements in common that distinguish them from the first: in all three the question is expressed, and perhaps strangely, it is not addressed to the actor.[11] The second episode was Jesus' eating with tax collectors and sinners (2.15ff.), which was considered improper for the pious. The scribes of the Pharisees asked his disciples why *he* did so, a question not necessarily hostile but probing his motivation. Jesus' reply was again confrontational. His "I have come to call not the righteous but sinners" implies that he had no business with Pharisees, who are thus excluded from his mission.

The third episode involves the question to Jesus why *his disciples* did not fast (2.18ff.). Fasting twice a week had become a mark of piety but was not obligatory.

The fourth episode (2.23ff.) has the Pharisees ask Jesus why *his disciples* plucked grain—worked—on the Sabbath, which was unlawful. Jesus' reply was not to the point and would not be persuasive to the Pharisees. Scripture (Exodus 16.25f.) forbade reaping on the Sabbath, and by interpretation plucking grain was reaping. The rule being based on Scriptural law was thus *halakah*. Jesus' legalistic response was that there was a precedent: David and his companions ate the consecrated bread. Still, this behavior was not a rule but an example, a matter of religious importance that did not affect the law. It was thus *haggadah* that could not prevail over halakah. Besides, the precedent was not in point: it did not concern a breach of the Sabbath. And what was permitted to David need not have been permitted to others.

The disciples' plucking grain on the Sabbath should probably not be regarded as a serious offense.[12] Still, to the Pharisees it could be surprising, given

Jesus' emergence as a figure of religious importance. What was more offensive was Jesus' claim, "The sabbath was made for humankind, and not humankind for the sabbath: so the Son of Man is lord even of the sabbath" (3.27).

This second group of four episodes differs in other ways from the first group. They all have Jesus using language indicating that he believed he was someone very special. More important, they now have the Pharisees following Jesus about to discover what kind of a person he is.

The legal episode at the beginning of chapter 3 (3.1ff.), the curing of the withered hand on the Sabbath, marks an ending and a beginning. It is connected with the episodes in chapter 2: the Pharisees were still watching Jesus, Jesus is still the one who began the confrontation, and he again used an inappropriate argument about law. But the episode marks a new phase: the Pharisees watched him *with hostility*, and then they plotted with the Herodians (3.6) to kill him.[13] They had decided he was not like them and could not be coopted.

Jesus was being watched to see whether he would cure a withered hand on the Sabbath; healing on the Sabbath was contrary to custom.[14] He asked, "Is it lawful to do good or harm on the Sabbath, to save life or to kill?" The question was palpably unfair. There was no prohibition on doing good on the Sabbath, only on working. Even more to the point, it was lawful to work on the Sabbath in order to save life.

The other episode in this chapter is relevant for the tightness of Mark's structure and its understanding of law in a different way (3.19ff.). People were saying that Jesus had gone mad and his family came to restrain him, as was proper under Jewish (and other ancient) law.[15] When he was told that his mother, brothers, and sisters were looking for him, he neatly replied, "Whoever does the will of God is my brother, sister and mother." He thus denied that his blood relatives had legal authority over him. The legal point that gives the episode its meaning is lost in Matthew 12.46ff.

There are two legal episodes in chapter 5, and surprisingly they are intertwined (as they also are in Matthew 9.18ff. and Luke 8.40ff.). Such intertwining of episodes occurs nowhere else in the Gospels.

Jairus, a leader of the synagogue, begged Jesus to lay hands on his little daughter, who was at the point of death (5.23). Jesus went with him, and a large crowd followed (5.24ff.). Now the second episode intrudes. A woman who had been hemorrhaging for twelve years touched his robe, believing that if she did so she would be healed. She was cured, and when Jesus asked who had touched him, she told him *the whole truth* "in fear and trembling." Then Mark reverts to Jairus's daughter. Before Jesus reached the house, he was told that she was dead (5.35). Inside, he claimed that she was only asleep, told her to rise, touched her, and she did rise (5.39ff.).

What these episodes have in common is that in both Jesus is rendered unclean by contact with a woman. For the structure of Mark we should notice that there is again a marked escalation. The hemorrhaging woman, by touching Jesus, made him unclean according to Scripture (Leviticus 15.19ff., especially 15.25), and this uncleanliness lasted until evening (Leviticus 15.19). That is why the woman was terrified by what she had done when she told him the whole truth, a point not noted in Matthew though it is in Luke 8.47. Jesus, by touching the dead girl, made himself unclean for seven days (Numbers 19.11). The escalation is not just that in the second episode the period of uncleanliness is longer but also that in the first it was the woman who made Jesus unclean, whereas in the second it was Jesus who made himself unclean. But the fact of uncleanliness is not mentioned for either episode. Mark, by intertwining the stories, is making the point that Jesus was unconcerned about ritual purity. It must be emphasized that the importance of ritual purity was established expressly by God, not simply by pharisaic interpretation.

At the beginning of Mark's chapter 7, Jesus is asked by the Pharisees and scribes why, contrary to tradition, his disciples ate without washing their hands.[16] Jesus took this as an opportunity to attack the Pharisees quite unjustifiably. He accused them of abandoning the commandment of God and holding to human tradition (7.6ff.). He illustrated with a contrast between God's command to honor father and mother on the one hand and Corban—improperly understood as an offering to God—on the other, which would deny its use for parental support.[17] But the strictness of the necessity for keeping an oath was enjoined not by pharisaic tradition but by a commandment of God set out in Deuteronomy 23.21ff., Leviticus 27, and Numbers 30.2. In fact, the Pharisees actually tempered the inviolability of oaths (Mishnah Nedarim 2.3). We should note in passing that for the Pharisees there would be no difference between Scripture and their interpretation of it. Jesus' verbal response would be more offensive than his disciples' behavior.

Subsequently in the same chapter (7.14ff.), Jesus declared that no food makes one unclean.[18] The pronouncement was made with an absence of clarity, and only privately did he expand on his meaning to the disciples. Jesus thus again apparently pronounced against the express commandment of God in Leviticus. Indeed, God's command against unclean food is expressed in strong language: the food is "detestable" or "abominable" (Leviticus 11.10ff.). It should also be stressed that the uncleanliness of the partaker cannot be cleansed by any purificatory rite or the passage of time. I offer a modified interpretation. Jesus declared that what goes into a man defiles (7.15). In the circumstances of the time he did not consider that Jews would consume food prohibited by God. Rather, I suggest that he was again attacking pharisaic interpretation. He was claiming that food not declared detestable by God did not become unclean by contact with an unclean substance. In other words, as we have them, his words were more inflammatory than his meaning.[19]

At Mark 10.2ff. Jesus in effect condemned divorce, though Moses allowed it (Deuteronomy 24.1ff.). It is sometimes claimed by modern scholars that Jesus was not changing the law: after all, the argument goes, Moses did not command divorce. The argument is false. There is a vast legal difference between a system that permits divorce and one that forbids it. I will return to the subject of divorce.

The so-called cleansing of the Temple is told in Mark 11.15ff. in a way that is much more muted than in John 2.13ff. Still, Jesus' atrocity toward Pharisees, Sadducees, and all observing Jews alike shines through. Jesus threw out those buying and selling in the Temple, that is, in the Temple precincts (11.15). But the sales, as we know from John (2.14ff.), were of the sacrificial animals: cattle and sheep and doves for the poor. The sale of such things was permitted in the Temple by the Temple authorities—indeed the sale of doves was directly under their control (Mishnah Shekalim 6.5). Only religiously clean animals could be offered for sacrifice, and apart from sales in the Temple precincts, these would not be easy to find, especially by pilgrims to Jerusalem for the festival. God, moreover, had centralized worship, and sacrifice could be offered only in one place, Jerusalem (Deuteronomy 12:16.5f.). Thus Jesus was inhibiting the necessary sacrifices to God, at the one place where they were permitted and, at that, just before Passover, among the holiest days of the Jewish year.

Jesus also overturned the tables of the money changers. Their function was religious or quasi-religious: to enable the Temple tax to be paid. Roman denarii with the portrait of Tiberius on the obverse, and the graven image of a false deity—Pax in the form of Tiberius's mother Livia—on the reverse could not be offered. Similar objections applied to Greek didrachms. The money changers gave unobjectionable Tyrian coinage in exchange. So Jesus was preventing the payment of the Temple tax.[20]

Such are the passages in Mark that relate to Jesus' behavior and the law. It must be stressed that Jesus' hostility is not just to pharisaical interpretation but to the laws of God themselves. There are six observable stages in Jesus' behavior. At stage 1, Jesus thinks he is beyond the law, but he behaves with discretion and does not disclose the fact. At stage 2, Jesus is confrontational, and the Pharisees follow him about to find out what kind of a person he is. At stage 3, Jesus is even more confrontational, and the Pharisees become hostile. At stage 4, Jesus displays open indifference to ritual purity. At stage 5, Jesus becomes still more confrontational, violently attacking the Pharisees verbally. At stage 6, Jesus is physically violent in obstructing the Passover sacrifice and payment of the Temple tax.

Something very odd is going on. The legal passages relate to Jesus' hostility to the prohibition of working on the Sabbath, to laws of purification, to dietary restrictions, to sacrifice in the Temple, and to the payment of the Temple tax. In effect, they concern those matters that in the annual round of life show a Jew that he is a Jew. But this cannot be because Jesus wanted to assimilate Jew and Gentile. In Mark, Jesus' mission is decidedly not to the Gentile. Though Mark ignores this issue, the Gospel's stance is obvious from Jesus' reaction to the Syrophoenician woman who wanted her daughter cured (7.24ff.): the symbolism is obvious, the children are the Jews; Gentiles are dogs.[21]

But what about the laws in Leviticus that had a moral content? They are ignored by Mark's Jesus, except for divorce. Jesus not only forbade divorce but declared, "Whoever divorces his wife and marries another commits adultery against her; and if she divorces her husband and marries another, she commits adultery" (Mark 10.11f.). So Jesus was presumably in favor of the Seventh Commandment, which forbade adultery. There is also the blanket condemnation of evil coming from within in Mark 7.20ff. "And he said, 'It is what comes out of a person that defiles. 21. For it is from within, from the human heart, that evil intentions come: fornication, theft, murder, 22. adultery, avarice, wickedness, deceit, licentiousness, envy, slander, pride, folly. 23. All these evil things come from within, and they defile a person.'" But this language is unspecific and does not take us very far. And even this much was explained only privately to his disciples.

But otherwise in Mark there is nothing about Jesus' attitude to God's laws in

Leviticus that might be regarded as having a moral content, such as those against incest (Leviticus 18.6ff.); against sacrificing offspring to Molech (Leviticus 18.21); against male homosexuality (Leviticus 118.22); against bestiality (Leviticus 18.23); those to benefit the poor (Leviticus 19.9f.); those condemning theft, fraud, and lying (Leviticus 19.11–13); those against stealing; harsh dealings with poor employees and the deaf and the blind (Leviticus 19.13f.); and so on. This omission cries out for an explanation.

Mark's Jesus has no precise and clear moral, social, or spiritual message except for any that is inherent in his miracle cures. But these miracle cures may have had a different function, such as to demonstrate his powers or to show that he was the Messiah. At the very least one should say that there is no emphasis in Mark on a specific spiritual message from Jesus.

But then why the stress on Jesus' opposition to those commandments of God that had no obvious ethical content? The only explanation that seems plausible to me is that Jesus as the charismatic religious leader believed from the beginning of his mission that he was above or beyond these laws, that when he recognized his inevitable opposition to the institutional religious leaders, the Pharisees, he set himself up to confront them, becoming more and more hostile. Eventually, in the cleansing of the Temple he also roused the anger of the Sadducees and brought about his own death.

To the trial(s) and execution of Jesus I devote a later part of this chapter.[22]

JOHN

John's Gospel is also dramatic and rhetorical but very differently from Mark. John also begins with the start of Jesus' ministry.

Again there is manipulation of the timing of the events that involve law, but this manipulation is strikingly different; there is no escalation of Jesus' hostility to the Pharisees. The first episode involving law shows Jesus at a high point of this hostility; the second shows him at the peak of his rage.

The manipulated structure for law in John is, as I have argued extensively elsewhere, his dependence on a pharisaical anti-Christian source that was so much part of a strong tradition where John was writing that he could not ignore it but had to deal with it.[23] This hostile tradition is the basis of the episodes in John that do not appear in the Synoptics or that appear there in a very different way. The tradition was rich in realistic details—a noted feature of John—that portrayed Jesus in a bad light. John's defense (or attack) was to defang the episodes by adding a spiritual dimension in a very few words. But the original hostility still shines through.

This source, *S*, dictated much of the structure of John's treatment of legal episodes in John. The manipulation of timing was already in *S*. This hostile source is why the so-called "Cleansing of the Temple," behavior abominable to all right-thinking Jews, is placed at the outset of Jesus' ministry and why the raising of Lazarus from the dead is at the end to justify the handing over of Jesus to the Roman oppressors.

The rhetorical structure from *S* is then, as I see it, the following. Jesus at the wedding feast at Canna behaves appallingly by preventing the purification jars from being used for their designated purpose. He obstructs the performance by others of their ritual obligations. There is no outcry. Jesus next in the cleansing of the Temple obstructs the obligatory Passover sacrifices and the necessary payment of the Temple tax. Jesus suffers no unpleasant consequences from his outrage. Jesus continues to be antagonistic to established pharisaic values. More than that, he is unnecessarily hostilely arrogant to the good, warm-hearted Pharisee Nicodemus, who only seeks enlightenment. Pharisaic hostility dramatically—yet surely not unreasonably—mounts, but it is brought to an "official" conclusion only when Jesus' behavior presents a dire threat to the survival of the Temple and the Jewish nation.

It is within this setting of the sources, especially *S*, that one must place John's treatment of law in literature.[24] The rhetorical stress is dictated by *S*.

At the wedding feast at Canna (2.1ff.), Jesus has the stone purification jars filled with wine. There were six of them, each holding twenty or thirty measures—customarily interpreted as gallons—so Jesus provided on my reckoning somewhere between 727 and 1,090 extra bottles of wine.[25] This is an extraordinary amount for a village wedding and may be understood as God's superabundance or as a call to drunken excess. Whichever interpretation is adopted, Jesus is ruining the feast. The jars can no longer be used for their appointed purpose—and one, indeed, that is spelled out in the Gospel—of purification. Purification was regarded by many as needed before breaking bread or eating wet fruit. Modern scholars may dispute how far purification by handwashing was regarded as a Jewish religious requirement in Jesus' time—it was not among later Christians—but the very presence of purification jars shows that purification was important. And the feast was a wedding feast, where proper religious observances would be stressed. The steward of the feast, when he did not know where the wine had come from, praised it. To great rhetorical effect, we are not told the dismay of observant guests when they found no water for purification. Jesus has gone out of his way needlessly to offend those sympathetic to Pharisaism.

Jesus next cleansed the Temple (2.13ff.) in an account that is more detailed than the Synoptics. John tells us that he drove out both buyers and sellers, so his objection was not to excessive prices. John relates that the objects for sale were sheep, cattle, and doves, the obligatory creatures for sacrifice at Passover. It will be remembered that in Luke, Jesus' parents took him to Jerusalem as an infant for the purification rites and offered two doves for him (Luke 2.22ff.). The creatures had to be ritually pure, so where else could pilgrims easily find them if not in the Temple precincts where the sales were sanctioned by the religious authorities, who even had a monopoly on doves? By driving out the money changers, Jesus, as I mentioned when dealing with Mark, was obstructing the payment of the Temple tax. In John, Jesus is out of control. He whipped these people out of the Temple precincts. He even whipped out the sacrificial animals (2.15). This outrageous behavior in John is at the beginning of Jesus' ministry, but it has no harmful consequences for him. To rhetorical effect—the result of S—we are not told of any hostile reaction.

There can be no escalation in John after this beginning. But the Gospel continues to portray Jesus' behavior as outrageous. With the Samaritan woman at the well he has no concern that, as a Samaritan, she must be unclean, and so will be her clay water pot, from which Jesus wishes to drink (4.7ff.). Moreover, there are strong teasing sexual overtones in the dialogue between the woman and Jesus.[26]

When Jesus cured the sick man at the pool of Beth-zatha he did so on the Sabbath. As an ingredient of the cure ("Do you want to be made well?") (5.6), the man must break the Sabbath ("Stand up, take your mat and walk") (5.8). And the man is then accused by "the Jews" of Sabbath breaking. In John much more than in the Synoptics, Jesus pressurizes others to break the law as seen by the Pharisees. The episode is artfully crafted. It begins as a healing miracle. Only when the cure is complete is it revealed that the cure was on the Sabbath and that Jesus had caused the sick man to breach Sabbath observance. When the Jews blamed Jesus for breaching the Sabbath, he equated himself with God, whom he called his father: "My Father is still working, and I also am working" (5.18). The claim is that Jesus works in the same way as God. It can be no surprise that they wanted "all the more to kill him."[27]

Two episodes where the Jews tried to stone Jesus for supposed blasphemy need only a mention: when Jesus claimed or admitted he was greater than Abraham (8.31ff.) and where Jesus claimed "the Father and I are one" (9.30ff.). The purpose is to highlight the extreme tension between Jesus and some other Jews.

More important for us is the episode sandwiched between these two, giving sight to the man blind from birth. This is very artfully contrived (9.1ff.). When the disciples asked who sinned, the man or his parents, Jesus replied neither: he was blind so that God's work might be revealed to him.[28] This is a lead-in to "We must work the works of him who sent me while it is day; night is coming when no one can work" (9.4). We do not yet know, we have not been told, and will not be told until much later in the story, that it is the Sabbath. Hence the repeated emphasis that it is day: "Night is coming when no one can work." More to the point for us, we are reminded that when Jesus healed the paralytic on the Sabbath at the pool of Beth-zatha he claimed to work in the same way as his Father, which caused the Jews to want all the more to stone him. Jesus here ups the ante. He is no longer just working in the same way as God; he is working (on the Sabbath) the works of God. For rhetorical effect we are given the details of the healing. Jesus "spat on the ground and made mud with the saliva and spread mud on the man's eyes, saying to him, 'Go, wash in the pool of Siloam' (which means Sent)" (9.6f.). Then we are told again in detail of the interchange between the former blind beggar and his neighbors, and they bring him before the Pharisees. Only at this point are we told that the day was the Sabbath (9.14). We are meant to be reminded of the cure of the paralytic at the pool. The blind beggar is about to have problems. The two episodes are to be understood together, but it is the differences in telling that is significant. The paralytic was in trouble because he worked—carried his mat—on the Sabbath. Only later in that story does Jesus' working—like God—come to the fore. This time the blind beggar has problems because Jesus "does not observe the sabbath" (9.16). The man's problems are specifically because he maintains the greatness of Jesus (9.24ff.). The rhetoric continues, much more markedly than in the Beth-zatha episode. "The Jews" question the blind man's parents, and they equivocate (9.18ff.). They question the blind man again, he replies with grim humor and maintains Jesus, and they drive him out. We are not told of punish-

ment for the paralytic at the pool, but we are for the blind man. Jesus rails at the
Pharisees (9.40f.), but again rhetorically, we are told of no response on their part.

The final legal episode before Jesus' arrest and trial—to be dealt with below
in this chapter—is the raising of Lazarus from the dead (11.1ff.). The whole
point is to justify the Jews in arresting Jesus and handing him over to the Romans for trial and execution. This is another episode that does not appear in the
Synoptics, and consequently I assign it to S. Accordingly, Jesus does not appear
in a wholly sympathetic light. Certainly, he raised Lazarus from the dead, but
he waited unnecessarily for him to be mourned for three days. This is the one
event in the Gospels that we can be sure did not occur. It relates Jesus' greatest
miracle but—astonishingly, if it were true—is omitted from all three Synoptics. The centerpiece in John, the response of Jewish leaders, is muted, as dramatically it should be (11.45ff.). We are given no details of the meeting of the
Sanhedrin, of the chief priests and Pharisees. We have only "What are we to do?
This man is performing many signs. If we let him go on like this, everyone will
believe in him, and the Romans will come and destroy both our holy place and
our nation" (11.47f.). The council faced a real dilemma. If Jesus could raise one
man, he could raise an army. If the people believed Jesus was the Messiah, they
would rally to him; and then if he were not in fact the Messiah the Romans
would indeed destroy the Temple and the nation. It is no wonder that Caiaphas
says, "It is better for you to have one man die for the people than to have the
whole nation destroyed" (11.50).[29] The subsequent desire of the chief priests to
kill Lazarus is also understandable (12.9ff.). I would not sympathize with statements condemning "the viciousness of those who would not only kill Jesus but
also Lazarus."[30] A second death for Lazarus would be important. If Jesus did
not raise Lazarus from the dead a second time, then his miracle would have been
pointless, and the threat from the Romans would diminish. (And if Jesus did
raise Lazarus a second time, then maybe even the chief priests would begin to
think of Jesus as the Messiah.)

MATTHEW AND LUKE

The literary use of law in Jesus' life in Mark and John is highlighted when we
turn to Matthew and Luke. If one accepts, as I do, the general opinion that Matthew and Luke made use of Mark, then it follows that at least one reason for

the evangelists writing was dissatisfaction with Mark. I can think of only two possible causes. First, they felt that Mark was insufficiently spiritual, and indeed, love, theology, and spirituality are much more prominent in Matthew and Luke. Second, they disapproved of the ordering of events in Mark.

This second cause brings us to a full awareness of Mark's use of law to bring out Jesus' personality. Matthew and Luke though dependent on Mark do not show the escalation of Jesus' hostility to organized Judaism. Certainly, the reason is in part that they lack Mark's sensitivity to rabbinic law, but lack of sensitivity cannot be the whole answer.

Another part is that their literary intention does not hinge on Jesus and the law. Still, when this has been said, it must be emphasized that Matthew, on whom I will concentrate in this section, has as his first legal episode the beautiful Sermon on the Mount (Matthew 5.21ff.). This is a model of legal interpretation but has no counterpart in Mark. The sermon contains six antitheses, but it is not wholly apposite to regard them as contrasting the Jewish law "with Jesus' authoritative teaching altering or radicalizing this law."[31] Rather we have, as David Daube has pointed out, a structure of rabbinic exposition.[32] The structure has two parts. In the standard case, the rabbi gives his supposed interpretation. Then he gives a second, which is to prevail. Jesus in his turn gives one supposed narrow interpretation of the law, then he gives his own. But Jesus is not altering the law: he is giving his interpretation of it. Indeed, he says, "Do not think that I have come to abolish the law or the prophets: I have come not to abolish but fulfill" (Matthew 5.17).

At Matthew 8.1ff., Jesus' cleansing of the leper is recounted much as in Mark 1 except that it is no longer part of a group of episodes stressing that Jesus is nonconfrontational. Indeed, when Jesus cures Peter's mother-in-law (Matthew 8.14ff.), there is no sign of the detail so vital in Mark that the healing was on the Sabbath. When in Matthew 9.2ff. Jesus heals the paralytic who has been let down through the roof, it is no longer, as in Mark, Jesus who is confrontational. The confrontation begins with the scribes who said to themselves "this man is blaspheming."[33]

Then follow various episodes involving law that are also in Mark but are not remarkable: Jesus eating with tax collectors (Matthew 9.9ff.); his curing of the hemorrhaging woman and the raising of Jairus's daughter (Matthew 9.18ff.);[34] his disciples plucking grain on the Sabbath (Matthew 12.1ff.).

But we must pause at the episode where Jesus' mother and brothers were looking for him. In Mark, they were doing so because people were saying he had gone insane, and close relatives had a legal obligation to look after and control those who were mad. The legal point is entirely lost in Matthew 12.46ff. His relatives were simply looking for him.

We need trace law in Matthew (and in Luke) no further. Law is prominent in Matthew. But it is not used for any specific literary effect. The falling away of Matthew from Mark highlights the latter's use of law for dramatic effect. "Law and literature" are very much an integral part of Mark. As, for a very different effect, they are indeed for John.

THE TRIAL(S) AND EXECUTION OF JESUS

The marked differences in style between Mark, John, Matthew, and Luke continue into the trial or trials and execution of Jesus. With very different goals, Mark and John (using or abusing his hostile pharisaic source) present coherent, rhetorical, and vastly contrasting accounts.

To start this time with John. Jesus was arrested by a detachment of Roman soldiers and police of the chief priests and Pharisees (18.3, 12). Only in John are the Romans involved, and this fact I would attribute to S, which wished to downplay Jewish involvement. But the Romans were not much interested: they did not arrest Jesus' followers, and Jesus himself was taken to the house of Annas, father-in-law of Caiaphas, who was the high priest, not as might be expected to the Roman praetorium (18.13). Jesus was questioned in the house of Annas and then in that of Caiaphas (18.19ff.). But there was no trial before the Sanhedrin, again a feature that I would attribute to S. Again the evangelist subsequently obtrudes: the Sanhedrin did not try Jesus because it could not impose the death penalty (18.31). This claim, as I have argued at length elsewhere,[35] is demonstrably false. The evangelist John, with the tradition of S before him, which he is unwilling to challenge directly, tries to mutilate it. Yes, he says, the Jews did not try Jesus but only because they could not execute him. They are not to be excused.

The Jewish leaders then took Jesus to Pilate's headquarters. Despite a direct question, they refuse to charge Jesus with a specific crime. "They answered, 'If this man were not a criminal, we would not have handed him over to you'" (18.30). They are passing the buck. They had done so already when they would not enter Pilate's headquarters (18.28). This refusal was to avoid ritual defilement, which would mean they could not observe Passover, but it also distances them from Pilate. This stance diminishes pharisaic direct involvement with Jesus' crucifixion, but *S* has a very neat twist to portray the Pharisees in a good light. Nicodemus, who is emphatically a Pharisee (3.1, 7.50, 19.39) and was nastily rebuffed by Jesus (3.15ff.), nonetheless provides an exceptional quantity of spices for his burial and makes himself, by contact with the corpse, unclean, thus unable to share in Passover (19.39ff.). All in all, if my understanding is correct, John's Gospel presents us with a wonderful literary balancing act, between *S* and not-*S*.

But nothing in John surpasses in literary magnificence the stages in the trial of Jesus before Pilate. The Jews bring Jesus to Pilate, they refuse to enter his headquarters, they refuse to make specific accusations but insist Jesus is a criminal. It is up to Pilate to act. Pilate, well aware of what is going on, asks Jesus whether he is King of the Jews, and Jesus responds that his kingdom is not of this world (18.33ff.). Pilate seeks to release Jesus, but the crowd protests (18.38ff.). Pilate again seeks to release Jesus (19.4ff.). This time the Jewish leaders who had not tried Jesus and who made no specific accusations against Jesus were adamant to Pilate for his death: "The Jews answered him, 'We have a law, and according to that law he ought to die because he claimed to be the Son of God'" (19.7). They were still insisting that Jesus should be executed by Pilate, but they have changed their ground: Jesus' offense was religious and merited death according to Jewish law. Pilate still wanted to release Jesus, but the Jews applied still more pressure: "If you release this man, you are no friend of the emperor. Everyone who claims to be a king sets himself against the emperor" (19.12). Pilate was afraid (19.8). No wonder. His governorship was not a success, and he was eventually recalled to Rome to defend his actions on other matters.[36] Pilate gave way and had Jesus executed. Still, in John Pilate insisted on having the last, offensive word (19.21f.): "Then the chief priests of the Jews said to Pilate, 'Do not write, "The King of the Jews," but, "This man said, I am King of the Jews."' Pilate answered, 'what I have written I have written.'"

John's Gospel is a literary masterpiece. The treatment of law is perfectly coherent and cohesive but cannot be factually accurate. The very offensive "cleansing of the Temple" could not have occurred at the beginning of Jesus' ministry with no adverse consequences for him. Again, this Gospel, in opposition to the Synoptics and most implausibly, does not represent the Last Supper as a Passover meal (13.1ff.). The genius is all the greater if I am correct in my claim that in much of the narrative John was turning the flank of a hostile, pharisaic source.

Mark is also spectacular as literature. In complete contrast to John, Mark's focus is very pointedly on a trial before the Sanhedrin, an illegal trial at that and one with blatant irregularities. Jesus was arrested at night by a crowd from the chief priests, the scribes, and the elders (14.43). Nothing indicates that Roman soldiers were involved. Jesus was taken to the high priest: and all the chief priests, elders, and scribes were assembled (14.53). They looked for testimony to put Jesus to death (14.55). So we have here a formal meeting of the Sanhedrin. Since it was night and the case was capital, the trial was contrary to law.[37] False testimony was given—we are not told in Mark that the Sanhedrin actually sought fake evidence—but the witnesses did not agree (14.56ff.). The evidentiary requirements were very strict[38] and were not met.

The High Priest intervened and asked Jesus for his response (14.60). Jesus made none (14.61).[39] The High Priest asked whether Jesus was the Messiah, and he replied that he was (14.61f.). The High Priest then tore his clothes and asked why witnesses would still be needed when they had heard his blasphemy, and he asked for their decision. All condemned Jesus as deserving death (14.63–65). These three verses are particularly significant. They indicate, to begin with, that up to this point the evidence against Jesus was insufficient. But the High Priest took the initiative and continued with the claim that Jesus' admission that he was the Messiah was blasphemous. This statement of Jesus probably was technically blasphemy at that time.[40] The High Priest continued his initiative and tore his clothes. The point here is that the members of the council were obliged to rend their garments when someone was being found guilty of blasphemy. This action is a sign of mourning. It is sometimes suggested that the High Priest's action is not significant with regard to a verdict, because Jews tore their clothes at other times of mourning. This interpretation is impossible. In a trial in which the High Priest declared the accused to be blasphemous, the only possible symbolism of his tearing his clothes is condemnation of the accused. But then, it has been argued, all the judges should have torn their garments, not only the High Priest. And he has done so at the wrong time, before condemnation to death at the second morning session, which is the point of time specified in Mishnah Sanhedrin, 7.5. Just so. The drama of Mark's account has been missed. The scenario is this. Although the meeting of the Sanhedrin was illegal, the judges insisted on observing the proper standards of evidence. On this basis, they could not reach a conviction. The High Priest took matters into his own hands. He claimed that Jesus' admission in front of the council that he was the Messiah was blasphemy, asked what was the point of hearing other witnesses, and tore his clothes. He was acting as if Jesus were condemned to death! And the Sanhedrin acquiesced in his conduct and decided that Jesus was worthy of death. High-handed bullying by the boss paid off, as it so often does. The underlings had the choice: face up to the hard-nosed chief and cause a confrontation, or go along. This choice in itself is always difficult, and in this case the chief priests had no reason to be enthusiastically in favor of Jesus anyway.

But there is much more to the issue of the High Priests' high-handedness. The High Priest was forbidden to rend his garments and not as a result of the interpretation of Scripture but by Scripture itself. Leviticus 21.10 reads: "The priest who is exalted above his fellows, on whose head the anointing oil has been poured and who has been consecrated to wear the vestments, shall not dishevel his hair, nor tear his vestments." [41] The High Priest's behavior is outrageous. He engages in a show of grief that is forbidden him but is obligatory for his fellows. On this basis, only the most bitter and obdurate of the judges would refuse to follow him.

When it was morning, the chief priests held a consultation with the elders and scribes and the whole council (15.1). This is presumably in terms of the very important rule of Mishnah Sanhedrin 5.5, "If they found him innocent, they set him free; otherwise they leave his sentence over until the morrow." The same rule stated that they should come together early in the morning. Mark does not tell us what sentence was decided upon, or even whether they decided upon a sentence at all. But they delivered Jesus, bound, to Pontius Pilate (15.1).

At this point I should like to pause again to show that there is no indication in Mark that Jesus was in any way an enemy of the Romans. Indeed, the evidence is all to the contrary.[42] In Mark, Roman soldiers were not involved in Jesus' arrest. No real attempt was made by the arresters to catch the disciples, which they would have done if the arresters had been soldiers and the disciples had been the band of a revolutionary leader. Jesus' main hostility was directed against the Pharisees rather than the Sadducees, yet the latter were more openly collaborators with the Romans. In fact, the Pharisees were intent on preserving a particular Jewish way of life and separateness: this was at least part of the reason that the crowds admired them. Then Jesus, when directly asked, did not reply that it was illegal to pay tax to the Romans. Yet the supposed illegality of paying the tax appears to be the first ground of the Zealots' hatred of the Romans. Significantly, too, Jesus had a disciple called something like Simon the Zealot (3.18). Such a name would be impossible if they were all Zealots. One would not call a Scot living in Scotland "David the Scot," but if David emigrated to the United States he might be thought of there as "David the Scot." Such appellations indicate a characteristic that separates the individual from his fellows.[43]

To return to the narrative, Jesus was delivered to Pilate. According to Mark, Pilate took the initiative and asked Jesus whether he was king of the Jews (15.2). So Pilate must have had some prior knowledge of what was afoot. Of course he had. The procurator's consent was needed in fact before the Sanhedrin could meet. Jesus replied, "You say so." Basically this response is no different from refusing to answer. The chief priests then accused him of many things (15.3). Mark does not state, however, that they told Pilate that they had tried him, or had found him guilty, or had condemned him to death. Pilate then wanted him to respond to what he termed the "many charges they bring against you" (15.4). The words indicate that for Mark the chief priests had not claimed to have convicted Jesus but had simply brought to Pilate accusations against him. Jesus made no answer to Pilate (15.5). The next few verses show that the immediate procedure had ended and that Pilate had made his decision.[44] Jesus, as we shall shortly see, is clearly treated as a prisoner who might be mercifully released but in fact is crucified and at that for sedition, treason against the Roman emperor.

But can it be claimed that there has been a proper Roman trial of a non-Roman before a provincial governor? The answer is a strong positive in view of Pliny the Younger *Epistulae* 10.96. Jesus was not a Roman citizen, so Pilate had no need to respect the niceties reserved for them in a capital trial.

What is going on at this stage in Mark is clear. When the Sanhedrin met in the morning to give their official verdict, enough of the judges were ashamed of the illegality of the trial, of the failure of appropriate evidence, of their acceptance of the High Priest's outrageous bullying, and of the wrong verdict of blasphemy, or they were afraid of the mob that they refused to convict. No other scenario would explain why they did not put Jesus to death by stoning but instead handed him over to Pilate, for whom blasphemy was no crime. The charge brought against Jesus by Pilate was treason to the Roman emperor, and he was properly tried and put to death. But in the final analysis he was not convicted of any capital offense by the Sanhedrin, and he was not executed by the Jews. In

Mark, the failure of the Sanhedrin to convict is played down. (Indeed, the evangelist may not have been conscious of it.)

Pilate had a custom, Mark says, of releasing one prisoner to them at Passover, whomever they wished (15.6). The crowd asked him to follow his custom and to release Barabbas, a captured brigand (15.7f.). Pilate offered instead "the king of the Jews" because he knew that the chief priests had delivered Jesus out of jealousy (15.9f.). But the chief priests stirred up the crowd to demand Barabbas (15.11). When Pilate asked what should be done with "the man you call the king of the Jews," they insisted upon crucifixion (15.12). Barabbas was released; Jesus was flogged (15.15), a step that was the normal preliminary to a crucifixion. Jesus was crucified at nine in the morning (15.25). The charge against him was inscribed "The King of the Jews" (15.26).

The whole account of the arrest, trial, and execution of Jesus in Mark, ending with a Roman provincial trial on the charge of a Roman crime, ending in a Roman execution, is entirely internally consistent, a remarkable literary feat.[45]

One final point. To me the account in Mark is entirely plausible, but it seems much less so to others. The difficulty, I think, lies in a reluctance to believe that responsible judges and public personages can act illegally, even cruelly, yet feel they are fully justified. But they do it all the time. No doubt important persons who overstep the law to preserve—as they see it—the state cannot be wholly exonerated from a charge of acting in self-interest. The safety of the status quo is much to their advantage. Their main conscious motive may nonetheless be an urgent desire for the well-being of the nation, people, or religion.

CHAPTER THREE

LITERATURE IN LAW
Thomas R. R. Cobb

Thomas R. R. Cobb's *An Inquiry into the Law of Negro Slavery in the United States of America to which is prefixed A Historical Sketch of Slavery*, published in Philadelphia and Savannah in 1858, is one of the remarkable law books of the nineteenth century. That it is not better known or appreciated is due, I believe, to two factors. Slavery having been abolished, slave law is an obsolete subject. And slavery being regarded as so obnoxious, slave law, which is an integral part of slavery, can scarcely be treated as an objective scholarly discipline.[1]

A remarkable feature of the book is that it was ever written at all. Cobb was born in rural Georgia in 1823 and had an exceptionally active professional life as attorney and as a political and public figure, primarily in Athens, Georgia, until the Civil War. He was one of the founders of the University of Georgia Law School in 1859. The writing of a book of this kind presented difficulties that others would have found insurmountable. Cobb opens his preface:

> I enter upon an untrodden field. Stroud's "Sketch of the Law of Slavery" is and was intended only as an Abolition pamphlet; Wheeler's "Law of Slavery" professes to be only a compend of abridged decisions on prominent questions. An elementary treatise, purporting to define the Law of Slavery as it exists in the United States, has not been brought to my notice. . . .
>
> This work has been prepared at leisure hours, in the midst of a laborious practice. These have varied in length from a few moments to a few days. The natural result—disconnection and incoherency—may be detected by experienced eyes.

He continues:

Residing in an interior village, I have felt the want of access to extended libraries. I have taken advantage of occasional sojourns in the cities of Washington, Philadelphia, and New York, to examine references previously noted, and such books as related to my subject. I have added also a number of works to my own library, which I could not otherwise examine. . . .

From the causes before stated, I have been forced to rely on the accuracy of others for some of the references made. In almost every case I have noticed, at the time, the person on whose authority I cite.

The book does betray a frequent reliance on secondary sources when Cobb was unable to read the primary sources. The library difficulties were extreme, and the scope of the book was enormous: slavery from the time of the Patriarchs, among the Jews, in Egypt, in India, and so on up to modern times. The many who find such wide-ranging works on a particular topic to be valuable must expect that the author would have to rely on secondary literature. No one person could command the languages necessary to read the original texts. Inevitably the author will rely on sources that correspond to his interests. To the inaccuracies of these sources he will add his own exaggerations and occasional misunderstandings. My concern here is not Cobb's statements of the law—though I believe he is more precise than were most professional scholars of his time—but his artistry. In contrast to most law texts, Cobb's book may reasonably be regarded as a work of art, as literature.

THE *SKETCH*

The artistry begins with the title. To say that *A Historical Sketch of Slavery* is "prefixed" to *An Inquiry into the Law of Slavery in the United States of America* is deliberately misleading. Cobb wants to give the impression that the prefix is a flourish, a mere introduction to his theme. In fact, it is an integral part of his hidden, political agenda. In the simple number of pages it takes up around two-fifths of the whole. But this figure is misleading, because the typeface is smaller: the real proportion of substance is closer to one-half. Then also on the title page we have the claim of "Vol. 1."[2] The prefix is being further distanced from the *Inquiry*.

This distancing continues. Thus in the prefix the pages are numbered in Roman figures, in the *Inquiry*, in Arabic. There are two separate indexes, one for each part, though both appear at the end of the combined book.

The *Sketch* is not intended as window dressing or as evidence of the author's learning. It is much too detailed, and must have consumed too much time, for that. It is constructed to conceal the author's real aim, a justification of slavery in the slave states. Cobb ends his preface: "My book has no political, no sectional purpose. I doubt not I am biased by my birth and education in a slave-holding State. As far as possible, I have diligently sought for Truth, and have written nothing which I did not recognize as bearing her image. So believing, I neither court nor fear criticism; remembering that '*veritas saepius agitata, magis splendescit lucem.*'" And he is described on the title page as "Thomas R. R. Cobb, of Georgia." Cobb is declaring his allegiance. Still, the function of the prefix is to prove that he "diligently sought for Truth." The prefix is to show that slavery has existed everywhere among civilized peoples. Slavery in the United States is not a barbarous anomaly. It is a part of the human condition, is "natural," and (in the conditions that exist in the South) is morally right.

Cobb sets the scene in the first paragraph of his introduction: "Philosophy is the handmaid, and frequently the most successful expounder of the law. History is the groundwork and only sure basis of philosophy. To understand aright, therefore, the Law of Slavery, we must not be ignorant of its history." [3] If I understand him correctly, Cobb's claim is that one cannot understand or explain law without philosophy and that philosophy can be securely grounded only upon history. History of law, comparative history at that, is necessary for an understanding of law. [4] Immediately thereafter he makes his big claim: "A detailed and minute inquiry into the history of slavery would force us to trace the history of every nation of the earth; for the most enlightened have, at some period within their existence, adopted it as a system; and no organized government has been so barbarous as not to introduce it amongst its customs. It has been more universal than marriage, and more permanent than liberty. All that we can propose for ourselves here, is a limited and brief glance at its existence and condition during the several ages of the world." Every organized government has at one time or another recognized slavery as a social system within its boundaries. This statement includes the most enlightened states, and indeed no state has been so barbarous as to fail to introduce it. With true rhetoric, to shock the complacent reader, Cobb compares slavery to the two most revered institutions of his day, marriage (and the family) and freedom (the rallying cry of the United States), to their disadvantage. Slavery has been more universal than the family, and more long-lasting than freedom.

Cobb has admitted to being possibly biased in favor of the southern way of life but insists that he seeks only for the truth. Now he proposes to show that slavery is a natural part of the human condition, and on this he will be merely seeking objective truth. To this end he separates the two parts of his treatise, the second alone being about slave law in the South. Cobb is to be a disinterested scholar, not an advocate, and insofar as he is an advocate, he is an advocate without a client. In the *Sketch* as a whole he carefully avoids drawing conclusions about slavery from slave conditions in the South.

The third paragraph of the Introduction reads: "Its beginning dates back at least to the deluge. One of the inmates of the ark became a 'servant of servants;' and in the opinion of many the curse of Ham is now being executed upon his descendants, in the enslavement of the negro race. From the familiarity with which Noah spoke of the servile condition of his youngest son, it seems probable that the condition of servitude must have existed prior to the flood." Thus slavery is ancient. It existed by the time of Noah,[5] who alone had "found favor in the sight of the Lord."[6] Noah caused his son Ham and his descendants to be slaves, and this would be under the auspices of God. Still, Cobb observes that from the ease with which Noah spoke of slavery, the status must have existed before. Ham and his descendants were black; hence God, at best at one remove, had inaugurated black slavery.

Cobb has done a remarkable job in three short paragraphs: to understand law, one must have a philosophical standpoint, and this can be established only by history; history shows that slavery has been accepted to a remarkably extensive degree and, from the earliest times, approved by God, and, specifically, approved for the enslavement of blacks.

The final and longest paragraph of the introduction is more relaxed, even reassuring in tone. Bondage naturally arose, it was a benefit to the poor and less intelligent, was frequent among the early Israelites, and was generally mild. Around the middle of the paragraph Cobb includes a fundamental sentence with implications for part 2 of the book: "Certain it is, that Abraham had his man-servants and maid-servants, born in his house and bought with his money; and that Sarah, his wife, was a hard mistress to Hagar, her handmaid, who became a fugitive from her hand, and returned only by the direction of the angel

of the Lord." Slavery was beneficial and mild, but on occasion an owner could
be cruel. Though Cobb does not say so here, he accepts that this cruelty is a consequence of the defenseless position of slaves. Still, even where this is the case,
even where the slave becomes a fugitive, slavery is so much part of God's order,
that his angel directs the runaway Hagar to return to her slavery.

Chapter 1 is, almost inevitably, "Slavery among the Jews": slavery was acceptable to, and prevalent among, God's chosen people. This was the obvious place
for a Christian upholding slavery to begin. Cobb slips in a few intriguing sentences: "The negro among the Jews, as everywhere he is found, was of a pro-
scribed race. He was even forbidden to approach the altar to offer the bread of
his God. The treatment of this class of slaves, among the Hebrews, was extremely rigorous."[7] There is no obvious need for the ostensible purposes of this
chapter of Cobb's to characterize some of the Hebrew slaves as black. Even less
to the ostensible purposes was needed "as everywhere he is found." Cobb is ad-
verting indirectly to southern reality. Nor is it apparent from Leviticus 21.18
(which Cobb cites) that blacks could not approach the altar. He says in a footnote, "The flat-nosed must refer to the negro." But I find nothing in the Hebrew about "flat-nosed." Cobb adduces no other evidence.

The sentence at the beginning of the second paragraph in my quotation of
Cobb with "this class of slaves" refers to slaves who were not Hebrews, not specifically to black slaves. But its conjunction with the short paragraph on black
slaves is significant: we are meant not to be surprised that treatment of black
slaves may be rigorous.

It is not necessary to trace out Cobb's description of slavery in other countries. His prime purpose is always the same, to show how universal slavery
has been.

At chapter 9 he comes to "Negro Slavery and the Slave-Trade." From there
to the end of the volume with chapter 18, the subject is black slavery and the
consequences of the emancipation of black slaves. He is coming ever closer to
the main thrust of his work: the defense of slavery in the southern states. But
the slow and careful buildup increases the feeling of objectivity and reasonable-
ness. It is almost enough to state the main thrust of these 104 pages: manumission has been misguided, and blacks revert to barbarism. But a little more
should be said about chapter 17, "Slavery in the United States."[8]

Cobb claims that the history of abolitionism in the United States has been the history of fanaticism. Slaves have been generally well treated, so slaves are not inclined to revolt. Individual manumission had been frequent, but the lazy habits of free blacks, coupled with agitation for abolition by northern fanatics, have induced legislatures to prohibit domestic emancipation.[9]

He then discusses the benefits and evils of black slavery. I quote extensively: [10]

Both politically and socially negro slavery has its benefits and its evils. To the negro himself the former greatly preponderate. To the owners, the masters, the question is a greater problem, and there is more room for honest differences of opinion.

Politically, slavery is a *conservative* institution. The mass of laborers not being recognized among citizens, every citizen feels that he belongs to an elevated class. It matters not that he is no slaveholder; he is not of the inferior race; he is a freeborn citizen; he engages in no menial occupation. The poorest meets the richest as an equal; sits at his table with him; salutes him as a neighbor; meets him in every public assembly, and stands on the same social platform. Hence, there is no war of classes. There is truthfully republican equality in the ruling class.[11]

The laborers being slaves, there is not the same danger of conflicts between labor and capital, nor the same liability to other excitements in crowded masses, which end in riots. These are unknown in pure slaveholding communities.

Raising their own laborers, there is no inducement for foreign immigration into slaveholding communities. Their citizens imbibe freedom with their mother's milk.

The leisure allowed to the slaveholder gives him an opportunity of informing himself upon current questions of politics, and his interest being identical with his neighbors, in preserving existing institutions, the Southern politician addresses always a body of men having a common sentiment, and not to be influenced to so great an extent by the "humbugs" of demagogues. This is an influential element in forming public opinion, and acts thus *conservatively* upon the public men of the South.

Official position is not very consistent with the interest of the slaveholder, and hence is never sought for its pecuniary emoluments. It is coveted only by those ambitious of distinction. Hence, the public men of the

South do not find themselves supplanted by unprovided aspirants, but their services are frequently gratefully received by their constituents. Born to command, and habituated to rule, they frequently commend themselves to the nation by their firmness, their independence, and their fearlessness. These are important elements in the character of a statesman.

Slavery is a protection from *pauperism*, the bane for which the wisdom of civilized man has not yet prepared an antidote. In America, affliction, old age, and idleness, are the only sources of pauperism. Where the laborers are slaves the master is compelled by law to provide against the former, and is authorized to protect himself against the latter. The poorhouse, therefore, is almost unknown.

The severities of winter and the depression of financial crises, bring no horrors to the laborers of the South. The interest of the master as well as the law of the land protect the negro against the former, while a change of masters is the worst result which can befall him from the latter.

As already intimated, there is perhaps no solution of the great problem of reconciling the interests of labor and capital, so as to protect each from the encroachments and oppressions of the other, so simple and effective as negro slavery. By making the laborer himself capital, the conflict ceases, and the interests become identical.

On the other hand, a slaveholding State can never be densely populated. The slaves, moreover, occupying the places of free laborers, and three-fifths only of their number being estimated under the Constitution of the United States, for representative purposes, the result is inevitable that the slaveholding States must ever have a smaller voice, politically, than the same territory would command with free labor. To this extent slavery destroys their political equality in the nation.

Another result of a sparse population is, that a perfect system of thorough common school education is almost an impossibility. Extensive plantations, occupied by slaves only, independent of the exhausting crops cultivated and annually adding to barren fields, render a perfect system of common schools impossible. . . .

As a social relation, negro slavery has its benefits and its evils. That the slave is incorporated into and becomes a part of the family, that a tie is thus formed between the master and slave, almost unknown to the relation of master and hireling, that in consequence even the young spend-thrift experiences a pang in sundering a relation he has recognized from his infancy, that the old and infirm are thus cared for, and the young protected and reared, are indisputable facts. Interest joins with affection in promoting this unity of feeling. To the negro, it insures food, fuel, and clothing, medical attendance, and in most cases religious instruction. The young child is seldom removed from the parent's protection, and beyond doubt, the institution prevents the separation of families, to an extent unknown among the laboring poor of the world. It provides him with a protector, whose interest and feeling combine in demanding such protection.

To the master, it gives a servant whose interests are identical with his own, who has indeed no other interest, except the gratification of a few animal passions, for which purpose he considers it no robbery to purloin his master's goods.

In short, the Southern slavery is a patriarchal, social system. The master is the head of his family. Next to wife and children, he cares for his slaves. He avenges their injuries, protects their persons, provides for their wants, and guides their labors. In return, he is revered and held as protector and master. Nine-tenths of the Southern masters would be defended by their slaves, at the peril of their own lives.

The evils of the system are equally unquestionable. That it engenders in the youth of the South that overbearing and despotic spirit, ascribed to the relation by Mr. Jefferson, is not true to the extent he alleges. The fact, that Northern men are sometimes the most exacting masters, is well known. The reason of this is that they expect from the slave the amount of work which they have received from a hireling. *This he never will do,* and the Southern-bred master does not look for it. The security of his place, as well as the indolence of his nature, do not furnish the necessary stimulus. It is true, however, that the young man of the South *is accustomed to rule,* and even the son of a poor man, without a slave, to a certain extent, commands obedience from the negro population. The result is a spirit of independence, which brooks not opposition. Within a proper limit this is not an evil. Indulgence makes it a sin.

A good consequence of this is, a more perfect equality in social life, among the rich and poor, than can be had where the menial servants are of the same color. An evil consequence is a too great sensitiveness on questions of personal honor, and a corresponding disposition to settle them "by wager of battle."

An evil attributed to slavery, and frequently alluded to, is the want of chastity in female slaves, and a corresponding immorality in the white males. To a certain extent this is true; and to the extent that the slave is under the control and subject to the order of the master, the condition of slavery is responsible.

Every well-informed person at the South, however, knows that the exercise of such power for such a purpose is almost unknown. The prevalence of the evil is attributable to other causes. The most prominent of these is the natural lewdness of the negro. It is not the consequence of slavery. The free negro in Africa, in the West Indies, in America, exhibits the same disposition, perhaps not to the same degree when living in a Christian community. Another cause is the fact that the negress knows that the offspring of such intercourse, the mulatto, having greater intelligence, and being indeed a superior race, has a better opportunity of enjoying the privileges of domestics; in other words, *is elevated* by the mixture of blood. Her sin does not entail misfortune but good fortune on her children. Nor does she lose any social position even with her own race. Under such circumstances the prevalence of this sin is not surprising.

It is undoubtedly true, that from this cause the poor white females of the slaveholding States are not subject to as great temptations and importunities as they would be under other circumstances. That the ignorant poor, under the heating Southern sun, would compare unfavorably with those of colder climates in this particular, except for this institution, is manifested by the immorality of some ignorant districts in slaveholding States, where but few negroes are found. How far such a result counterbalances the evil admitted, can be weighed only by the great Arbiter of the universe.

That the marriage relation between slaves is not recognized or protected by the law, is another evil to the negro attending the system, and to a qualified extent it is an evil. In practice, public opinion protects the relation. The unfeeling separation of husband and wife, is a rare occurrence. It never happens when both belong to the same master. To regulate properly this relation by legislation, so as to prevent inhumanity on the one hand, and not to bind too much the owner's power of selling an unworthy or unruly slave on the other, requires great sagacity and prudence.

With great clarity and simplicity Cobb has openly admitted that there is the possibility of evils befalling slaves but has claimed that for slaves the benefits outweigh the evil.[12] The preponderance of good or ill for the owners is less clear. But Cobb holds that whatever the advantage or disadvantage to the individual owner, the free persons benefit by living in a society that contains slaves.

I have set out this very long quotation from Cobb to illustrate his rhetorical skill. The ostensible subject of his book is slave law in the United States. But his real purpose is a defense of slavery in the South. Slavery is good for the slaves; less clearly so for the owners. Cobb wants to show his evenhandedness. The slave-owning society is not an exploitative one.

In this volume 1 Cobb has not been addressing law directly and for the most part has steered clear of discussing slavery in the southern United States. But now he has reached the substantive part of his treatise.

THE LAW

In volume 2—never so called—Cobb turns to slave law in the United States. Still, the first two chapters, decidedly on law, are introductory and are vitally important in Cobb's scheme of things.

Chapter 1, "What is Slavery, and its Foundation in the Natural Law," begins by distinguishing Absolute Slavery, where one person has absolute power over another, who is viewed merely as property, from Slavery in its more limited significance, where the person in servitude possesses various rights as a person "and is treated as such by the law." Absolute Slavery no longer exists among civilized nations, but the other Slavery has been found in every social system that history records. Cobb's purpose is to instill the idea that southern slave law is essentially moderate.

In §2 he begins his discussion of slavery and natural law. He observes that Justinian's *Institutes* declared slavery to be *contra naturam*, "contrary to nature," [13] that slavery has so often been asserted to be contrary to the law of nature that even most slaveholders acknowledge that it is so, and "even learned judges in slave-holding States, adopting the language of Lord Mansfield, in Somerset's case, have announced gravely, that slavery being contrary to the law of nature, can exist only by force of the positive law." [14] At §4 Cobb tells us that it is very important to understand what is meant by "the law of nature," which jurists have asserted is the only true basis of law. At §5:

> Yet we find it very difficult to cull from them all, a clear, concise, tangible definition of what is meant by the *law of nature*. The Roman lawyers and others applied the term to that "law which nature teaches *all living creatures*," thereby causing it to include all animals, beasts as well as men. To this others have demurred, and insist that *law* can be applied only to creatures who have *reason* and *will*, to perceive an obligation and to adapt their acts accordingly. And Potgiesseri very properly observes, that even when applied to men it assumes a double aspect: "Vel, ut concipiuntur omnes et singuli homines in naturali libertate, nullique imperio subjecti vivere; vel, ut intelliguntur cum aliquibus tantum in societatem civilem coivisse, cum reliquis autem nullo, nisi communi humanitatis vinculo colligari." [15]

An equally great difference of opinion exists, he says, about the rules that can be deduced from the law of nature. And he cites four differing views, those of Hobbes, Montesquieu, Cicero, and Ward. The last will turn out to be fundamental for Cobb's argument: "Yet Ward, after examining its claims with great attention, is forced to conclude, in the language of another writer, that 'To speak of one fixed, immutable, and universal law of nature, is framing an imaginary scheme, without the least foundation in the nature of things, directly contrary to the present order of the whole creation.'" Cobb then discusses the views on the law of nature of a large number of writers, showing vast learning in the process—the large number of writers and his own learning are vital to his enterprise—to conclude at §10:

> These varying definitions might be multiplied to almost any extent. Sufficient have been adduced for our purpose, viz.: first, to show that as a general rule, men have very indefinite ideas, when they speak of the law of nature, and would many times be puzzled to explain their own meaning; second, to deduce from these the most satisfactory idea of this law, for

the investigation which we undertake. From what has been said, it is evident that whatever definition we adopt, the nature of man enters as a very important element, and if that nature is subject to any variation, from race, or climate, or history, to that extent the consequences of the law of nature must vary when applied to him.

His conclusions are in three parts: what the law of nature is, is by no means clear; whatever it is, the nature of man is a very important element in the concept; and, finally, if the nature of man varies from whatever cause, including race, which he lists first, then the law of nature as applied to him must also vary.

Cobb then goes on to distinguish rightly between the state of nature and the law of nature and says at §11: "A celebrated Scotch commentator applies this distinction clearly and philosophically to the subject of slavery: 'It is indeed contrary to the state of nature, by which all men were equal and free; but it is not repugnant to the law of nature, which does not command men to remain in their native freedom, nor forbid the preserving persons at the expense of their liberty.'" [16] This distinction is already in Justinian's *Institutes* 1.3.2, where we are told that slavery is part of the ius gentium—that is, law found everywhere—but is contrary to nature, contra naturam. As Cobb observes, this distinction was followed by the celebrated Roman law scholar Heineccius.[17] And Heineccius was one of the two Roman law scholars most highly regarded in America. It was also, he records, the view of Vinnius. And Vinnius was the other most highly regarded Roman law scholar in America.[18] Cobb reasonably translates: "This is contrary to that common condition of all men, which they had, by nature, from the beginning, although it is not repugnant to natural justice to become a slave, either by contract or by crime." To the same purpose he cites the Frisian jurist Ulrich Huber, whose writing on conflicts of laws was the foundation of the American law.[19]

Cobb then at §14 supports this position by referring to writers on religion who also claimed that some persons would benefit from being slaves, and he concludes at §14:

With these preliminary remarks, we adopt, as the law of nature, when applied to man in his intercourse with his fellow-man, that obligation which reason and conscience impose, so to shape his course as to attain the greatest happiness, and arrive at the greatest perfection of which his nature is susceptible. Consequently, whatever interferes with the attainment of this happiness and perfection does violence to the law of his nature, and whatever promotes or is consistent therewith is sanctioned by the law of his nature. In this view, *natural rights* depend entirely upon the nature of the possessor, not of the right; for, it is the former and not the latter that determines the question of right. Hence, to speak of the natural right to personal liberty is unphilosophical, until the previous question is settled, that such liberty will conduce to the happiness and perfection of the possessor.

Cobb's scholarly authorities are chosen with erudition and great literary skill: the German Heineccius; Vinnius from Holland; the Frisian Huber; Bishop England from Ireland, who became the Roman Catholic bishop of Charleston, South Carolina, was regarded as a friend of slaves, and opened a school for free blacks;[20] Thomas Aquinas of Italy; and the Byzantine St. Basil. They come from various states. With the sole exceptions of St. Basil and England, none had a personal acquaintance with slavery, none was a slave owner or slave trader. None had much exposure to slavery. Above all, none, apart from the slave sympathizer England, was American. Cobb wants to appear, and does appear to be, wholly objective. He is simply stating facts: great jurists and great theologians from all over the civilized world do not regard slavery as contrary to natural law, and indeed for them it can be beneficial to the enslaved. So objective is he being that he does not rely upon, or even refer to, southern authorities! His literary triumph is that he never at this stage indicates the international character of his witnesses or that he is leaving out his fellow southerners who might be thought to be biased on the issue of slavery.

Cobb has now reached the point (at §15) at which he was aiming all along: "In this view, is Negro Slavery consistent with the Law of Nature? We confine the inquiry to negro slavery, because, upon the principles already established, it is undoubtedly true, that the enslavement, by one man or one race, of another man or another race, physically, intellectually, and morally, their equals, is contrary to the law of nature, because it promotes not their happiness, and tends not to their perfection. Much of the confusion upon this subject has arisen from a failure to notice this very palpable distinction." Once more he is pointedly not relying on southern experts. At great length he sets out the weaknesses, as he sees them, of negroes and claims these are innate and not the consequence of slavery

(§§30–50). Indeed, "In mental and moral development, slavery, so far from retarding, has advanced the negro race."[21]

Thus for Cobb, the slavery of blacks in the South is justified, is in harmony with the law of nature, and is even beneficial to the slave. His erudite conclusion rests, he makes it appear, on solid, acceptable, worldwide scholarship, and he has not invoked the opinions of fellow southerners, however learned, who might be thought to be biased.

Chapter 2, "Slavery Viewed in the Light of Revelation," appears with the inevitability of the denouement of a Greek tragedy. Chapter 1 was to show the consistency of negro slavery with the law of nature; this second chapter opens with the claim we saw in the first chapter of the present book, made by St. Augustine, that the law of nature is the will of God.[22] He returns to the Old Testament. The last of the Ten Commandments (Exodus 20.18) not only shows God recognizing the right of property in male and female slaves but protects it from covetousness.[23] God not only *gave* (Cobb's emphasis) slaves to Abraham, but (§54)

He commanded the Jews to make slaves of the heathen round about them: "Of them shall ye buy bondmen and bondmaids. Moreover, of the children of the strangers that do sojourn among you, of them shall ye buy, and of their families that are with you, which they begat in your land, and they shall be your possession; and ye shall take them as an inheritance for your children after you to inherit them for a possession. They shall be your bondmen forever." This command being given very shortly after the escape of the Israelites from Egypt, was probably before they owned a slave, was the charter under which they enslaved the Canaanites.

Cobb is guilty of an atypical exaggeration here. God at Leviticus 25.44ff. does not command the Jews to make slaves of the heathens around them. The Jews may have slaves—there is no command that they must have slaves[24]—and they are to be from the heathen around them. The exaggeration, which I am ready to believe was accidental, is revealing. For Cobb, God wills that certain people enslave certain other people: for "Jews" read "southerners," for "heathen" read "blacks." He then proceeds to show (§§58–64) that Jesus not only accepted slavery: "he recognized distinctly and approved the master's superiority" (§60). Into detail we need not go. For present purposes what alone is important is the central position in his argument that Cobb gives to revelation: an argument that would be given serious weight by his contemporaries. He concludes the chapter at §65:

> From this investigation into the law of nature, the will of God, our conclusion is, that until the nature of the African negro becomes by some means radically changed, there is nothing in his enslavement contrary to the law of his nature. In this, we speak of the limited or qualified slavery, such as exists at present in the United States, and not of absolute or pure slavery, as defined by us. For the latter includes the power over life, the *jus vitae et necis;* and as it cannot be said that the physical, intellectual, or moral nature of the slave, can be improved, or his happiness promoted, by the existence or exercise of such a power as this, so we find in the law of nature no justification of or foundation for this power.

Southern slavery is justified: it is in accordance with the nature of the African Negro, the law of nature, and the will of God, and it is mild.

Cobb comes at last in chapter 3 to deal with what is ostensibly the subject matter of the book, "The Law of Negro Slavery in the United States of America." But he has already taken up more than half the space he allots himself! I do not wish to examine here in detail his discussion of the rules, which is in general excellent, with much citation of even European authority. Rather, I want to concentrate on two points that I think indicate his whole purpose.

First, of the remaining twenty chapters, seven are concerned with conflicts of laws, that part of a state's law that deals with situations in which relevant facts have a connection with another legal system. The issue is, the law of which state to apply. Cobb's emphasis on it seems disproportionate, but it was *the* political-legal issue that concerned him. The real, difficult question was the effect of passage through or sojourn in a free U.S. state of a slave from a southern state. Cobb rightly saw that the failure of some northern judges to respect the law of southern states was disruptive of the Union. Earlier, his brother, Howell, who was governor of Georgia, had asked Thomas to write an opinion on the New York case *Lemmon v. The People.*[25] Howell incorporated it in his annual message of 1853:

> If it be true that the citizens of the slaveholding States, who by force of circumstances, or for convenience, seek a passage through the territory of

a non-slaveholding State with their slaves, are thereby deprived of their property in them, and the slaves *ipso facto* become emancipated, it is time that we know the law as it is. No court in America has ever announced this to be law. It would be exceedingly strange if it should be. By the comity of nations the personal status of every man is determined by the law of his domicile. . . . This is but the courtesy of nation to nation founded not upon the statute, but absolutely necessary for the peace and harmony of States and for the enforcement of private justice. A denial of this comity is unheard of among civilized nations, and if deliberately and wantonly persisted in, would be just cause of war.[26]

That failure to observe comity of nations could be a casus belli was proved by the aftermath of the Dred Scott case.[27] Cobb's main purpose in these chapters is to underscore the unreasonableness of northern abolitionists, given that southern slavery was mild and in accordance with the law of nature.

Second, we have Cobb's final paragraph of the book in §391: "Having concluded our view of the negro slave *as a person,* we shall hereafter consider of those rules of law to which *as property* he is subject. In that investigation we shall find that his nature as a man, and his consequent power of volition and locomotion, introduce important variations in those rules which regulate property in general."[28] He appends a note: "This branch of the subject will be considered in another volume." It never was, and I doubt if this second volume was ever in serious contemplation.[29] Cobb had made the case he wanted to make.

CONCLUSION

If a work of rhetoric is to be judged by the extent to which it was persuasive, then Cobb's book was a failure. He was intent on persuading not his fellow southerners but northerners. Most northern reviews were unsympathetic.[30] If Cobb had hoped for anything else, he was unrealistic. But his rhetorical skill must be admired.[31]

It should be emphasized that Cobb was not the only defender of southern slavery. There was a mass of pamphlets and books.[32] The difference was that Cobb was ostensibly writing an objective legal treatise.

In two ways Cobb was successful. First, he laid stress on comity of nations

and conflict of laws, which was a flash point at which the northerners could easily be seen to be at fault in the wider field of national unity. He brings out the
political, legal issue very clearly as a legal issue. Cobb is on the offensive but gen-
tly. His treatment of conflict of laws contrasts markedly with that of Joseph
Story, whose *Commentaries on the Conflict of Laws* (1834) was *the* book on the subject.
Story—carefully and deliberately, I think—says not one word about the effect
on the status of a slave brought from an American slave state into a free state.[33]

Second, to some extent at least, for nonlawyers, Cobb would turn attention
away from the law reports. The southern case law shows slave law in a much
less favorable light. This is, of course, inevitable. Case law is always concerned
with a failure or breakdown of human relations, and this will be nowhere as obvious as when the parties are of vastly different status.

Cobb's art was to appear artless. He does not use irony or sarcasm against
opponents. He does not stress his (apparent) reluctance to use artifice. He successfully hides his passionate nature and convictions.[34]

CHAPTER FOUR

LAW AS LITERATURE, LITERATURE AS LAW

LAW AS LITERATURE: WITHOUT REALITY

It is a characteristic of treatments of a legal situation that they oversimplify. Certain facts that are vital to the human understanding of the situation are omitted. This is true of law reports, whether from the United States or (a more extreme example) France.[1] It is true to a remarkable extent of the opinions of the Roman jurists. Facts are not allowed to obtrude upon the law. In most instances we cannot even hazard a guess as to whether the discussion relates to a real episode or is entirely fictitious. Sometimes, when the treatment contains details that are irrelevant to the law, we may assume a real episode.[2]

The juristic treatment is bloodless. In this chapter I will give a few examples chosen mainly from discussions of the *lex Aquilia*, the Roman statute of around 287 B.C. that dealt with damage to property. The choice is dictated by two considerations: first, the human interest of the situations; second, in chapter 5 I will look at the subsequent history of the statute into modern times in South Africa. For the present chapter, the scope of the law and its development in Roman times are irrelevant. What matters is the treatment of the factual situation.

CASE I

> D.9.2.30pr. A man who kills another's slave caught in the act of adultery will not be liable under this law.

The text from the third-century jurist Paul does not say so, but we must understand that the woman is the killer's wife. It focuses on one issue and one issue only: did the husband act wrongfully, *iniuria*, in killing the slave and so become liable to a civil action under the lex Aquilia for damaging or destroying another's property? But all sorts of issues spring to mind. Did the husband know the adulterer was another's slave? If so, how, and what would it mean for the relationship of the husband and the slave? Was the slave a domestic servant or a field laborer or even a bank manager, a doctor, or a celebrated actor? Was the husband's anger more justified because the adulterer was a slave? Even if the slave was, in practical terms, wealthy? How had the wife come to know the slave? Were the husband and slave business associates? Did the wife incite the slave? Did the husband know of previous infidelities? Was the whole episode set up by the husband? Was the wife even a nymphomaniac? How did the husband deal with his wife? All the issues that would lend human color to the issue are ignored. No doubt if the slave's owner sued, rhetorical images might be used to argue that *in this case* the husband had behaved *iniuria*.

CASE 2

D.9.2.33pr. If you killed my slave I do not think that personal feelings are to be estimated. For instance, if someone killed your natural son whom you wished to buy at a high price, but for the amount he would be worth to everyone. Sextus Pedius also says that the prices of things are judged not by affection nor usefulness to individuals, but in a general way. And so, he who possesses his natural son is not on that account richer because if another person possessed him he would redeem him at a higher price; nor does he who possesses another's son have as much as he could sell him for to the father.

This is another lifeless example, again from Paul. Under the lex Aquilia, one who wrongfully killed another's slave had to pay the highest value the slave had had in the past year. The jurist, Paul, begins with the unexceptionable proposition that the value of the slave must be objectively assessed. But he moves on to a proposition more open to question. You own my illegitimate son. I have, let us say, made an offer to purchase him at a sum twice his normal market value, and you have not yet decided whether to accept. Then Marcus kills him, and you bring a suit against Marcus under the lex Aquilia. It is not difficult to imagine the range of arguments that in reality might surface. You might argue that, though feelings might be ignored, here the value I put on your slave was the objective value for you, because you could sell at that price. Marcus might respond that I might withdraw my offer or die. The fervor of a court battle is excluded, even though Paul is not just setting out an abstract rule but gives poignant illustrations.

CASE 3

D.9.2.27.34. If a man hired a slave to drive a mule and entrusted it to him, and the slave tied the mule by his halter to his thumb, and the mule broke away so that it tore off the slave's thumb and dashed itself over a height, Mela writes that if an unskilled slave was hired out as experienced, an action on the lease may be brought against the owner for the disabling or damaging of the mule. But if the mule was excited by someone striking or frightening it then the owner, that is of the mule, and of the slave would have an action on the *lex Aquilia* against the person who excited it. I [Ulpian] think that in the case where there is an action on the lease there is also an action on the *lex Aquilia*.

The basic factual situation discussed by Ulpian, also of the third century, is dramatic: a slave loses a thumb because he had tied a mule's halter to it, and the mule hurls itself over a cliff. No doubt the drama determined the choice of example. But again the issues that would concern practitioners—how to win the case—are lacking. How would the hirer prove that the slave was represented as skilled? How could it be proved that someone frightened the mule? What is lack of skill? Should the notion be applied only to tasks involving specialist training? Slave testimony was restricted in any event, but what weight could be given to the evidence of a mule driver stupid enough to tie the halter to his thumb?[3]

CASE 4

D.9.2.31. If a pruner when he threw down a branch from a tree or a man operating a crane killed someone who was passing, he is liable on these conditions: if it fell in a public place, and he did not call out so that the accident could be avoided. But Mucius said, even if the same happened on private property, an action could be brought for negligence. For he said it was negligence that what could be foreseen by a careful person was not foreseen, or a warning was given when the danger could not be avoided. On this reasoning it does not much matter whether the person was making his way on public or on private ground, since often, commonly, persons make their way through private ground. But if there is no path, he ought to be liable only for wrongful intent; for negligence is not to be attributed to him when he could not have guessed that someone would pass through that place.

The jurist Paul, and the much earlier Mucius, whom he cites, are concerned with the broad principles of the law, though they deal with examples. Orators would have a field day with such a case. The legal issue is negligence and what could be foreseen. If the injury was on public land and a shout was given, did it matter that the victim was infirm, deaf, or a child? What defense attorney would not argue that, though there was a path on private ground, this accident took place in the heat of the day when no sensible person would be walking on the path? Or yes, there was a path, but the victim was not actually on it but sleeping in the shade of the tree. Or yes, there was a path, but strangers were forbidden to use it and could not be expected to be there. Or yes, there was a path, but it was used only by cows, and the victim was a human slave.

CASE 5

D.9.2.11pr. Again Mela writes: if when people were playing at ball, one of them hit a ball rather hard and knocked it against the hands of a barber, so that a slave whom the barber was shaving had his throat cut because the razor was forced against it: in whichever of them was negligent the action on the *lex Aquilia* will lie. Proculus says the barber is at fault; and certainly if he were shaving in a place where people were accustomed to play or where there was heavy traffic some blame will be attributed to him: though it is well said that if anyone entrusted himself to a barber who had his chair in a dangerous place he has only himself to blame.

No comment on the absence of human excitement in Ulpian's arguing of the case seems needed.

I could go on, multiplying case after case, from the lex Aquilia, and from theft, sale, hire, wills, and so on, but I hope I have made my point. The Roman jurists were a self-selecting group. They wished to gain a reputation among other jurists by their skill in legal interpretation. As jurists they were unpaid and had no official position. In the later Republic they were wealthy, aristocratic gentlemen who might, and often did, seek high elected office. In the first two and a half centuries of the empire they were largely imperial bureaucrats. But they wrote their books to win prestige, to show they were able jurists. They were not without literary art. When it was possible, they chose, even invented, titillating scenarios. They made up intriguing scenarios, but then they ignored human realities to reach their interpretation of the law.[4] They were not interested in winning lawsuits, in the hurly-burly of the courts, in advocates' tricks and dodges, or in rhetorical skill to influence the masses. We are a world away from Mark Antony's speech in Shakespeare's *Julius Caesar*.[5]

But law and legal practice developed at Rome in a decidedly strange way.

LEGAL RHETORIC WITHOUT LAW

"But law and legal practice developed at Rome in a decidedly strange way" is how I ended the previous section, and so it did.

By a strange quirk of fate, juristic interpretation—a major factor in Roman legal development—developed almost entirely without the use of rhetoric. I have set out the detail elsewhere,[6] and here the merest sketch will suffice. Rome became a republic in 509 B.C., and disputes soon broke out between the patricians and plebeians. The former had a monopoly of state offices, including the public priesthoods. The plebeians' grievances centered on law reform, and eventually they compelled the patricians to issue a law code, the Twelve Tables, of around 451/450 B.C. The patricians skillfully gave a monopoly of interpretation of this code to the College of Pontiffs, the body of public priests entrusted with maintaining the right relationship between the gods and the Roman state and its leaders. The pontiffs' functions were therefore primarily religious legal interpretation. They carried over to private law their legal skill in religious matters. In religion their function was interpretation, and interpretation was the only function entrusted to them for private law. The pontiffs, who tended to be leaders also in other high public office, chose one of their number each year to be the interpreter of the civil law. Thus it became one mark of a civic leader to be able to interpret private law. When the pontiffs eventually lost their monopoly of interpretation, their place was taken by those prominent citizens whom we know as jurists. The jurists were, as I mentioned in the first section of this chapter, a self-selecting group motivated primarily by a desire to gain the prestige among their peers. But this prestige was won by skill in interpretation, and they were not much interested in other law jobs. Above all, for present purposes, court pleadings were seldom a matter for them. From this fixation on interpretation comes the nature of juristic writings.[7]

Thus the jurists were not pleaders, and they were not orators. But pleaders are needed, and this necessity was one of the roots of Roman oratory. For the modern reader the distinction between jurist and orator is most vividly apparent in the politician and orator Cicero, who is openly contemptuous of juristic skill.[8]

Into the early history of Roman oratory we need not go; legal pleadings are certainly not the only root.[9] But pleadings in lawsuits are a very proper place for the exercise of rhetoric. A prime subject of inquiry for modern scholars of declamation in the early Roman empire is the extent to which the subject is fantastical, or reflects Greek conditions, or relates to Roman conditions. In the judgment of S. F. Bonner, "If one were to descend to detail, one would discover in the Senecan declamations a wealth of evidence of contemporary Roman life, which has been all but neglected by historians of the subject, owing to the all-too-prevalent suspicion towards everything savoring of rhetoric."[10]

I regard Bonner's work as the most satisfactory on Roman rhetoric,[11] so I will take my starting point from him on a detail where I disagree. I will choose my examples from Seneca the Elder's (ca. 55 B.C.–A.D. 40) Controversiae, on which Bonner concentrates. This L. Annaeus Seneca has long been regarded as one of the greatest exponents at Rome on the teaching of rhetoric.

Bonner rightly criticizes earlier writers for holding that Seneca's declamatory laws have little connection with Roman law.[12] Several are. This is not the point on which I would disagree with him. Rather he overlooks the point that I would stress, that in the Controversiae the arguments usually do not turn on the interpretation of the law. The arguments are not upon the wording of the law. I will quote only one example, Controversiae 3.6, which I select partly for its brevity:

THE HOUSE THAT WAS BURNT DOWN WITH A TYRANT IN IT

An action may lie for damage to property.

A man pursuing a tyrant in flight from his castle cornered him in a private house, and set fire to it. The tyrant went up in flames along with the house. The other man got the reward; the house-owner sues him for the damage caused.

For the "tyrannicide": Whom did you shut out, whom did you let in?—Why didn't the tyrant make for some other house? Everyone shut their doors as he approached.—I couldn't get into your house—though I had got into the castle.—Aren't you glad to have made some sacrifice for the people's liberty?—People say: "This is the man who owned the house where the tyrant was killed." You are pointed out as if you were the killer of the tyrant.—"Give me back my house." That means you hadn't lost it while the tyrant was alive. You were his friend, his hireling, at least (and this you cannot deny) his host.—I waited for a long time to see if the tyrant would get thrown out.—Better either blame yourself—*you* were so friendly to the tyrant that he chose your house particularly, *you* took him in—or blame the tyrant, who caused you damage by resorting to your house, or (to free you from guilt) blame Chance, which sent the tyrant to your house in particular.

The other side: The loss ought to be borne by the recipient of the reward. You may fairly be blamed for damage involved in something from which you drew the profit.—The tyrant didn't *choose* my house—he hadn't time. He burst in where he could, at a time when *I* wasn't there.—This man took the opportunity of doing me harm. He chose not to enter, but instead selected a method of killing the tyrant that was uncertain, slow and dangerous for the city.—He surely got a bigger reward on the understanding that he must repair the damage.[13]

Bonner claims, "This is clearly the Roman enactment regarding unlawful damage to property," and he relates it to the lex Aquilia, the statute on the subject.[14] He points to similarities of wording in the lex and the *Controversiae*, which I do not find a persuasive argument; they are not close enough. But that fact is immaterial. Let us assume that the lex Aquilia was in view; then what is significant is that it cannot be seen in the debate.

The lex Aquilia had two basic chapters, the first and the third. The third covered all financial loss resulting from damage to property, other than from the killing of a slave or herd animal. Hence any action on the lex Aquilia for the burning of the house would be under chapter 3. No reference is made in the *Controversiae* to chapter 3.

Under the lex Aquilia the action lay where the damage was caused *iniuria*, "wrongfully." The possible justification discussed for damaging another's house is overwhelming necessity: you pull down a neighbor's house in reasonable fear that the fire will spread to yours.[15] But in the *Controversiae* the justifications for no liability are: (1) the killer of the tyrant could not get into the house otherwise, (2) the tyrant who was admitted was a friend of the house owner, (3) the house owner should be glad to have made a sacrifice for the people's liberty, (4) at the time of the fire the owner had no house because the tyrant was alive. None of these has relevance for the lex Aquilia. The counterargument has even less relevance to anything in the lex Aquilia, basically that the killer of the tyrant should bear the loss because he got a reward for his deed.

I am not, of course, claiming that orators would not have used such arguments in an actual case. My point is that the lex Aquilia, if it was in view, is not in sight.

Other examples can be adduced, but one is enough. Bonner properly refers to *Controversiae* 10.1 as concerning the *actio iniuriarum*, the action for assault or insult.[16] A poor man whose father had been murdered followed his father's enemy while dressed in mourning. But any actio iniuriarum here would have been based on a specific clause of the praetor's Edict that allowed the action where the defendant's behavior was calculated to bring *infamia*, technical disgrace, upon the plaintiff. Of the particular scope of the action there is no indication in the *controversia*.

It may be mentioned in passing that Cicero, writing much earlier, had stressed the unimportance of law and knowledge of it and the importance of rhetoric for court purposes.[17]

Thus in this chapter we have two very different instances of law out of context. In Roman juristic writings the reality of legal proceedings scarcely appears; in rhetorical exercises on legal issues, the law disappears.

Roman law may fairly be described as the most innovative and successful secular legal system that the world has known. From the surviving legal sources, such as the writings of the jurists, the Romans appear the most legalistic people that the world of secular law has known.[18] But it should be remembered what we do not have: we have no official court records and very little information on what was argued in a private lawsuit. Rhetorical exercises on legal matters may suggest that, in practice, matters were very different. The same is suggested by legal speeches of Cicero such as *in Verrem* and *pro Milone*. The Romans, apart from the jurists, may not have been overly legalistic at all.

CHAPTER FIVE

THE LEX AQUILIA
IN SOUTH AFRICA

Recent South African case law is an ideal system to study for law out of context.[1] I say "out of context" because a basic foundation of the law is the law of Holland as it was on 7 April 1652, when Jan van Riebeck formally took possession of the Cape for the Dutch republic.[2] Apart from other considerations, the geography and climate differ markedly from Holland to South Africa. There seems no legal reason for the choice of law to be that of the province of Holland rather than of one of the other Dutch provinces such as Utrecht, but the significant fact for us is that Holland, with Friesland, was the province most penetrated by Roman law. The Roman law that is most important in this context is therefore not classical nor even Justinianic but the *Corpus iuris* as it was understood and accepted in Holland in 1652. A rigid standard has of course not always been adhered to in South Africa. There is at times a rejection of the *Corpus iuris* as Byzantine and an attempt to base a decision on classical law.[3] More frequently there is an attempt to look at interpreters of Roman law from outside the Dutch republic to find the true solution.[4] Roman-Dutch law is not the sole base of the recent law. There are also, unsurprisingly, statutes passed and cases decided in South Africa. After the British Articles of Capitulation of 10 and 18 January 1806 of the Cape, the British kept the existing law, but English law gradually and generally had an impact until at least 1961, when the Republic of South Africa was created.

For the present book, the object of study will be the main branch of torts law—Aquilian liability, as it is called. This is ostensibly based on the Roman statute the lex Aquilia, but the liability has changed virtually out of all recognition, and it is fashionable to speak of Aquilian liability rather than of liability under the lex Aquilia.

The Roman lex Aquilia seems to have been enacted in stages but reached its final form traditionally (and I think acceptably) in 287 B.C. It had three chapters. Chapter 1 gave an action to the owner for the wrongful killing of a slave or herd animal for the highest value he, she, or it had had in the past year. The second chapter was concerned with a point of contract law. Chapter 3 gave an action in classical law for wrongful damage to property that was not covered by chapter 1 and was caused by burning, breaking, or destroying (or breaking off).[5] The measure of damages for chapter 3 is disputed. I accept the view of David Daube, who argued that it was the amount of financial loss that emerged after thirty days.[6] The traditional view is that it was the value that the property had in the preceding thirty days. The injury came to be interpreted very strictly in early classical law, *corpori corpore*, "to the body by the body," and direct physical contact by the wrongdoer to the person or thing was needed. For less direct injuries where the jurists favored a remedy, an ad hoc action entitled *actio in factum* or *actio utilis* would be given. The same remedial actions were given when the plaintiff was not the owner but a deserving person, such as a possessor in good faith or one who had a liferent.

In a book of this kind there is little point in giving the law as it exists today; that is not the point of the exercise. So I have stopped at 1961, when South Africa became a republic. This date allows us to take into account the upsurge of fervor in the use of Roman-Dutch authority after World War II and the takeover of the government by the (Afrikaaner) Nationalists in 1948. Moreover, it enables us to notice the very different approaches taken by McKerron and Price.[7] Above all, the transformation of the lex Aquilia was complete by then.

The apparent emphasis of this chapter is Aquilian liability in modern South African law, but the point is its development from the law of Justinian. The lex Aquilia has undergone considerable modification—to such an extent in fact that in Germany in the eighteenth century (where the law was very similar to that of seventeenth-century Holland) it was doubted whether there had ever been a reception of the statute.[8] How far at any given time the lex was removed from its original scope is not always an easy matter to discover. Only too frequently does one find that a work that is consulted gives the law of an earlier period as it was then understood. Gerard Noodt (1647–1725) is an extreme example,[9] but other writers, for example, Johannes Voet (1647–1713),[10] and indeed most of the commentators, comment on aspects of the statute that had long been obsolete in their day. And moreover, the same thing applies to the lex as we find it in the *Digest*. For example, by the time of Justinian the normal mode of bringing an action was by the process known as the *cognitio extraordinaria*—which did not distinguish rigidly between the limits of one action and those of another—but we still find texts discussing in all seriousness whether a direct action or an actio utilis or an actio in factum lay. We have come across this problem before, in chapter 1, where the compilers' method of working on the *Digest* meant they were not stating the law as it was in their day. Furthermore, it is extremely difficult to see how wide the scope of the lex at that time was, since all of the cases in the *Digest*, which is our main source, almost of necessity have a classical basis. Hence a situation that was so far removed from the lex Aquilia in the early third century after Christ that there could be no question of discussing it under that heading would find no place in the *Digest* exposition even if it was covered by the lex in Justinian's time. Perhaps it is as a result that there is no sign in the *Digest* of the difficult problems arising where there is liability for mere pecuniary loss without physical injury.

There can be no question but that the lex Aquilia is regarded in South Africa as the basis of liability for financial loss as the result of another's wrongful act. But we should note the thesis by Christianus Thomasius entitled *Larva legis Aquiliae detracta actioni de damno dato receptae in foris Germanorum*.[11] In this work, he claims that the action *de damno dato*, "for loss inflicted," in Germany was as different from the lex Aquilia as a bird from a quadruped. First, he gives his opinion of what the ius gentium, the law that is found everywhere as the result of natural reason, on the subject would be. Then he demonstrates that this is very different from the provisions of the lex Aquilia. Next he shows that the law in use was vastly different from the Roman statute and argues that the lex was, therefore, never received. And finally he puts up a plea for the acceptance of the dictates of the ius gentium in those points where it differed from the law accepted in Germany. J. G. Heinecius (1681–1741) vigorously supports him, summarizing the points where *hodiernum ius*, "contemporary law," differs from the lex Aquilia:

Fourthly, it remains for us to investigate the present day use of this title. And here indeed, scholars, in an extraordinary way, commonly praise the use of this title. But if you examine the position accurately you will find almost no trace of it in the courts. We have an action for financial loss. The action is brought to recover the loss and to exact a penalty. But the Turks and the Chinese do the same and they never received anything from Roman law. But, I ask you, do we nowadays distinguish between slaves and four-footed beasts that go in herds, from other things? Or do we take the value of the thing at the highest value it had, undamaged, in the previous year or thirty days? Or do we inquire minutely whether the injury was done by the body to the body, or by the body but not to the body, or neither by the body nor to the body? Or lastly, do we increase the damages if the defendant denies liability? Of course, no one would say we do. And therefore, who can say that the action on the *lex Aquilia* has been received? Therefore, the contemporary action for financial loss is based on natural law and local statutes, not on the *lex Aquilia*.[12]

The general accuracy of these observations as to the substantive law will be confirmed in the course of this section. But the modifications had taken place in most countries of Western Europe at an early date and were not the result of statute. Antonius Matthaeus II (1601–1654) in the chapter in his book *De criminibus* on the municipal law in his title *De damno iniuria data* says, "De Damno paucissima in Statutis civitatis reperio, quae praesenti loco tradi possint," that is, "In the statutes of the Republic I find very few things that can be dealt with in the present place." Yet the rest of the chapter[13] shows how far removed the law was from the lex Aquilia. The changes, in fact, were mainly the result of preexisting custom. François Petrus Van den Heever's criticism[14] of Heineccius that the latter observed a change in the law but gave the wrong reason—the right reason being that although the lex Aquilia was received, "We have jettisoned the Roman pattern of stenciled legal remedies and lay stress on substantive law"— is certainly unjust. Whether one approaches a legal problem from the angle that one has a right and therefore one should have an action, or vice versa, namely that one has an action and therefore one has a right, should be totally irrelevant to the decision. Above all, the approach chosen should have no effect on the quantum of damages. Aquilian liability did, in fact, undergo substantive alteration in the course of its reception, but I think no one would now deny that it was received.[15] Van den Heever was a judge who consistently stressed the Roman-Dutch background.

INJURIES COVERED BY AQUILIAN LIABILITY

The wrongs covered by modern Aquilian liability may be divided into four classes.

PHYSICAL INJURY TO AN OBJECT CAUSING
FINANCIAL LOSS TO ITS OWNER

This first category was the main field of operation of the lex Aquilia in Roman and Roman-Dutch law, and no authority need be given. It is still very important, and if any authority is wanted, see *Richards v. Richardson* 1929 E.D.L.D. 146, a case concerned with the destruction of a wall.[16] Originally the manner in which the injury was done was a matter of great importance. Under chapter 3 of the lex Aquilia, which in classical Roman law covered nonfatal injuries to slaves and four-footed animals that went in herds, and all injuries to other animate and inanimate objects, the action was only available "quod usserit fregerit ruperit," that is, "on account of burning, breaking or breaking off." Now, however—as needs no demonstration, since the action is available for mere financial loss— the manner in which the injury is caused is irrelevant.

FINANCIAL LOSS CAUSED TO THE OWNER OF AN OBJECT
ALTHOUGH THERE IS NO PHYSICAL INJURY TO THE OBJECT

This second class may be subdivided.

Where the Object Is Lost to the Owner but Is Itself Unharmed. For example, in the Roman texts, if coins are knocked out of my hand into the sea or into a drain,[17] or if a silver cup is negligently thrown overboard,[18] or if a fettered slave is released to enable him to escape.[19] The first of these has the jurist Sabinus giving a direct action, but the others all give an actio in factum, which, it has been suggested, was in classical law modeled on the *actio de dolo*, the action for fraud, and was only later brought within the sphere of influence of the lex Aquilia. I have not found any modern cases on this subdivision, but there should be no doubt that the wrongdoer would be liable.

Where What Is Injured Is an Incorporeal Right. As early as classical Roman law, it was recognized that if one suffered financial loss because of wrongful interference with an incorporeal right, one had an action for the full measure of loss suffered, provided that some corporeal object—even one of much lower value—had directly suffered physical deterioration. The main case is in *D.9.2.41pr.*, where Ulpian tells us that if a will is destroyed, the heir or legatees have an actio legis Aquiliae. This action is obviously not for the value of the corporeal will, which would amount to very little, but for the financial loss inuring to the heir or legatees, probably because they were put to the expense of proving by other methods that they were such. This action has been extended in modern South Africa to cover situations where there has been no physical deterioration of an object at all. Thus, in *Nathan Bros. v. Pietermaritzburg Corp.* 23 N.L.R. 107, the corporation was held liable for withholding approval of the plaintiffs' building plans as a result of which the plaintiffs suffered loss. And in *Ntuli v. Hirsch and Adler* 1958 (2) S.A. 290 (W), the plaintiff successfully claimed damages for loss of rental arising from an unlawful sale in execution, on the defendants' instructions, without leave of the court, of the plaintiff's incorporeal right as lawful holder of a site permit.

An interesting question is liability for misstatements. There is no doubt that misstatements that are not defamatory but are made with the intention of injuring another person and do result in financial loss are now actionable under the lex Aquilia.[20] This case is best illustrated by *Bredell v. Pienaar* 1924 C.P.D. 203. A minister of the Dutch Reformed Church stated inter alia falsely and maliciously that the plaintiff, a farmer, was a man of immoral conduct and had committed adultery with a servant who had borne him a child. The minister also falsified some of the evidence given at a meeting of the Kerkraad. The farmer alleged that as a result of this he suffered expense. An actio iniuriarum, the action for assault and insult, being barred by lapse of time, Watermeyer, J., said:

> If, as stated by de Villiers, C.J., in Cape of Good Hope Bank v. Fisher (4 Juta at 378), and quoted by de Villiers, J.A., in Matthews v. Young (1922 A.D. 504) "in the time of Voet and Matthaeus, the Aquilian Law had received an extension by analogy to a degree never permitted under the Roman Law, the *actio in factum* being extended to every kind of loss sustained by a person in consequence of the wrongful acts of another" then it would appear more likely that this (the Aquilian action) would be the form of action, or at any rate that this would be *one* form of action.

I am not therefore satisfied that the plaintiff's cause of action in respect of patrimonial damages, alleged to have been caused to him by the publication of false words, not defamatory, is prescribed. [P. 213]

And judgment was accordingly given for the plaintiff. This is an excellent illustration of South African judicial reasoning from Roman-Dutch law. The obvious ancient remedy was the Roman actio iniuriarum. This was barred by lapse of time. But the judge wanted there to be a remedy, so he turned elsewhere, to the lex Aquilia. Instead of reasoning from other South African cases that there could be an action for financial loss where there was no physical injury, he argued from the lex Aquilia as it was interpreted in the seventeenth century. No action on the lex Aquilia would have lain in the time of Justinian.

More difficulty is found where the misstatement is made not willfully but negligently. R. G. McKerron has stated that "in principle there is no reason why in our law an action should not lie for a negligent statement which causes damage, and in *Perlman v. Zoutendyk*[21] the existence of such a cause of action was expressly recognized.[22] He then proceeds to restrict this to cases where the defendant owed the plaintiff a duty to speak carefully if he spoke at all and he says that in general a person must exercise care if the misstatement may result in physical injury to the persons or property of another. But, he goes on, where the misstatement can result in nonphysical damage only, the courts are reluctant to recognize the existence of a duty of care; and he concludes,[23] "It is clear that liability depends on many considerations, and it is therefore impossible to define with precision the circumstances in which it arises. Two considerations, however, would seem to be of paramount importance: (1) the existence of a relationship between the parties arising from contract or otherwise and (2) the fact that the plaintiff had no reasonable practicable means of protecting himself from any loss he might suffer through acting in reliance upon the statement."[24] This attitude is based mainly on the case of *Alliance Building Society v. Deretich* 1941 T.P.D. 203 and indeed, in an earlier edition[25] McKerron said, "It follows—as was held in *Alliance Building Society v. Deretich*—that ordinarily there can be no liability based upon negligence for a misrepresentation made not to the plaintiff himself but to other persons concerning him." It seems to me, first, that McKerron's attitude is contrary to the principles of Roman-Dutch law and introduces the technical concept of the duty of care, which has no place in South African law,[26] and second, that there were no decisions that, in fact, properly laid down the proposition that an action would only lie for a nonphysical injury resulting from a negligent misstatement made to another if there is some relationship between the parties. In fact, McKerron here as elsewhere consistently made South African law more English than it was.

As to the first point, we have seen that there was without doubt liability for financial loss caused by malicious misstatements made to third parties—*Bredell v. Pienaar*—and this is the natural and rightful consequence of the extension of the lex Aquilia. But there is not the slightest indication that in Roman law any distinction as to liability under the lex Aquilia was ever drawn between cases involving dolus and cases involving culpa. Indeed, all the evidence is the other way. The lex Aquilia punished *damnum iniuria datum,* "financial loss wrongfully caused," and in the course of time, *iniuria,* which was always the operative word, was interpreted as meaning *culpa aut dolo,* "by negligence or malice." There was no room for further distinctions. F. H. Lawson, however, in his discussion of *D.*9.2.27.10 [27] suggests that only an actio in factum may have been given where your neighbor carelessly places a movable stove against a common wall and the wall is burned down, whereas if someone deliberately set my house on fire and the fire spread to yours, you had a direct action (*D.*9.2.27.8) because the damage in the second case was the result of a willful act, whereas the damage in the first was caused by negligence. But this reasoning seems incorrect. First, there is no reason for the jurists to be more willing to give the direct action if there was malice. After all, in classical law, the actio de dolo would have been available if there had been no other remedy. Nor has it ever been convincingly shown that an actio in factum was less satisfactory than the direct action. More important, Lawson's argument does not explain why in the first case the jurist Proculus gives as the reason for his decision (and this must be the key to the problem) that one could not have brought the action against one who had a fireplace. The situation is clarified by an examination of *Collatio.*12.7.8, which is the same text in a less abbreviated form. The meaning of the latter text is this. Proculus refused to give a direct action where your neighbor had his stove against a common wall, because you could not sue him if he had a fireplace. The reason for this is that in both cases your neighbor was acting within his rights, and Proculus was writing at a time when *iniuria* in *damnum iniuria datum* still signified *non iure,* "without right," rather than *culpa aut dolo.*[28] The wall was, of course, burned, although Proculus did not say so, doubtless because he regarded it as obvious that it had to be damaged if there was to be any question of the action. Lawson mistranslates "Sed non proponit exustum parietem" as "But he does not put the case of the wall being burnt down." [29] In abstracto the sentence could mean this, but it need not mean anything more than "But he does not say that the wall was burnt down." And the subsequent discussion, especially the sentence "Fortassis enim de hoc senserit Proculus," "Perhaps that was what Proculus felt," would be inexplicable if Ulpian knew that in fact Proculus was discussing the case where the wall was not burned down. The difficulty in the text arises from Ulpian's failure to appreciate Proculus's reason. By the time of Ulpian, *iniuria* had come to mean culpa and dolus, and there could be little doubt that the neighbor had acted negligently. Hence for this later jurist, the direct action was appropriate, and Ulpian's lack of historical knowledge led him to try to explain the earlier decision on another ground. For this reason he raises the question whether an actio in factum would be appropriate where one feared future damage, and he suggests that this might have been what Proculus was thinking of. But he himself rather takes the view that a *cautio damni infecti*, the guarantee against threatened damage, would suffice. This text is very accurately summarized in D.9.2.27.10 with the cunning substitution of *puto* for *putat*, which allows the discussion to be considerably simplified. The differing decisions in D.9.2.27.8 and 10 are explicable on the ground that in the former the direct action is given by Ulpian, while in the latter, although only actio in factum is given, this is directly attributable to Proculus, a much earlier jurist. The latter text is no authority whatever for the view that the direct action was more readily given where there was dolus.[30]

As to the second point, until 1941 it would have been agreed that no case turned on whether there was liability for financial loss caused by negligent misstatements, although there were obiter dicta on both sides. But in that year was decided the case already mentioned of *Alliance Building Society v. Deretich* 1941 T.P.D. 203, on which McKerron relied for his conclusion that generally there would be no liability for negligent misstatements made to another unless there was some relationship between the parties. T. W. Price, who took the opposite view,[31] held that *Alliance Building Society* turned on the point, but he says, "Based as it is upon English authority only, [it] cannot, with every respect, be accepted as South African authority, ignoring as it does the basic principles of our law of delict." I agree with the second author that the case is not good authority for Aquilian liability, but here our agreement ends. I suggest that the case is not good authority for two additional reasons. First, the decision turned essentially on a different point, and second, it involved an extreme example of a non sequitur. Barry, J., after saying (p. 216) that it was not necessary for him to decide whether *Perlman v. Zoutendyk* went too far in imposing a duty to take care because it could be distinguished from the present case, and that no authority was cited to impose a liability on the facts of the present case where the plaintiff relied on culpa and not on dolus, went on:

> Moreover the pecuniary loss was caused by the tenants' leaving, resulting in a breach of contract by the tenants *vis-à-vis* the plaintiff. The tenants may have an action against the defendant, but may be met by the defense of contributory negligence, and the plaintiff would have an action against the tenants. But the only action that the plaintiff could have against the defendant would be one for inducing breach of contract. There is no liability for negligently interfering with contractual relations; it is only actionable if done intentionally and knowingly. See Ware and de Freville v. Motor Trade Association (1921, 3.K.B.40 at 91) and British Industrial Statistical Plastics Ltd. v. Ferguson (1938, 4 All E.R. 504). Kotze, J. in Solomon v. Du Preez (1920, C.P.D. 401) pointed out that "an interference with or violation of the legal rights of another, knowingly committed without justification, tending to injure the plaintiff is an actionable wrong by our law," and is so regarded in England and America. An averment in that case that "the defendant with knowledge of the existence of the contract between plaintiff and L, unlawfully and wilfully induced L to break her contract with the plaintiff" sets out a sufficient cause of action. See also, New Kleinfontein Co. v. Superintendent of Laborers (1906, T.S. 241). The plaintiff in this case, would therefore have to base her action on *dolus* and not on *culpa*. [P. 216]

Before examining the decision more closely, we should note the—entirely proper—assumption in the case that if there was any liability on the plaintiff, it would be under the lex Aquilia.

As to the decision itself, it turned primarily on causation, and as Barry, J., said, "The pecuniary loss was caused by the tenants' leaving, resulting in a breach of contract by the tenants *vis-à-vis* the plaintiff." In other words, any liability for the financial loss of the plaintiff should attach not to the persons giving the order to quit but to the tenants who quit the premises. And this interpretation is in accord with the position in Roman law.[32] From *D.9.2.37pr.* especially, it is clear that if you have the right to command me, and on your instructions I do some wrongful act, you will be liable (and I will not be unless the act was particularly heinous), but you will not be liable if I act on your instructions where you have no right of command. In the first situation, your command is the *causa causans;* in the second it is my act. And such, I suggest, was also the modern position and was the basis of the decision in the present case. It must, however, be admitted that there is a great deal of old authority contrary to this position.[33] But I think that this authority is not conclusive against the present view for the following reasons. First, as far as I have been able to see, no Dutch jurist took this stand. Second, the reason for this old position was, in most cases, the fact that the jurists were considering criminal responsibility—for example, where a mandate was given to commit murder—which was not at that time clearly separated from civil responsibility. Third, where they were not discussing criminal responsibility, they relied on the delict of iniuria, where the principles of liability are different from those of the lex Aquilia. A request made *animo iniuriandi,* with the intention to injure, to spread a false report would clearly be actionable as a straightforward case of iniuria. But if the old authority should be regarded as authoritative, then *Alliance Building Society v. Deretich* was wrongly decided, since there is nothing in the authorities to suggest that it mattered for liability under the lex Aquilia whether the misstatement or request to do a wrongful act was made fraudulently or merely negligently.

On the other hand, the authority of the case is considerably weakened by a glaring non sequitur. Barry, J., in the passage quoted above, referred to the remarks of Kotze, J., in *Solomon v. du Preez* that knowingly to interfere with the legal rights of another would ground liability. And he concluded, "The plaintiff in this case, would therefore have to base her action on *dolus* and not *culpa.*" But *Solomon* was concerned solely with dolus, and culpa was not discussed. It was therefore inappropriate to conclude that because there was liability for dolus there could not also be liability for culpa.

Despite this last point I suggest that the case was rightly decided and that there should be no Aquilian liability. But I would disagree with McKerron's conclusion that ordinarily there will be no liability for negligent misstatements resulting in purely pecuniary loss where there was no relationship, contractual or otherwise, between the parties. At the very most, all the case lays down is that where *A* negligently induces *B* to act wrongfully in respect of his contractual obligations to *C,* whereby *C* is caused financial loss, *C* as a result of the intervening wrongful act has a right of action not against *A* but only against *B.* I suggest that if a case similar to *Bredell v. Pienaar* arose, differing only in that the minister acted negligently and not willfully, the minister would be liable on an action on the lex Aquilia. McKerron consistently overemphasized English legal input.

FINANCIAL LOSS CAUSED THROUGH

PHYSICAL INJURY TO A FREEMAN

Wounding of Plaintiff. From at least the time of Justinian, a freeman who was wounded had an action termed *actio utilis* for his loss.[34] An action was likewise granted in Roman-Dutch law[35] and in modern law.[36] Damages cover the financial loss: for example, loss of earnings and medical expenses.

Wounding of Another.[37] Roman law gave an action to a father whose *filiusfamilias* was injured.[38] This action was based on the father's *potestas*,[39] domestic power, and so was limited in its application. But with the altered position of sons in Roman-Dutch law—the lifelong power of fathers had disappeared—the basis was obscured and came to rest simply on financial loss, and so at the same time the action was restricted to injuries to minor children.[40] The changed basis in turn allowed a husband to sue for financial loss caused by injury to his wife. Thus in *Abbott v. Bergmann* 1922 A.D. 53, De Villiers, J.A., said:

> In Warneke's case I took occasion to point out that, in spite of the rule of the Roman-Dutch law that a money value could not be placed upon the body or limb of a free man, the Romans allowed a father to recover the medical expenses and the loss of services of a son who was wounded, and this extension of the *lex Aquilia* was recognized by our law in respect of sons as long as they were minors (Voet 9.2.11 and Grotius Introd. 3.34.3). As in the case of the death of a wife, our law is, however, silent whether a husband can recover from a person who has through *culpa* injured his wife, though not fatally. But no reason can be suggested why a husband should not be allowed to recover the actual pecuniary loss sustained by him under these circumstances. . . . For, in principle, no distinction can be drawn between the two cases.

This conclusion would not be justified in Roman law but is in modern South African law. It would not be justified in the former system because the basis of the action was that the filius was in the potestas of his father and so was akin in some respects to a slave, whereas the wife in classical Roman law and later would not be in the *manus*, matrimonial power, of her husband.[41] But with the change of the basis of the action in modern law to loss of support and straightforward financial loss, he would have an action [42] especially where the marriage was in community of goods. And indeed, it has been held that even where the marriage is out of community, since the wife owes her husband a legal duty to help in his business if such assistance is essential to the upkeep and maintenance of the joint household, then the husband where he is deprived of his right through a wrongdoer's negligence and has suffered financial loss has an action for the recovery of his damages: *Plotkin v. Western Assurance Co., Ltd.* 1955 (2) S.A. 385 (W).

In Roman law the owner could sue on the lex Aquilia for financial loss as a result of injury to his slave, and this was perhaps the most common application of the statute. In Roman-Dutch law this right of action was extended to cover financial loss caused by injury to a free domestic servant.[43] And recently there was an unsuccessful attempt to extend the rule to cover all cases where an employer has a pecuniary interest although the injured employee was not a domestic servant.[44] It was also suggested in this case that the rule as applied to domestic servants might now be obsolete.

Causing the Death of Another. A fortiori, an action lies at the suit of the head of a household for financial loss caused by negligent killing of his wife or children. And furthermore, the wife and children have an action, based on loss of support, where the husband or father is killed.[45] But their action is excluded as long as the husband or father is alive.[46]

PAIN AND DISFIGUREMENT OF A FREE PERSON

Disfigurement alone did not give rise to an action in Roman law.[47] The Roman-Dutch jurists did give an action,[48] although they admitted that this was contrary to Roman law.[49] This was the result of a fairly slow development that began at least as early as the fourteenth century (Albericus ad Ravennas), but we need go no further back than Gomez, apparently the earliest jurist who, on this point, is commonly cited by the Roman-Dutch writers. After saying that a free man has no action on account of a scar, he goes on, "Adde tamen quod in muliere bene aestimaretur praedicta cicatrix et deformitas, saltem quando non est nupta, quia per hoc difficilis, et cum maiori dote inveniret maritum, cui nubere possit." [50]

That is, when at least an unmarried woman is disfigured there is an action which at first was presumably intended to cover the amount by which her dowry had to be increased in order to find a husband. The qualification *saltem*, "at least," suggests that the rule was being widened, and it is not surprising to find that Farinacius,[51] who cites Gomez, gives it on account of a woman who is disfigured *especially* where she is to be married and her dowry has to be greatly increased ("longe maiorem dotem constituere"). Then Gothofredus in his comment on the word *deformitas* in *D*.9.3.7 makes it apply to women generally but not to men. And the Dutch go further. Matthaeus[52] says disfigurement should be taken into account, especially in the case of unmarried women, and Groenewegen[53] declares that the Dutch and French rightly make no distinction between the sexes. Even earlier, of course, Grotius simply said, "De smert ende ontciering van't lichaem, hoewel eighentlick niet en zijn vergoedelick werden op geld geschat, soo wanneer sulcks versocht werd" (*Inleidinge* 3.34.2), that is, "Pain and bodily disfigurement, though properly speaking incapable of compensation, are assessed in a sum of money, if such is demanded."[54] Thus, at first, an action for disfigurement was granted in a limited set of circumstances because the father of an unmarried girl had to increase her dowry if she was disfigured, that is, if there was pecuniary loss, but this rule was then extended to all cases of disfigurement although no financial loss was suffered.

Not only disfigurement but also pain willfully inflicted gave rise to an action in Roman-Dutch law,[55] and this is still the case.[56] But one could not get damages for the mental suffering or loss of comfort and society caused by the negligent killing of a close relative as in Scotland.[57]

THE IMPORTANCE OF CHAPTER 2

Chapter 2 of the lex Aquilia in classical law gave an action against an *adstipulator*—a person to whom payment on a contract of *stipulatio* could be made rather than to the creditor—who fraudulently released the debtor,[58] or better, who released the debtor properly but retained the sum exacted.[59] By Justinian's time chapter 2 was obsolete though not stated to have been abolished, and no direct evidence as to its nature existed until the discovery of the Verona Codex of the *Institutes* of Gaius in 1816. In the interim there were many conjectures as to its nature, none of which came near the truth.[60] Very few jurists were like Noodt, who refused to make a guess as to its nature. Indeed, even the careful Noodt,[61] and he was not alone in this, went so far as to suggest that there were more than three chapters.[62]

These conjectures, although all wrong, should not be neglected, because they gave further opportunity to the Roman-Dutch jurists for widening the scope of the lex Aquilia. When a jurist had given his opinion on the nature of the second chapter, he would be tempted to say that it could apply at the present day. Voet, who believed that the action was for the corruption of slaves, is a good example. He points out[63] that the second chapter was not repealed but fell into disuse (because there was a better remedy), but, he says, it is still possible, and sometimes useful, to bring it. Later in the same section he suggests that it could, by analogy, be extended to cover the moral corruption of filiifamiliarum, monks, subjects, vassals, and so on.[64]

MEASURE OF DAMAGES

In Roman law, the measure of damages under the first chapter of the lex Aquilia was the highest value that the slave or animal of the class of pecudes had had in the past year.[65] The reason was probably, as F. P. van der Heever suggests,[66] that slaves as well as pecudes were primarily used in farmwork when the lex was passed, and so it was fairest to fix the damages as the highest value in a full cycle of agricultural operations. Incidental value, for example, where a mule was one of a matched pair, or where a slave was left an inheritance but was killed before entering upon it, came to be included[67] but probably only where the incidental value was still in existence at the time of the killing. This point is never directly stated in the texts, but it appears from the stress laid on the fact that the slave who was left an inheritance died before entering. Otherwise it should not matter whether he had entered or not.[68] In Roman law a person named heir under a will who was not in the power of the testator became heir only when he accepted the inheritance.

Under the third chapter, as already mentioned, the original measure of damages was the loss that became apparent within thirty days from the date of the injury.[69] But by classical law this rule had been slightly altered to become simply the interesse, and where the object was completely destroyed, this was calculated as the highest value the object had had in the previous thirty days.[70] And Justinianic law retained this position. Most of the Roman-Dutch jurists misinterpreted the chapter as meaning that, however slight the injury to the thing, damages would be the value that the thing had had in the past thirty days. They, however, never put their interpretation into practice.[71]

Two modifications are found in Roman-Dutch and modern law. First, the measure of damages was always the loss caused by the wrongful act (plus damages for pain and suffering). Second, and as a result, the distinctions between the chapters ceased to matter, and one simply brought an action under the lex Aquilia, not under any particular chapter. The change in the Roman-Dutch law was almost certainly the result of local law existing before the reception, local law being regarded as better on this point. The change is found not only in the Netherlands but elsewhere, for instance, in France and Germany.[72] Originally, fixed penalties had to be paid for injuries to humans, and almost certainly a trace remains of this practice in the rule that for physical injury to oneself, one can recover, over and above the pecuniary loss, a sum of damages with respect to pain and suffering.

In modern law, where property is completely destroyed, the measure of damages will be the value of the property. Normally, where an object is damaged, the damages will be the difference between the value of the object before and after the injury. And a common method of arriving at this amount is to prove the reasonable cost of repairing the injury.[73] It does not matter whether the repairs are in fact done, and it is irrelevant that the plaintiff has himself carried out the repairs.[74] Where this standard is adopted, any factor external to the injury that reduces the plaintiff's loss is immaterial, for example, that he was insured[75] or that a friend did the repair gratuitously.[76] In *Richards v. Richardson* 1929 E.D.L.D. 146, the plaintiff suffered damage owing to the collapse of his wall through the defendant's negligence. The municipality rebuilt the wall on the plaintiff's agreeing to allow the wall to be set back so as to give a wider pavement. No evidence was led as to the value of the land surrendered to the municipality. It was held that even if there were a substantial difference in the plaintiff's favor between the value of the land surrendered and that of the rebuilt wall, this could not operate in mitigation of damages, since it had not come about as part of the occurrence but had resulted through intervention of a new agency.[77] Where the injury can be repaired by installing new parts and this results in an increase in the total value of the object damaged, the increased market value must be deducted from the cost of repairs. Conversely, where parts are repaired, but the repaired object will still have a lower value than it had before the injury, the difference between the values before and after the injury must be added.[78] But in all cases it must be proved that the damages claimed are reasonable. It is not enough to show simply the cost of the repairs.[79] Where an accurate assessment of pecuniary loss is not possible, the court will, nevertheless, make an estimate of the loss suffered.[80] Sentimental value, of course, cannot be considered.[81]

On occasion, the normal method of assessing damages is impossible or is ousted by a superior approach. In *Witwatersrand Gold Mining Co. Ltd. v. Cowan* 1910 T.P.D. 312, Innes, C.J., said: "It is admitted that the true measure of damages in a case of this kind is the diminution in the value of the ground caused by the flood. Under ordinary circumstances we should take the market value immediately before that occurrence, and compare it with the market value in the condition in which the flood left it; and the difference between the two would be the damages which under ordinary circumstances the Court would award" (p. 314). But this approach could not be used in this particular case, where such a proportion of the topsoil of an area used for agriculture (for which it alone seems suitable) was swept away as the result of the breaking of the defendant's dam that it was impossible to estimate its market value for agricultural purposes after the injury. There it was held that the correct measure of damages was to be calculated on the loss of crops, and the estimated cost of replacing the denuded area with similar soil. It was further held that it was not incumbent on the plaintiff to calculate his damage on the basis that he was bound to shift the surface soil from another part of his land to the denuded area in the absence of proof that it would not injure his land at the place from which it was taken. Another illustrative case is *Oates v. Union Govt.* 1932 N.P.D. 198. In this case the trees in the plaintiff's apple orchard were destroyed by fire caused by the negligence of the defendant's servants. The trees were of a kind that did not bear fruit for thirteen years, and they had in fact been planted for sixteen years. It was held that the plaintiff was entitled to damages that would place her in as good a position financially as she would have been in before the fire. Evidence was led that showed that a different type of apple tree that took only six years to bear fruit would give at least a similar yield, and it was held that damages were the total cost of the restoration of the orchard with such trees (including fertilizing, etc.) plus plaintiff's loss of income pending the restoration, that is, for six years.

Where damage is caused by a negligent act, a right of action accrues immediately for all damage flowing from the act, and the right includes prospective damage; see *Oslo Land Co. Ltd. v. The Union Govt.* 1938 A.D. 584. There the plaintiff suffered financial loss from the spraying of locust poison in April 1934, and some of his stock died that month. Later he suffered additional losses from the same act. It was held that his right of action arose immediately after the spraying and that further losses did not give rise to new grounds of action; consequently the plaintiff's action failed because his right had prescribed under Act 26 of 1908 (T) s.6, since he had not taken out the summons within three years of the spraying. Watermeyer, J.A., distinguished this case from Voet *Ad Pandectas* 9.2.7. (relying on D.9.2.46), where an action was brought under the third chapter of the lex Aquilia for the wounding of a slave who later died and whose master was then enabled to sue under the first chapter. In this latter case there is no question of suing twice on the same claim; the first action is under chapter 3 for wounding, the second under chapter 1 for killing—and "Voet is merely giving a particular instance in which the *lex Aquilia* provided for two different causes of action arising out of the same wrong and is not laying down a principle of general application when a claim for damages is made under the *lex Aquilia*." A particular instance, it should be noted, that could no longer apply since the fusion of the chapters of the lex.[82] All in all, the rigid assessments of the Roman law have been altered out of all recognition to give a flexible modern system.

Where an action is brought for personal injuries, damages are awarded under three main heads: (1) disfigurement, pain and suffering, and loss of amenities (including loss of expectation of life) generally; (2) expenditure and financial loss up to the time of action; and (3) future expenditure and loss of earning capacity.[83]

Disfigurement, pain and suffering, and loss of amenities. It is impossible to fix a certain relationship between pain and suffering and money, and usually all the relevant circumstances are taken into account and a sum is arbitrarily awarded. The damages are given for noneconomic reasons, and the standing and race of the plaintiff are irrelevant,[84] but sensitivity to pain should probably be considered. But although the injured party is entitled to damages for pain and mental suffering, he cannot, where the exercise of his work is made more difficult by the injury, swell his damages because of a peculiarly personal attachment to his work or demand punitive damages for being deprived of this pleasure.[85] The damages are awarded not only for past but also for future pain and suffering.

Expenditure and financial loss up to the time of action. This category is straightforward and includes items such as loss of earnings and medical expenses. Here, too, matters collateral to the injury should not be used to mitigate or increase damages. Although this principle was accepted in *Van Heerden v. African Guarantee & Indemnity Co. Ltd.* 1951 (3) S.A. 730 (C), it would seem to have been wrongly applied. There the plaintiff sued for damages caused by injuries due to the negligence of the driver of a truck insured with the defendant, and although he received his wages during the period he was out of work from his employers, who need not have paid them, he nevertheless claimed that amount. After accepting the principle stated above, Van Zyl, J., said:

> The payment of plaintiff's salary by his employer during the time he was out of work cannot be said to have arisen out of the unlawful act complained of. The question therefore arises did the payment of salary during this period result from the supervening of a new cause, or did the payment of salary result from the circumstances left undisturbed by the injury, viz. that plaintiff was not injured in this respect. The amount of £87 . 10s. od. was paid to plaintiff as wages and he received them as wages. His employer intended them as wages. Notwithstanding the collision and the injuries plaintiff suffered and notwithstanding his not being at work he was nevertheless paid his wages. The payment cannot be said to be due to the supervening of a new cause. It would have been the supervening of a new cause had the plaintiff received a sum of money as charity but it is not charity when it is given as wages. Under these circumstances I come to the conclusion that plaintiff was paid his wages and consequently did not suffer a loss of wages, and therefore he cannot recover the £87 . 10s. od. claimed as wages. [P. 732]

The decision, I suggest, was wrong, because the judge overlooked the point that although the sum given by the employer was equal in amount to what would have been the plaintiff's wages and may even have been termed such, there was no legal reason for the payments, which in fact amounted to a gift and, accordingly, were collateral. McKerron notes that in England and America the position would have been the same if the employer had been bound by contract to pay wages, although this time the reason would be different, for the employer's "duty is deemed to have been purchased, much like insurance." [86] But the rationale is different.

Future expenditure and loss of earning capacity. As far as future expenses are concerned, these are general damages and need not be pleaded at all, and further particulars need not be given.[87] As for loss of future earnings, a good guide would be a sum awarded on the basis of what would be required to buy an annuity equal to the income lost.[88] But other relevant factors, too, should be considered. Where the injured party has his expectation of life reduced, this is immaterial to the calculation of future earnings. As Ettlinger, A.J., said in *Goldie v. City Council of Johannesburg* 1948 (2) S.A. 913 (W.L.D.): "It was argued that the plaintiff's loss of earnings must be computed only for the period that he will still live. In my opinion this is an erroneous view of the position. Damages are to be awarded for actual patrimonial loss sustained as a result of the defendant's wrongful act. In so far as loss of future earnings is concerned, this would *prima facie* be the present value of the anticipated loss of earnings during the period of the prospective life the plaintiff would have had but for the wrongful act. This is what the plaintiff, or his estate, has lost" (p. 920). Nevertheless, a shortened expectation of life does operate to reduce the damages in that the cost of maintenance of the injured party is deducted for the period during which he would have lived but for the accident and is not now expected to live.[89]

Where an action is brought on account of a physical injury to another who was under a duty to support the plaintiff, the plaintiff must in general[90] show that he was unable to support himself.[91]

The Aquilian action for personal injuries would be unrecognizable to a Roman jurist.

THE PLAINTIFF IN THE AQUILIAN ACTION

WHERE AN ACTION FOR PERSONAL INJURIES IS AVAILABLE TO A PERSON OTHER THAN THE PARTY INJURED

Roman Law. Under the lex Aquilia the owner had an action where his slave had been wrongfully killed or injured.[92] This was one of the most basic cases and was given to the *dominus* for the injury to his property. Later, although it is not

clear when it was introduced or whether the action was originally direct or praetorian, an action, as already mentioned, was given to a paterfamilias whose filius
was injured.[93] This action was certainly based on the father's potestas. Even in
late law there was little, as far as paternal or dominical power was concerned, to
distinguish a filiusfamilias from a slave, the former owning only the *peculium castrense* (funds acquired through military service) or *quasi castrense* (funds acquired
through certain public services), all other acquisitions going to his father. Thus,
in a sense, injury to a filius could be regarded as injury to the property of the
pater. The action was not based on the loss of support that a filius had the duty
to provide for his father. Otherwise, since an actio utilis was given to a freeman
who was injured, it is difficult to see why, when a pater was killed, his filius had
no actio utilis based on loss of support. Moreover, if loss of support were the
ground of liability, it would not matter whether the filius were in his father's
potestas or not. This is not to deny that in Roman law there was a mutual duty
for ascendants and descendants to support one another in need[94] but only that
it was not important for Aquilian liability.

Roman-Dutch Law. Roman-Dutch law granted an action for injury to a domestic servant. This action was based not on the ownership by the master of his servant, since the latter was free, but on the injury to the master's patrimony caused
by the loss of services.[95] It is, in fact, an action to make good the damages arising from the injured person's inability to fulfill a contract, given to the other
contracting party, but there is no evidence that the rule was widened to cover
other similar cases.

   Again, an action was given to parents with respect to injuries to their minor
children for medical expenses and loss of services.[96] This is a survival of Roman
law—though there it was not restricted to minor children—and seems to be
grounded in the dependent position of the children, hence its restriction to injuries to minor children. This too is not based on the child's duty to support his
parents; otherwise the rule would apply even where the child was of full age.
This point is important, because where the action is for loss of support, it can
succeed only if it is shown that the parents could exact the duty, that is, that
they were indigent.

   But another action was made available that did not come from Roman law.
We are told that "modern practice" (probably derived from Germanic custom)
allowed an action to the wife, children, and parents of a free man who was killed

to the extent that the free man had been able and accustomed to support these relatives and was bound to do so.[97] Action by one relative did not bar a subsequent action by another, but each was entitled to sue for what he had lost. This action, too, was for patrimonial loss. What, however, is not clear from the texts is whether the action was always available when relatives of the above groups were in fact supported or whether it was available only when an action could have been brought by such a relative to compel the deceased to support him, that is, when the relative was unable to support himself.

Modern Law. In modern South African law, as already stated, there has been a recent unsuccessful attempt to extend the Roman-Dutch rule that a wrongdoer who injured a domestic servant was liable to the master for the latter's pecuniary loss, to cover all cases where the employer had a pecuniary interest in the life and health of his employee.[98] It was also suggested in that case that the rule, as applied even to domestic servants, might now be obsolete.

Then the right of the father to sue for injuries to his minor son based on loss of services seems to have lapsed. But there is a general action for loss of support. Where the injured party owed another a duty of support that, as a result of the wrongful act he is unable to perform, the other can bring an Aquilian action against the wrongdoer, provided the plaintiff can show that he was unable to support himself, since only then can there be proof of patrimonial loss.[99] The main field for such cases is where indigent parents are supported by a grown son who is wrongfully killed. It has been held that where the parents are married in community, the father may sue on behalf of the joint estate, and there need be no express allegation that he is suing as administrator of such.[100] No case seems to have arisen where the indigent parents were supported by a son who was wrongfully killed and where the defendant argued that the parents had another son who was equally capable and bound to support them and that therefore they had suffered no loss.

A further ground of liability that has no direct authority in Roman-Dutch law has grown up as a result of *Union Govt. (Minister of Railways and Harbours) v. Warneke* 1911 A.D. 657. In this case the wife was wrongfully killed, and the husband brought an action on the grounds of: (1) loss of comfort and society of his wife and (2) loss of her assistance in the care, clothing, and upbringing of their seven children. The action on the first ground failed, but Lord de Villiers, C.J., argued that in Roman-Dutch law, Voet tells us[101] that where a free man was

killed through negligence, his wife or children or other relatives whom he had
supported has a right of action for their loss and that although Voet does not
expressly say that the husband was entitled to sue on his wife's death, it was not
intended to deny any such right to a needy husband whose wife had been accustomed to support him. The chief justice then went on:

> It would be no undue extension of this right to hold that, where a wife
> during her lifetime actively assisted her husband in the support and edu-
> cation of their children, he would be entitled, upon her being killed
> through negligence, to claim such pecuniary damages as he can be proved
> to have sustained by reason of the permanent loss of such assistance. It is
> one of the duties of the wife to render such assistance. According to Voet
> (25.3.6) the duty of supporting (*alendi*) children was in his time common
> to both parents unless one of them was destitute, and by supporting he
> meant (25.3.4) not only feeding and clothing, but also looking after their
> health and education according to their position in life. If in the present
> case the plaintiff's wife was accustomed, during her lifetime, to see to the
> "clothing and upbringing" of his children, she did no more than her duty
> towards him and them, and, if by reason of her premature death his ex-
> penses in the care and education of the children are increased, there would
> be a clear case of *damnum rei familiaris*.

Thus, the ground of liability not being the general duty of support, which only
comes into operation where the plaintiff is indigent, but the more particular
duty of mutual aid arising from the marriage bond, a husband or wife suing for
loss resulting from the death of the other spouse need not show he or she is indigent, *Gildenhuys v. Transvaal Hindu Educational Council* 1938 W.L.D. 260. In this
case, Schreiner, J., said, "The relationship may itself be a fact that creates, *prima
facie* at least, the duty to maintain" (p. 262). A similar situation exists where a
minor child sues for the death of a parent.[102] The action is available not only
where the spouse is killed but also where he or she has merely suffered injuries.[103] Nor does it matter that the parties are married out of community.[104] But
where the marriage is a customary union in accordance with native law and custom, there is no action because there is no duty to support, since the relationship
is not a lawful marriage in accordance with common law.[105] This ground of
liability—for mutual aid, not based on indigency—is not justified on Roman-

Dutch authority, which makes no distinction between the duty to support a wife and the duty to support parents.[106]

Where an action arises for an injury to another party, the plaintiff's right is for the loss he himself has suffered and is not based on the right of the injured party. Therefore, where a person is wrongfully killed and an action is brought by dependent relatives, they are not suing as heirs of the deceased, and so defenses that would have been available against the deceased do not bar the action. Thus before the Apportionment of Damages Act it was no defense to show that the deceased was guilty of contributory negligence (and the measure of damages was the full amount of the loss)[107] or that the deceased had excluded the wrong-doer's liability either by contract[108] or by subsequently accepting a sum in full compensation.[109] However, in *de Vaal N.O. v. Messing* 1938 T.P.D. 34, the full bench of the Transvaal Provincial Division refused an action by the wife and minor children where the husband had been guilty of contributory negligence and was only injured, not killed. Since the wife and children were suing on their own right, which is irrespective of the right of the injured party, the decision is impossible to understand in Aquilian terms. But the decision might be explained on the ground that the right of action came not from the lex Aquilia but from Germanic custom, which restricted the right to cases where the injured party was killed, and that the modern court merely refused an extension. But if a rule from an external source is introduced into the law, which could be, and is, interpreted as an extension of the ordinary law of the land, it is hardly justifiable to refuse to apply it in all circumstances as part of the general system on the ground of its foreign origin.

ACTIONS BETWEEN SPOUSES

In Roman law, an action lay on the lex Aquilia where one spouse wrongfully damaged the property of the other. This, indeed, is one of the points showing that the actio legis Aquiliae was not purely penal but was rather a mixed action, that is, it included damages as well as a penalty. This position was accepted by the Roman-Dutch writers, an action lying, as Voet tells us, because it did not involve infamy.[110] At Rome, actions that brought *infamia*, technical disgrace, on a defendant who lost were prohibited between husband and wife. But the clarity of the law was obscured by general statements that delictal actions did not

lie between husband and wife and by the fact that naturally no actio legis Aquiliae could be brought in Roman-Dutch law between husband and wife where
they were married in community, which was normally the case. Thus we have
statements such as Groenewegen *De legibus abrogatis* on *D*.9.2.27.30, "Non obser-
vatur. Autumnus Cens. Gallic hic propter consuetudinarium, quae est inter con-
juges, bonorum communionem," that is, "Not observed. See Autumnus *Cens.
Gallic at this*, because of the customary community of property between spouses."
This type of statement has induced some modern jurists, wrongly, to hold that
the actio legis Aquiliae was excluded between spouses even when they were not
married in community.[111] And it has been felt to be contrary to the public
interest that there should be such an action.[112] But the case of *Rohloff v. Ocean
Accident and Guarantee Corp. Ltd.* 1960 (2) S.A. 291 (A.D.) held that where the parties are not married in community, such an Aquilian action is competent, and
Malan, J.A., said that in fact such an action is in the public interest.[113] On the
other hand, where the delictal action is such as would, in Roman law, have
brought infamia on an unsuccessful defendant, for example, the actio iniuriarum, there is authority to the effect that it is not competent between spouses
who are living together, *Mann v. Mann* 1918 C.P.D. 89. But Malan, J.A., said in
Rohloff, obiter, that since these consequences of the Roman action no longer applied, delictal actions in general would be competent between spouses.[114] Infamia, as already mentioned, did not exist in Roman-Dutch law.

WHERE THE PLAINTIFF IS NOT THE OWNER
OF THE DAMAGED OBJECT

In Roman law an analogous action was granted in several cases to a person who
was not the owner. We have texts giving the action to the bona fide possessor
(almost certainly they referred originally to the bonitary owner),[115] the usufructuary and usuary,[116] and the pledge creditor,[117] all to the extent of their interest. So also the *colonus*, the tenant farmer, has an action where his crops are damaged[118] but not the borrower of a movable[119] or one who has the right to have
the ownership of the thing transferred to him.[120] There is considerable doubt
as to how far the foregoing represents classical Roman law. Difficulties are especially caused by the cases of the pledge creditor and the colonus, the latter of
whom had only a personal right to the object, and the relationship of their action to that of the owner is obscure. The Roman rules were adopted by the

Roman-Dutch jurists and to some degree extended.[121] Voet *Ad Pandectas* 9.2.10 tells us that even a borrower for use or a fuller will have the action if, as a result of their negligence, they are liable to the owner. And he goes further and says that the *commodatarius* will have the action, even if he has not been negligent, to recover the damage he has sustained through being deprived of the use of the object before the time for which he was entitled to it had elapsed. This is a wide extension and at the least means that anyone in rightful control of an object has an action for his loss if it is wrongfully damaged by another.

Modern law seems to follow Roman-Dutch law exactly. *Erasmus v. Mittel and Reichman* 1913 T.P.D. 617 established that the bona fide possessor had an action. There a native chief in whose name land was registered on behalf of his tribe gave R. the right by verbal agreement to cut grass on the land. R. did not know that the land belonged to the tribe and honestly believed that it belonged to the chief personally. E. negligently caused damage to the grass cut by R. It was held that R. was the bona fide possessor of the grass and was entitled to recover damages from E. to the full value of the loss sustained. In *Hudson's Transport (Pty) Ltd. v. Du Toit* 1952 (3) S.A. 726 (T), a secondhand car was delivered to the purchaser before the certificate of roadworthiness was obtained (prohibited by Ordinance 17 of 1931 (T) s.13 (bis)(1)) and was involved in an accident. The purchaser brought an action, but it was held that he was not a bona fide possessor and so could not recover damages. Here the plaintiff could not even be said to have been in rightful control of the car. On the other hand, in *Maraisburg Divisional Council v. Wagenaar* 1923 C.P.D. 94, it was held that a plaintiff who had hired a car that had been damaged by the defendant's negligence was not entitled to recover as damages the cost of repairs to the vehicle, since he was not the owner and was not liable to the owner. He did, however, recover the expenses he incurred in hiring another car to take the place of the damaged one. In *Spolander v. Ward* 1940 C.P.D. 24, the contractual relationship of the plaintiff and the owner of the car was even more tenuous. The plaintiff claimed damages on the ground that the defendant negligently drove a car that collided with and damaged the car driven by the plaintiff. The car was bought under a lease-purchase agreement in the name of the plaintiff's brother for use by members of the family who lived together. Plaintiff had agreed with his brother that when he used the car he would be responsible for its good condition and would be liable to make good any damage. It was held that since the plaintiff was liable to make good the damage, he had the right to claim damages from the defendant.

CULPA AND THE DUTY OF CARE

PRELIMINARY

The whole topic of liability for negligence is so obscured in the modern law of both the United Kingdom and South Africa, mostly as a result of the ambiguities centered on the concept of the duty of care, that even before we examine the texts and cases we must look at the various possibilities of legal liability. First, let me define negligence in such general terms that the definition would be acceptable as a starting point in any developed system of law. "Negligence occurs where a lawful act is performed with such deviation from the norm that it should have been foreseen that damage to another might ensue from the deviation." This and the immediately following discussion omit the question of liability for omissions and do not go into the question where "should have been foreseen" means "foreseen by a reasonable man" or "foreseen by the defendant." Neither point is of immediate importance, and both will be dealt with later. This definition immediately rules out certain situations that are at times explained on the ground of the duty of care. For instance, where an airplane is flown at the height required by the regulations, and that is customary by a pilot who is not under the influence of drugs or alcohol and who behaves in all respects as a reasonable pilot should, but the noise of the airplane so frightens mink on a mink farm that they eat their young, there cannot be said to be negligence, and no liability attaches to the pilot or owner of the aircraft.[122] The decision should be the same even where the pilot was aware of the mink farm, knew that the noise could have such an effect, and did not alter course, but it could not of course be the same where he deliberately acted with the intention of injuring the owner of the farm.[123]

Accepting this definition, a legal system may adopt one of the following as a general test of liability.

Situation A. When there is negligence, the wrongdoer is liable for all loss that results from it whether foreseeable or not, until there is a definite break in the causal nexus.

Situation B. When there is negligence and some loss to *A* was foreseeable, the wrongdoer is liable for all injury to *A*, even for the part that was not foreseeable, until there is a break in the causal nexus, but there is no liability for loss to *B* that was not at all foreseeable. For instance, if on a part of my land where no outsider is usually found but where my neighbor's cattle are permitted to graze, I cut off a branch of a tree and allow it to fall without looking to see if there is a cow under the tree, I am negligent and will be liable if I killed my neighbor's cow but not if I killed an outsider who, unknown to me, had decided to take a nap in the shade.

Situation C. There is negligence, but there is liability only for injuries that could be foreseen. It is dangerous to talk of remoteness of damage: that is ambiguous. Sometimes "damage is too remote" is used to mean that it was not foreseeable and sometimes that there was a break in the causal connection.

Situation D. There is negligence, but there is liability only for damage to a person to whom one owed a particular duty of care.

Situation E. There is negligence, but there is liability only for damage to a person to whom one owed a particular duty of care, and only for that injury which was foreseeable.

On this analysis, the concept of the duty of care (situations D and E) is important for the legal decision only where there was a negligent act and damage to a person was foreseeable but that person was not allowed an action. The importance of the concept has been exaggerated because (1) it is discussed in cases where there has been, in fact, no negligence, and (2) it is frequently used as synonymous with foreseeability. Even in English law, where it undoubtedly applies, its use as a separate consideration is restricted to a small number of situations, the decision in some of which seems unjust and in others based on special considerations of public policy.[124] Which of the above five situations was the one adopted in Rome and the Netherlands is not easy to discover. Certainly the Roman texts that discuss liability seem to suggest that liability extends until there is a break in the chain of causation.[125] Foreseeability is never raised apart from the initial question of negligence. This rule would tend to exclude situation C. Since there is not the slightest hint in any text that there was liability only if the plaintiff was owed a particular duty of care, situations D and E must be excluded. Ruling them out leaves A and B, and no text gives any guidance. As far as I can discover, no Roman-Dutch writer takes the matter further.

Two other preliminary points should be discussed. First, is the standard of foreseeability that of a reasonable man or that of the defendant? In other words, is liability objective or subjective? It should be noted that in theory there is a vast difference between them, but in practice the difference amounts to very little. When one takes the objective viewpoint, characteristics, for example, blindness, of the class of persons of which the defendant forms part are inevitably brought in, and the question becomes what a reasonable blind man would do in the circumstances. When one takes the subjective test, since one cannot judge a man's inmost thoughts, one thinks in terms of what a person who was similar to the defendant would do. It is all a matter of degree. An example shows how little practical significance the distinction has. In *J*.4.3.8 and *D*.9.2.8.1, a mule driver lacked the strength necessary to hold in his mules, and damage resulted, and he was held liable. Did his negligence consist in the fact that a *diligens pater familias*, a careful head of a family, who was used to driving mules would have foreseen that a person with the strength of this mule driver would not be able to hold in his mules or in the fact that *he* should have foreseen that *he* lacked the strength? No answer can be given. Even the extreme cases do not help. In *D*.9.2.5.2 we are told that if a lunatic does damage he will not be held liable. Strictly, this decision would be correct on the subjective view but wrong on the objective. But as Lawson points out, this statement is not conclusive, since it is "possible for an adherent of the objective theory to treat the exemption as a well-defined exception admitted, it may well be, on grounds of hardship, and . . . to reduce its scope if the greater hardship proves to be on the injured party."[126] Perhaps the really significant case would be where the defendant had no specific disability such as deafness or lunacy but was well below average intelligence without being a mental defective. If his degree of intelligence were considered, the standard would appear to be subjective; if it were not, then objective. However, no text or case turns on this point.

Second, if there is negligence when there is a derogation from the norm of a lawful act, and injury to another could be foreseen as resulting from the derogation, or as Mucius Scaevola put it in *D*.9.2.31, "culpam autem esse quod cum a diligente provideri poterit, non esset provisum," "There is negligence when what could have been foreseen by a diligent man was not foreseen." Then there can be no value in distinguishing degrees of fault. Either there is negligence or there is not negligence. As far as Aquilian liability is concerned, there is no point in asking whether *levissima culpa*[127] equals the contractual *culpa levis in abstracto*.[128] The point may possibly be of value in contract, but there the fundamental question is significantly different. It is not "Has there been negligence?" but "Has there been so much negligence as to result in a breach of contract?"

COMMON SITUATIONS WHERE THERE IS INJURY

Fires Starting in the Open. In *D*.9.2.30.3 we are told that a man is liable if he sets fire to his stubble and the fire spreads to a neighbor's crop or vineyard provided that there was negligence in that the stubble was set alight on a windy day or he did not take care to prevent the fire from spreading. But he is not liable if he did everything he should have done, or if a sudden gust of wind spread the fire. This rule is approved by Voet *Ad Pandectas* 9.2.12, who gives the additional case of liability where a person discharges a gun at a bird that had alighted on a thatched roof or on a corn or hay rick. This Roman and Roman-Dutch rule has been adopted in its entirety in South Africa.

In *Glass v. Grahamstown Council* 18 E.D.L.D. 244, it was held that where the defendant kindled a fire to burn off his grass on a windy day and the fire spread, he was liable although the wind had freshened.[129] In *Van Tonder v. Alexander* 1906 E.D.L.D. 186, the defendant lit a fire to burn out a polecat on a day when a light wind was blowing but did not provide a competent staff to check the fire if occasion arose. The wind freshened and veered, and the fire spread to a neighbor's land. It was held that since the fire was lit in a wind and no sufficient precautions were taken, the defendant would have been liable for damage caused by the wind merely freshening, and the simple fact of the wind having veered did not relieve him of liability. It is also negligence on a windy day to leave a bucket containing unextinguished fire twenty yards from dry grass.[130] But the fact that a fire starts on a man's land and spreads is not enough to ground liability. There must be direct proof of negligence in starting or dealing with the fire.[131] An instructive case is *Van Reenen v. Glenlily, Fairfield and Parow Village Management Board* 1936 C.P.D. 315. There the plaintiff sued for the loss he suffered through a fire that started on the defendants' property and spread to his. The plaintiff argued: (1) the defendants had negligently allowed quantities of dry inflammable material to be on or near the boundary of his land, (2) the defendant failed to supervise adequately people using or frequenting its property to prevent them making fires, and (3) the defendant, knowing of the outbreak of the fire, failed to take adequate steps to extinguish it or stop it from spreading. There was no evidence as to who caused the fire or how it began. It was held (1) that there was no liability under the (English) rule in *Rylands v. Fletcher*, first because, as Centlivres, J., said, it was extremely doubtful whether the doctrine ever formed part of South African law; second, there was no evidence that the defendant brought the fire onto its land; and, third, that allowing woodcutting to take place on the farm, which resulted in some debris being left behind, was not a nonnatural use of the land; (2) that it was not culpa not to exercise supervision over the persons allowed on the land, and there was no presumption that the fire was caused by someone on the land with permission (or even by the servants of the defendant); and (3) there was no duty on the defendant to extinguish the fire, since there is no liability for omissions. The defendant was therefore not liable.

Fires Starting Indoors. It is more likely that a fire starting inside a building has been caused by negligence than one that starts out of doors. Consequently, it is possible to hold that the fact of a fire's starting inside a house and spreading is prima facie evidence of the negligence of the owner or occupier. There is no evidence whatever for Roman law that the mere fact that a fire started inside a building and spread prima facie established a case for delictal liability. The matter was discussed only in connection with contract. The Roman and Roman-Dutch law was excellently expounded by Juta, J.P., in *Daly v. Chisholm* 1916 C.P.D. 562 at 566 – 568. In that case fire began inside leased premises, and the owner brought an action against the lessee for negligence.

> The questions of law which arise are, upon whom is the *onus* of proof of the negligence; if the plaintiff is entitled to succeed what are her remedies, and is the lease at an end. In the Roman law the passages generally relied upon are D.19.11.1 [*sic,* but should be 19.2.11.1.]; 19.9.3 [*sic,* but should be 19.2.9.3.]; 1.15.31 [*sic,* but should be 1.15.3.1.]; 18.6.11 [*sic,* but should be 18.6.12.(11).]; Cod.4.24.5.; D.54.17.23 [*sic,* but should be 50.17.23]; 44.7.14. and the law is summed up by Winschied [*sic,* but should be Windscheid] Pand. Sec. 265 thus, that the lessee is liable in case the house hired by him is burnt down unless he proves that he used all the care of a good house-father. But it is not clear for what he is liable. In D.9.2. sec.9 (*de Lege Aquilia*) [*sic,* but should be D.9.2.27.9] it is said, that if a slave of a tenant in the country went to sleep by the fireside and the villa was burnt down, "Neratius wrote, '*ex locato conventum praestare debet*' if he was negligent in looking after a fire." As a note to *conventum* in the *C. Juris* of Gothofredus is added *an et sequentium annorum? an vero etiam totius villas* [*sic,* but should be *villae*] *aestimationem?*" which are the very things the plaintiff claims here.

In the Roman-Dutch law the question of *onus* of proof is not always kept clearly distinguished from the liability and the form of action which is itself not always kept in view. The distinction is not clearly observed whether the action is the *actio locati* by the letter for restitution of the house by virtue of the contract of lease or whether it is one under the *Lex Aquilia* for damages for the injury caused to the letter by an unlawful act. This distinction may be of great importance. In the cases of deposit, loan, hire, of a movable, e.g. of a horse, where there is a duty on the depository, borrower, lessee to return the thing deposited, lent or hired, and he cannot do so, he cannot escape liability without proving that his inability does not arise out of his own negligence. *Madallie & Schieff v. Roux* 20 S.C. 438: *Liluli v. Omar* 1909 T.S. 192; *Parsons v. MacDonald* 1908 T.S. 809; *Mposelo v. Banks* 19 S.C. 370. The law is the same in the case of a pledge. Grotius 3.8.4; Van der Keesel, *Thes.*, 540. Special reference is made in the authorities to the case of a house burnt down. Zachineus (*Cont. lib.* 1. Contr. 87) is of opinion that the onus lies on the hirer to prove his innocence of *culpa*, which proof he gives by showing the diligence of a good house-father. He does not say anything about the form of action. Gaill (*Prac. Obs.* 2.21) discusses the question, which he calls *nodosa et tristis* but does not always distinguish between the liability of the lessee and the onus of proof, with the result that he is taken to task in some respects by Vinnius (*Select. Quaest.*, II c.33) who argues that if the vendor of a lodging house burnt before delivery is bound *ex empto* unless he proves his diligence, then a lessee of buildings must be bound *ex locato* if they are destroyed by fire, unless he proves that he has not been guilty of negligence. Grotius (3.8.4 and 3.19.11) considers that fire is regarded as negligence unless the lessee can prove unavoidable accident. Van Leeuwen (*Cen. For.* 1.4.10) says that a distinction must be drawn where the creditor (i.e. lessee) grounds his plea on something which is no one's fault, e.g. violence or enemies, inundation, in which case negligence must be proved by the debtor (i.e. lessor). But that implies that the onus of proving the inundation, *etc.*, is on the creditor. He adds that where the object of the obligation is lost by theft or fire, the lessee cannot be excused except on reasonable proof of "innocence," i.e. want of *culpa* or negligence. Burge (Juta's p. 226) says that by the civil law and the law of Holland the onus of proving that the loss was without any default is thrown on the hirer. Sande (*Dec. Fris.*, 3.6.9) is to the same effect.

Voet treats of this question of a house let being burnt down, and of the onus of proof, under the *Lex Aquilia* 9.2.20, and he holds that the plaintiff must prove what he asserts, *viz.,* the *culpa,* and that the defendant, the lessee, cannot be called upon to prove a negative. This view of the onus is held by Voet also in regard to a pledge (13.7.5) where he says that although proof of *culpa* in regard to the damage done to the pledge falls on the debtor (pledgor) the plaintiff, who affirms it; yet if the creditor (i.e., the pledgee) says that the thing was lost or destroyed by accident the onus of proving the loss is on him, and he cites Grotius and Van Leeuwen in the passages noted *suprà* as his authority. As van der Keesel in his Dictata (*Thesis,* 540) points out neither Grotius nor Van Leeuwen make such a statement. He adds that Voet's statement is no way out of the difficulty, because when the pledger claims the pledge he has not got to allege that the thing pledged perished by the *culpa* of the pledgee: all he has to do is to allege and prove that he delivered the pledge and that the debt has been paid, whereupon it is for the pledgee to prove that the thing pledged was destroyed by a *casus fortuitus;* and he adds, "But then comes into consideration the distinction drawn by the *Interpretes* and Grotius, between the different kinds of *casus fortuitus:* for if the pledge is alleged to have been destroyed by robbers, enemy, or inundation the presumption is in favour of the creditor, but if by theft or fire inside the house the presumption is against the latter, and the onus is on him to prove his '*innocence,*' and that that is what Van Leeuwen and Grotius say.

Now Voet is not necessarily in conflict with the other authorities although he cites, e.g. Zachineus in support, for he seems to be dealing with the question from quite another point of view, *viz.,* under the *lex Aquilia,* which is based on the commission of an act not on the omission to do something: though Voet points out that actions were allowed under that law for omissions where there was a duty imposed. It would seem that this point of view of Voet's is responsible for his opinion that even in the case of a pledge the pledgor has to prove the loss of the pledge by the *culpa* of the pledgee—which is quite contrary to the general view. The obligation *ex contractu* of the pledgee is to return the pledge when his debt is paid, and there is no more reason for holding that the pledgor must prove that the pledge was lost by the *culpa* of the pledgee who does not perform that obligation than in the case of deposit or of loan. The weight of authority is therefore much in favour of the view that the onus lies on the tenant to prove how the destruction took place, and that in case of a fire from the inside of the building but the onus lies on him to prove due diligence (Pothier 199; Frenkel v. Ohlsson's Cape Breweries 1909 T.S. 957; and see Holl. Cons., vol. I., C. 256.).

The case is a splendid illustration of the parameters of judicial reasoning. There is reliance in South Africa on Roman-Dutch law. In very large measure the lex Aquilia was not received. Still, where it was not obviously bypassed in Roman-Dutch law, the *lex* will be treated as basic to the modern law. The case also indicates the problem of exact citation of law when the authorities are in a foreign language. Whether the errors of citation are of the judge or the editor I leave open.

No later case takes us much further, and so it appears that there may well be a difference in the onus of proof when there is a contractual relationship between the parties and when there is not. In the former situation the onus is on the defendant, but it would seem from *McLaughlin v. Koening* 1928 C.P.D. 102 that if the defendant can show that the fire might have been started by someone for whom he was not responsible, for example, a guest at the hotel owned by the defendant, the onus would shift back to the plaintiff. In the latter situation, where liability is in fact Aquilian, the position is more doubtful, but there is at least Voet's authority for the view that the onus remains on the plaintiff.

Holes in the Open. In Roman law, there was liability under the lex Aquilia if pits were dug on footpaths to trap wild animals and someone fell in and was injured unless a warning of some kind had been given, but there was no liability if the pits were dug in places where it was the practice to have such pits, *D.9.2.28.* And this rule is followed by Voet.[132] Liability is therefore, as usual, based on culpa, and South Africa has taken over the same ruling as can be seen from two illuminating cases.

Transvaal and Rhodesian Estates Ltd. v. Golding 1917 A.D. 18 was a case in which the defendant, a mining company, left unfenced upon its property a hole used as a latrine. This hole was situated fifty-one feet from the public road, and the veld between it and the road (which had a good surface) was dusty and spotted with small bushes about three feet high. The plaintiff strayed from the road in the dark and fell into the hole. It was held that a reasonable, careful man would not have anticipated the accident, and so the defendant was not liable. Innes, C.J., said: "Now the basis of the Aquilian action was *culpa:* And the texts dealing with the liability of those who dig pits for the trapping of game, or who lop trees near a thoroughfare, show that the principle governing the equity in each case was whether or not the defendant had been guilty of *culpa.* See Digest (9.2.28 and 31) and Inst (4.3.5); see also Voet (9.2.18). The test which our law applies in these matters then is not nuisance but negligence; and the result is to impart greater elasticity to the enquiry."[133]

In *Webb v. Elgin Fireclays Ltd.* 1947 (2) S.A. 596 (T), the appellant and others grazed their cattle on land adjoining the workings of the respondent company, and on this land the company dug two prospect holes one of which was five feet deep and thirty-five yards from the road. No precautions were taken to prevent animals falling in. On a very wet day when the hole was filled with water and the surrounding land was waterlogged, a cow fell in and was drowned. It was held that the company had been negligent and was liable. Despite some talk of whether the respondent owed the appellant a duty, the decision clearly turned on negligence.[134]

Nautical accidents are the subject of many Roman texts, but since the position was much altered in the Netherlands by local legislation, and English law now applies in the republic, they will not be discussed here.

Imperitia. In Roman, Roman-Dutch, and South African law alike, a person who undertakes a task without having the necessary strength or skill and so does damage is liable.[135] There would seem to be no difference in principle (as perhaps there is in Scotland) between situations where a skill of a very special nature is required, for example, surgery, and situations involving a much lower degree of skill, for example, mule driving, although of course, in the former situation cases will normally turn on imperitia, since the other cases will often be treated as involving straightforward negligence. The skill demanded is that which is reasonably required of a person performing this type of work. How far local conditions are to be taken into consideration is the subject of opposing dicta in *Van Wyck v. Lewis* 1924 A.D. 438. Innes, C.J., said:

> And in deciding what is reasonable the court will have regard to the general level of skill and diligence possessed and exercised at the time by the members of the branch of the profession to which the practitioner be-

longs. The evidence of qualified surgeons or physicians is of the greatest assistance in estimating that general level. And their evidence may well be influenced by local experience; but I desire to guard myself from assenting to the principle approved in some American decisions that the standard of skill which shall be exacted is that which prevails in the particular locality where the practitioner happens to reside. The ordinary medical practitioner, should, as it seems to me, exercise the same degree of skill and care, whether he carries on his work in the town or country, in one place or another. The fact that several incompetent or careless practitioners happen to settle at the same place cannot affect the standard of diligence and skill which local residents have a right to expect.[136]

On the other hand, Wessels, J.A., said:

It seems to me, however, that you cannot expect the same skill and care of a practitioner in a country town in the Union as you can of one in a large hospital in Cape Town or Johannesburg. In the same way you cannot expect the same skill in these towns as you will find with the leading surgeons in the large hospitals of London, Paris and Berlin. You can only expect of surgeons in South Africa that degree of skill and that degree of care which is generally to be found in surgeons practicing in this country. It seems to me therefore that the locality where an operation is performed is an element in judging whether or no reasonable skill, care and judgment have been exercised. This principle has been recognized in the case of Small v. Howard (35 Am. Rep. 363) and kindred cases.

But of course, even where there was lack of skill, the plaintiff will fail unless it is shown that the injury was unlikely to have resulted otherwise. Thus in *Dhoma v. Mehta* 1957 (1) S.A. 676 (N), a plaintiff who sued his attorney for failing to note and prosecute an appeal did not succeed because he did not allege that he had reasonable prospects of winning the appeal.

LIABILITY FOR OMISSIONS

Four different types of situation are covered by the term "omission" in the law of delict.

Where There Is a Positive Action Followed by a Failure to Do Everything Necessary to Prevent the Positive Action That Itself Is Free from Negligence from Causing Harm. In Roman law, Roman-Dutch law, and modern South African law alike, an omission of this kind gives rise to an Aquilian action. Thus in Roman law, we are given examples of a doctor who operated but failed to continue the treatment[137] and of a farmer who set alight his stubble and then failed to take care that it did not spread,[138] and this precedent was followed by Voet[139] and Matthaeus.[140] In South Africa the same principle is applied, as can be seen from *Halliwell v. Johannesburg Municipal Council* 1912 A.D. 659. There it was held that where a road authority with permissive powers constructs or repairs a road properly, but through wear and tear the streets subsequently become dangerous, and an injury is caused, the road authority will be liable.[141] Innes, A.C.J., said: "For the decision of the present dispute it is sufficient to say that where, in consequence of some positive act, a duty is created to do some other act or exercise some special care so as to avoid injury to others, then the person concerned is under Roman-Dutch law liable for damage caused to those to whom he owes such duty by an omission to discharge it."[142]

Where a Duty Is Voluntarily Undertaken Followed by a Failure to Carry Out That Duty, Which Results in Injury. This too in all three systems creates liability. In Roman law, there is only one case, namely where a person undertook to look after a furnace that was already lit, but he fell asleep, and the country house burned down.[143] Voet, who denied that there was liability for omissions in Roman law,[144] gives two instances where omissions in the present sense of the word gave rise to no action. One is where the usufructuary does not plow the ground or fails to substitute new vines for those that die off,[145] but here the absence of liability is probably not because there was a failure to act, since this would leave the case just discussed inexplicable. For Aquilian liability, even by praetorian extension, there had to be a direct *corruptio*, for example, a blow or a fire, although this need not be immediately applied by the wrongdoer. A general deterioration through normal weather conditions and so forth, where there was a failure to plow, would not amount to such a direct corruptio. It is not the right sort of damage.

Voet follows the Roman law in the case of the man who fell asleep at the furnace and takes the position that he had assumed a duty and failed to perform it. South African law would almost certainly take the same attitude, although there appears to be no case except perhaps *Lance v. Mayor and Council of Pietermaritzburg* 2.N.L.R. 96. That was an action for damages for injury to an individual through the negligent want of repair to a street. Little stress was apparently put on the fact that the council, having permissive powers to keep the streets in good condition, was perhaps bound to do so, but it was emphasized that one who, for example for purposes of trade, invites the public to use a road is under a duty to see that the user will not be dangerous.

Where a Duty Is Imposed by Law, and It Is Not Performed, and a Person Suffers Injury. There is no Roman authority, or to my knowledge, Roman-Dutch, but it should follow from analogy with the preceding situation that there would be liability. Discussion of it could hardly be expected in Roman law, since only in a very limited number of situations could one talk of a direct corruptio. South African law clearly imposes liability in such cases. Thus in *Hume v. Divisional Council of Craddock* 1 E.D.C. 104, it was held that there was a legal duty on the Divisional Council to keep in repair the main roads entrusted to it, hence failures to do so that resulted in injury grounded liability. And in *Nathan Bros. v. Pietermaritzburg Corp.* 23 N.L.R. 107, it was decided that if a corporation was under a duty, expressly imposed by legislation, to decide whether building plans should be approved or not, and it wrongfully withheld approval, thus causing loss to the plaintiffs, the plaintiffs had an Aquilian action against the corporation.

Pure Omissions, That Is, Where It Could Be Seen That Failure to Do Something Would Injure Another Person But There Was No Special Reason for Imposing a Duty to Act. There is no authority in Roman law, a gap that, in this case, is probably the best possible evidence that there was no liability.[146] In Roman-Dutch law, however, we have the strong voice of Voet to the effect that there is no liability.[147] And this is followed in modern law.[148]

DUTY OF CARE

Until at least 1956, no cases decided in South Africa showed the acceptance of the duty of care as a separate element in determining whether or not there was liability. All the decisions could be explained on the ground of foreseeability or causation. Thus in South Africa, unlike England, a landlord is liable to third persons who are injured by defects in premises that are demised by him where the defects are due to his negligence, *Cape Town Municipality v. Paine* 1923 A.D. 207. In this case, Innes, C.J., said:

> It has been repeatedly laid down in this Court that accountability for un-intentional injury depends upon *culpa*—the failure to observe that degree of care which a reasonable man would have observed. . . . Once it is clear that the danger would have been foreseen and guarded against by the *diligens paterfamilias* the duty to take care is established, and it only remains to ascertain whether it has been discharged. Now the English Courts have adopted certain hard and fast rules. . . . Speaking generally, these rules are based upon considerations which, under our practice, also would be properly taken into account as affecting the judgment of a reasonable man; and the cases which embody them are of great assistance and instruction. But . . . there is an advantage in adhering to the general principle of the Aquilian law and in determining the existence or non-existence of culpa by applying the test of a reasonable man's judgment to the facts of each case. The large latitude allowed in such an enquiry is to be preferred to restriction within the more rigid limits of the English rules. [P. 216]

But in 1956 the case of *Union Govt. v. Ocean Accident and Guarantee Corporation Ltd.* 1956 (1) S.A. 577 (A.D.) was decided, which Price, the principal defender of the view that liability depends upon *culpa*, regards as wrongfully introducing the technical concept of the duty of care.[149] This, I think, is too pessimistic a view, and the judgment of Schreiner, J.A., should not be so read. The relevant passage is:

> So far as the question of principle in our law is to be considered, counsel for the Government relied upon the maxims *sic utere tuo ut alienum non laedas* and *ubi ius ibi remedium* for the general proposition that any person suffering patrimonial loss from the unlawful act of another can recover damages from the wrongdoer, as long as the causal relationship is not too remote. But wide general maxims of the kind referred to are commonly more ornamental than useful; they can frequently be countered by similar ones pointing, vaguely and imperfectly, it may be, in the opposite direction, such as, in this case, *qui suo iure utitur nemini facit iniuriam*, and *ubi remedium ibi ius*. . . .

To restrain the extravagances that might result from giving the widest conceivable meaning and effect to such generalizations as those contained in the maxims relied upon by counsel, it is usual to say that, to succeed in an action for damages for negligence, the plaintiff must show that the defendant owed him a duty of care and that the damage suffered was not too remote. Without venturing unnecessarily near to the problem whether remoteness rests upon foreseeability or upon directness, one must recognize some relation between remoteness and the duty of care. According to ordinary usage the former deals with the extent of the defendant's liability to the plaintiff, whoever he may be, the latter with the persons who are entitled to sue the defendant. The expression "duty of care" has sometimes been criticized as introducing an unnecessary complication into the law of negligence, but, apart from the fact that it is endorsed by considerable authority in this Court, it is so convenient a way of saying that it is the plaintiff himself and no other, whose right must have been invaded by the careless defendant, that the complication seems rather to be introduced by the effort to avoid its use. The duty of care is in our case law rested upon foreseeability and this gives rise to a measure of artificiality. But this is really unavoidable for, if there is to be control over the range of persons who may sue, the test must be that of the reasonable man; what he would have foreseen and what action he would have taken may not be calculable according to the actual weighing of probabilities, but the device of reasoning on these lines helps to avoid the impression of deriving an unreasoned moral judgement ex cathedra as to how the injurer should have behaved. The duty of care fits conveniently into the reasoning process and even if it is no more than a manner of speaking it is a very useful one.[150]

But it seems to me that this was an attempt to base liability or nonliability not upon the technical concept of duty of care ("even if it is no more than a manner of speaking") but rather upon foreseeability, which is expressed by saying that the defendant owed the plaintiff a duty of care (nontechnical) ("The duty of care is in our law rested upon foreseeability," etc.). And the decision that the plaintiff was not liable is perfectly understandable on the basis that loss to the plaintiff was not foreseeable. It is difficult to see how the private contractual relations of the injured man with a third party could be foreseen to the extent that the wrongdoer should know that an injury to the former would cause loss to the particular third party. Duties undertaken voluntarily cannot reasonably be foreseen, but general duties imposed by law can. Hence dependent relatives of the injured man whom he was under a duty to maintain have an action.

TEST OF LIABILITY IN MODERN LAW

Assuming that the above discussion of the duty of care is accurate, the modern test for liability may be that expressed in situations A, B, or C that I set out at the beginning of this chapter. Situation A would seem to be excluded by *Mulder v. South British Insurance Co. Ltd.* 1957 (2) S.A. 444 (W). There it was held that a person who witnessed an accident without having any apprehension of personal danger has no action against the wrongdoer for damage arising from shock or fright.[151] In the remaining situations B and C there would seem to be no clear authority. As McKerron has already pointed out,[152] Dove-Wilson, J.P., in *Frenkel and Co. v. Cadle* 1951 N.P.D. 173 rejected the foreseeability test, which, however, was applied by Villiers, J.P., in *Petersburg Municipality v. Rautenbach* 1917 T.P.D. 252.[153] Thus the law was not settled in 1961, but modern juristic theory would seem on balance to be in favor of making the wrongdoer liable for all of the loss flowing from his act.

The decision in *Cape Town Municipality v. Paine* could equally well have turned on a breach of the causal nexus. This was the basis of the decision in the Scottish case of *Reavis v. Clan Line Steamers* 1925 S.C. 725, from which Schreiner quotes on the score that it may prove useful. It could be argued that the cause of the loss to the plaintiff was not the injury but his contract with the injured party. An example may make this point clearer. It would be generally admitted, I think, that where the injured man was insured against such an injury, and he received a sum with respect to the injury from the insurance company, the company could not sue the wrongdoer in its own name for the sum paid out.[154] Its loss is only too obviously the result of the contract, which is, that is to say, the *causa causans*, while the injury is only the *causa sine qua non* of the payment.

Moreover, as Price pointed out, the action was completely misconceived, since the government did not prove that it had suffered any loss, but of course the court did not base its judgment on that score.

JUSTIFICATIONS

What Lawson[155] calls a "seemingly disproportionate number of the cases" in the *Digest* turn on justifications. The reason is to be found in the original nature of the lex Aquilia, which laid down that there was liability for "damnum iniuria datum," that is, damage caused *non iure*, or without right. To escape liability a person who had caused damage had to show, not that he had not been negligent, but that he had been acting within his rights. It was only in the course of the empire that *iniuria* assumed the other meaning of "culpa aut dolo." Hence, we have many Roman texts discussing self-defense, superior orders, public office, and so on. The justifications are of limited practical importance, and in later commentators we find that the more academic the jurist, the more space he devotes to a discussion of justifications, so that in Suarez de Mendoza they take up a considerable proportion of the whole, while in Grotius the discussion is limited to "Nood-weer ende onverzuimt werd hier, ghelijk in een doodslag, vrij ghekent. Wie oock in sijn huis werd aenghevochten, wat quetzing ofte schade hy uitewaerd doet, is beuten verbeurte."[156] "Necessary defense and accident without negligence, as in the case of killing, are free from liability. If a man is attacked in his house, and wounds or injures someone outside, he incurs no penalty."[157] In modern law there seems to be no important case under the lex Aquilia that has turned on justifications, although the defense is occasionally met within criminal law. Three cases may be given as illustrations.

Rex v. Werner and Another 1947 (2) S.A. 828. German prisoners of war on command of superior officer killed another German prisoner. It was held that during imprisonment the superior officer had no authority to give orders and the appellants were therefore under no duty to obey them, even if those orders had not been so obviously illegal that they should have been known to have been illegal. The prisoners were convicted of murder.

Rex v. Mahomet and Another 1938 A.D. 30. The accused were charged with obstructing the police in the execution of their duty, but they pleaded necessity and declared that their dominant motive was to protect themselves from an attack that they reasonably feared from a party of persons accompanying police. It was held that they had done no more than was reasonably necessary to protect themselves and that they were not criminally liable.

Rex v. Muller 1948 (4) S.A. 848 (O). A schoolteacher was charged with assault in punishing pupils. It was held that a teacher who exercises his right to corporal punishment does so in a quasi-judicial capacity. As long as he takes reasonable and proper steps by which he can establish facts that to a reasonable person justify a reasonable belief in a *veritas convicii*, it is unnecessary for him to prove veritas convicii.

ABUSE OF RIGHTS

W. W. Buckland and A. D. McNair[158] define abuse of rights as the "exercise of proprietary rights with intent or knowledge that the exercise will do harm to some other person or his property without any economic benefit to the doer." This definition, which I accept, means, of course, that the exercise would be perfectly legitimate if the doer had as his motive his own economic benefit; otherwise it would be difficult to speak of rights. And the question is really whether the act ceases to be legitimate if the doer has no such motive but simply intends harm to his neighbor. Cases are therefore excluded where, probably on the grounds of morality, an owner is forbidden by law, without regard to his motive, to act in a particular way with respect to his property. In Roman law there is little doubt that there was no general principle forbidding an abuse of rights.[159] And we are told in several texts that a person who is exercising his right cannot be committing a wrong.[160] Indeed, there is probably only one true case, which has been regarded as abuse of rights, where a person is not permitted to do something because he intends to injure another, something that he would be permitted to do if his intention were to benefit himself. One example is where a landowner interrupts a flow of water to his neighbor in order to injure him or diverts rainwater from his neighbor's land with the same intention.[161] It has often been felt surprising, first, that this case should be singled out and, second, that it did not give rise eventually to a general principle. But there may be a simple explanation. In the *Digest*, the right of the owner of the superior land to allow water that may injure his neighbor to flow on to the latter's land is said to be natural servitude, that is, a servitude imposed not by agreement between the parties but by the nature and situation of their estates, D.39.3.1.22, 23. Paul in D.39.3.2*pr.* says generally, "In summa tria sunt, per quae inferior locus superiori servit, lex, natura loci, vetustas," "In short there are three ways in which an inferior estate may be under a servitude to a higher, agreement, the situation of the place and long use." And no doubt, the right to divert water would be similarly regarded. But we know that the holder of an ordinary servitude has to use it *civiliter*, that is, to cause as little inconvenience to the owner of the servient tenement as possible, and only if the servitude benefited his land. He had no right to use it otherwise.[162] If the holder of a natural servitude were under the same restrictions it may be for this reason that the owner of a superior tenement is not allowed to divert water when there can be no benefit for himself and his intention is to injure his neighbor. And if so, this would not be a case of abuse of rights that could be generalized.

In Roman-Dutch law, there is comparatively little discussion of the problem, and the authorities conflict. Voet, who is on the majority side, says that if one cuts off a spring to a neighbor or directs water onto a neighbor's land, one is not liable if the intention was not to injure the neighbor but to benefit oneself.[163] Groenewegen says, on the other hand, that since the mind of men cannot be discovered and men always find justification for their evil deeds, the rule is not observed in practice to cut down the number of lawsuits.[164]

In South African law, there is likewise a dearth of real authority. There have been obiter dicta in a number of cases,[165] but the only case that may have turned on the point is *Vanston v. Frost* 1930 N.P.D. 121. The appellant and respondent owned adjoining properties. In 1925 the respondent erected an eight-foot fence on the boundary and in 1929 raised it to eighteen feet to shield his lavatory from the view of an attic window that the appellant had erected. It was held that although the heightening of the fence depreciated the appellant's property, the appellant could not recover damages even if the work had been done maliciously, which, it was said, was not a necessary inference. But how far the decision in this case would be extended is not clear. It may well be restricted to situations in which there is only financial loss without physical injury. No old authority was cited, and in any subsequent case that involves actual physical deterioration of the property it is unlikely that much weight will be attached to this decision.

CAUSATION

Since the Romans had neither explosives nor internal combustion engines, they were spared most of the difficult questions of causation that confront jurists today. Indeed, only three situations, none of which is especially important for us,

need be mentioned. First, where several people at the same time wound a slave
and it is not clear from whose blow he died, all will be liable for killing and will
have to pay the highest value that the slave had in the past year.[166] Now, in the
case of joint wrongdoers, they will be liable jointly for the injury, and payment
by one will release the others from liability to the injured party, although the
person paying will be able to claim contribution from the other wrongdoers,
Apportionment of Damages Act 1956 s.2 (6), (7). Second, if a ballplayer hit the
ball against the hand of a barber who was shaving a slave and as a result the razor
slit the slave's throat, we are told that an action lies against whoever was negligent. Hence, although it is not stated, if both the barber and the ballplayer were
negligent, it is reasonable to assume that both would be fully liable for the value
of the slave. For us it is enough to notice, if the foregoing is correct, that the intervention of the other party's negligence is not enough to break the causal connection and that the two are concurrent wrongdoers. The 1956 act abolished
the distinction between joint wrongdoers and several concurrent wrongdoers,
s.2 (1). Rule 12 of the Union Rules of Court provided for one action to be
brought against more than one defendant when it is uncertain which of two or
more defendants was responsible for the damage done to the defendant; compare *Jooste v. Ally* 1960 (4) S.A. 31. Third, and most interesting of all, what is the
position if one man mortally wounds a slave and he is finished off later either
by a blow from another person or from some other external act, *D.9.2.11.3; h.t.15.1;
h.t.51; h.t.21.1?* The Roman solution is not clear. Although the case was much discussed by the Roman-Dutch writers[167] and is important in the law of murder,
the situation is of no importance now for Aquilian liability because of the fusion of the chapters of the lex and since in any event the plaintiff can only recover from the wrongdoers what he actually lost.

It is difficult to say that any principle infuses the modern law, and the practical position is best seen by an examination of some of the cases.

Alliance Building Society v. Deretich 1941 T.P.D. 203. The owner of premises
claimed damages because the appellant, purporting to act as owner, negligently
gave notice to the tenants to vacate the premises. It was held that there was no
action, and the decision was at least mainly based on the fact that "the pecuniary loss was caused by the tenants leaving, resulting in a breach of contract by
the tenants vis-à-vis the plaintiff" (Barry, J.). It might be argued that with respect to causation there is no difference between this case and cases such as *Solo-*

mon v. Du Preez, New Kleinfontein Co. v. Superintendent of Labourers and *Isaanemon v. Miller*[168] and that therefore the absence of Aquilian liability in *Alliance Building Society v. Deretich* cannot be explained on the grounds of a break in the chain of causation. But it should be noted that these other cases just mentioned are not based on the lex Aquilia at all but on a rule introduced from English law that it is an actionable wrong willfully and without legal excuse to interfere with the contractual relations of another.

Brandfort Munisipaliteit v. Esterhuizen 1957 (1) S.A. 229 (O). The plaintiff claimed damages from the municipality alleging that she was the registered owner of a certain erf and that she had obtained permission from the municipality to make certain alterations to her dwelling thereon and had obtained approval for her plans. But, she claimed, after the roof was removed and a wall was broken down, the municipality unlawfully and mala fide forbade her to proceed with the alterations or to restore the dwelling to its original state, and as a result of this prohibition she suffered irreparable loss. It was held that since the plaintiff's allegation was that the municipality's prohibition was unlawful and mala fide, amounting to an allegation that it was a nullity, then if the plaintiff suffered loss through complying with the prohibition that was a nullity, her own act in doing so was the cause of her loss and therefore her action failed. The decision was upheld on appeal.[169]

Ntuli v. Hirsch and Adler 1958 (2) S.A. 290 (W). The plaintiff claimed damages for unlawful sale in execution, without the leave of the court, on the instruction of the defendants. The defendants claimed absolution partly on the ground that the plaintiff's loss was attributable to his long delay in bringing proceedings, but it was held that the delay affected not the cause of the loss but only questions turning on waiver of rights and for mitigation of damages.

Milward v. Glaser 1949 (4) S.A. 931 (A.D.). A widow sued her deceased husband's former mistress for £600 that the husband had left his mistress in his will and that the wife claimed would otherwise have come to her on intestacy. It was held that for the widow to succeed, she had to show that the loss of the expected gain of the £600 was *in consequence of* a wrong committed by the defendant, that the cause of the loss was persuasion by defendant plus exercise by the deceased of his liberality and right of testation. The consideration, it was said, for which he allowed himself to be persuaded was in law irrelevant and no link in the chain of causation, and hence the widow's claim failed.[170]

CONTRIBUTORY NEGLIGENCE

At common law, negligence on the part of the plaintiff ousted his claim unless it was based on intentional harm, but this rule was altered by the Apportionment of Damages Act 1956, which substituted the principle of apportionment.[171]

CONCLUSION

I have set out the South African law up to about 1961 in considerable detail because of the light it sheds on law out of context.

First, it shows that law out of context may be reasonably satisfactory. I doubt whether many scholars would seriously claim that the South African law in 1961 was markedly inferior to the torts law of the United States or of England. In this instance, and it is no minor one, law ostensibly based on a Roman statute traditionally dated to 287 B.C. has shown an enormous capacity to develop.

Second, to a great extent the purported transplant was a sham. It is not at all clear that the lex Aquilia was ever received in post-Roman Europe. By the seventeenth century at the latest scholars were openly claiming that the statute was not received. Its particular features: a division into three chapters with different liability for killing a slave or herd animal than for other injuries, damages determined (as later understood) without regard to the actual loss, a requirement that the injury be directly inflicted, "to the body by the body"—all were rejected. What was accepted was a remedy in general for financial loss that was wrongfully caused. Still, law requires authority. In the absence of a local statute—and none existed—the traditions of the time demanded the use of Roman law, or the lex Aquilia. Sham authority is standard.[172] Still, the influence of the lex Aquilia must not be denied. It was there, above all, that the Romans developed the notion of negligence that was to transform the law of Europe on delict and contract. The law of delict in post-Roman times was transformed, and judges and scholars came to prefer to talk of Aquilian liability rather than liability under the lex Aquilia. There could be an action by a free person for injury to himself, an action for loss of support when a close relative was killed, and even an action for mere financial loss in the absence of any physical injury.

Third, despite the foregoing, South African judges in the main held to the tradition that their law was based on that existing in Holland in 1652. By then, of course, Aquilian liability was vastly different from what it had been in Justinian's time. Still, as the quotations have shown, in an attempt to find out what the Roman law was or what the *usus modernus* was, the judges by no means restricted their gaze to jurists of seventeenth-century Holland or even to other parts of the Dutch republic or to the Netherlands (including for this purpose modern Belgium) but also included France and Germany even of a much later period. This is a general feature of South African law, not at all restricted to delict.

Fourth, it emerged in passing, without being stressed, that the weight given to historical analysis, and even the choice of sources to be used, varied greatly from one judge to another. This variation permitted a powerful element of flexibility in the law.

Fifth, a powerful factor for legal development, resulting from historical and political considerations, was the influence of English law. English law and Roman-Dutch law could have different approaches to a problem, and then it was not necessarily preordained which would prevail. Individual judges had their own proclivities: De Villiers very noticeably opted for a scholarly Roman-Dutch approach. Scholars did likewise: R. G. McKerron consistently favored an English law approach, and Price emphatically had a Roman-Dutch preference.

CHAPTER SIX

THE ASPIRING LAWYER
IN THE UNITED STATES

Sometimes it happens that, even without being transplanted, even without the passage of time, law is presented or represented in a way so skewed that it is irredeemably out of context from the very outset. Nowhere is this more obvious than in legal education in the United States.

FIRST- (AND SECOND- AND THIRD-) YEAR
LAW SCHOOL STUDENTS

The casebook method of teaching, which I believe is universal in American law schools and very rare elsewhere, is disastrous for an understanding of law. Casebooks, which are in prime use for almost all classes, from the first year onward, give a false picture. I would like to look at property law, which I believe is taught in the first year in every school.

Actual misinformation about law begins at the outset of the student's first semester. One of the earliest topics in a property class is usually "acquisition by find." At the very beginning of the second chapter of their famous casebook, Jesse Dukeminier and James E. Krier state: "Possession, as we saw in the preceding chapter, is a powerful concept in the law of property." [1] But they have not described possession in the preceding chapter, far less attempted a definition, nor will they do so in this chapter. What they have done is to quote a few cases and to pose a few questions. But it is not difficult to describe the concept at least tentatively. A description will readily be found, for instance, in Ray Andrews Brown, *The Law of Personal Property*. [2]

What is misleading in the standard approach is that in fact the law is not contained in a few cases but, in property as in other areas, is usually distilled from many cases. When only a few are studied, each appears out of context. The casebook does not put any of these into the general framework of the concept, say, that of possession, to give students the big picture. Students cannot tell how far a quoted case reflects general propositions or whether it stands at the very edge of a doctrine. They have no way of seeing how the law builds up. The role of authority is not clarified. Important aspects of a concept may not be discussed in any of the chosen cases. When a case is discussed in isolation, it is often impossible to know which facts are to be regarded as relevant. The issue is not that casebook editors ought to pick the right case. The law is to be gleaned from the effect of many cases.

The casebook method of teaching is, in fact, an exercise in futility. The students themselves are expected to build up a picture of law from the few generally disconnected scraps available to them and with virtually no tools. Students are left to guess what the *editors'* view of the law is rather than learning what the law is all about. Instead of looking at the reasoning of a case in the light of the developed conceptual thought that preceded it, instead of examining its place in a structured web of reasoned principle, they consider a single instance that justifies itself only by reference to particular features, leaving much to be understood. Much of importance to the case is left unsupported and unsaid because it rests on established principle.[3]

Dukeminier and Krier set out for discussion only three cases on acquisition by finding. Is all the relevant law to be found in them and in the few other cases that are mentioned? How is one to find the parameters of the law?

Their first case is *Armory v. Delamirie.*[4] A "chimney sweeper's boy" found a ring with a jewel in it. What rights did he have when a goldsmith's apprentice, to whom he handed it to find out what it was, removed the jewel from its socket and refused to return it? Lo and behold, the case, from 1722, is more than two and a half centuries old. Does it still have authority? Did it establish some principle? Odder still, it is not an American case but an English one. Has it any relevance here? Because it came before the Declaration of Independence? Or is there no issue of relevance, with the case chosen because of the piquant details? Dukeminier and Krier give no answers. I have been told that the point of the casebook method is to teach the student how to argue about law. But if the casebook method does this, it is teaching how to argue about law without thinking about law—for me a difficult concept. And it is teaching how to argue about law without thinking about law in the supposed context of teaching law. The casebook method is reminiscent of some cases in the *Controversiae* of Seneca the Elder (c. 55 B.C.–A.D. 40), a work that we looked at in chapter 4. Whether the law in a particular problem that is set out in that work existed or was correctly stated was not the point, which was to teach the student how to argue. The aim of the *Controversiae* was to teach young Romans the techniques of rhetoric, not law.

The second case is also English, *Hannah v. Peel*, from 1945.[5] Does modern English case law still have authority in the United States? If so, how much? Why? Is any remaining authority the result of the former colonial status of part of the country? Do Canadian cases have any weight here?

What is needed for the acquisition of possession? Is intention relevant? We are not told how old the "boy" in *Armory v. Delamirie* was, but chimney sweepers' boys tended to be very young, first because they had to be small enough to fit into chimneys, second because in that line of business they tended not to live long. Was he of an age to form the legally relevant intention, if intention is needed? We are not told. Nor does either of the other two cases quoted in the book[6] throw any light on whether intention is needed. Likewise none of the cases reveals anything of the kind of intention that would be relevant. Intention to possess, intention to act as owner, intention to exclude all others except the true owner, intention to hold on behalf of another? Is the place where the jewel was found relevant? We are not told where it was found, whether in a fireplace, within a house, or on the sidewalk. Whether any of these features are relevant to some general principle (and which one?) to be applied in other cases, and where to look for points of distinction, are not evident. The other two cases quoted show that the place is relevant, but this one does not. Should we assume that in 1722 the place was not relevant? If the jewel was found in the chimney while the boy was working, did this give the chimney sweeper any right to it? Neither of the other cases tells us anything about possession acquired by an employee "in the course of employment." Nor do any of the cases indicate whether bad faith has an impact on the finder's possession. Dukeminier and Krier report that the action is trover. Does that action still exist?[7] If not, has the right of action been affected? What difference does it make to the students' understanding of the case that the references to authority in the original report are omitted by the casebook authors? Last, the authors do not indicate whether the term "possession" has the same meaning in all contexts.

My point is emphatically not that learning the law would be much easier— it obviously would be—if concepts and rules as they had developed in hundreds of cases were set out briefly and were then followed by discussion of a few cases chosen to illustrate the rules, their parameters, and issues raised by borderline situations and that this is something necessarily desirable. Perhaps there is a virtue, as some colleagues think, in making first-year law study unnecessarily difficult.[8] My point is that the standard approach misrepresents the way law is, how it develops, and its relation to society. Concepts and principles are badly downplayed. So are rules and their authority and stability. Cases are removed from their legally relevant context, and the authority of the context is dismantled. Oddly, perhaps, a further result of this approach is that often cases are removed from their social context. The judges' yearning for authority and the future judges' respect for it are downgraded. So is the nature of the authority that is requisite or desired.

My stance is the classic one, enunciated for instance by Sir John Holt (1642–1710) though in a different context: "The law consists not of particular instances and precedents, but in the reason of the law." [9] And Lord Mansfield (1733–1821): "The law does not consist of particular cases: but in general principles which run through the cases and govern the decision of them." [10] The study of a few cases, torn out of context, has little if any educative value.

But the misrepresentation of law in general, and of its development, is only part of the problem. When a few cases for study are removed from their legal context, the individual case itself and what is going on in it are also misrepresented and become largely incomprehensible. The absence of theoretical underpinnings is a fatal flaw in the casebook approach. I would like to illustrate my argument by just one New York case that is usually studied in the first week of law school: *Pierson v. Post.*[11]

Post was hunting a fox on a beach with his dogs and was in sight of it. Pierson, knowing what was going on, killed and carried off the fox to prevent Post's having it. Tompkins, J., delivered the court's opinion in favor of Pierson. He cited Justinian's *Institutes* 2.1.13, Fleta 3.2 p.175, Bracton 2.1 p.8, Puffendorf 4.6.2, and Bynkershoek for the proposition that actual corporeal possession of animals that are wild by nature is needed to acquire ownership by occupancy. He also stated that Puffendorf affirmed with hesitation that a mortally wounded beast or one greatly maimed cannot be fairly intercepted by another while the person who inflicted the wound is in pursuit. He further recorded that Barbeyrac, in his notes on Puffendorf, affirmed that bodily seizure was not necessary in all cases for the acquisition of ownership.

Why are the authorities cited? We are not told. A first part of the answer is that in general judges require authority to bolster their opinion. It does not accord with good judicial practice just to say, "This is my decision because I like it." But this feature of legal writing should alert us to the belief, erroneous or not, that behind a case stands law. A case may make law but within the context of previous cases that made law.[12] If one denies that the previous cases were law, then the instant case also cannot be law. A true search for authority is always backward-looking. Law as expounded by judges has a built-in tendency toward conservatism. Even radical judges, if they wish to make their decisions acceptable, must seek to make their reasoning look conservative. But then we have to know what it is in a case that is important for future decisions. And the casebook never tells us.

But why these particular citations? Justinian's *Institutes* is, after all, a Byzantine emperor's textbook for first-year law students, issued in 533 with the force of statute and largely based on the second-century Roman model of Gaius. Bracton's (c. 1210–1268) famous book is entitled *De legibus et consuetudinibus Anglie* ("On the Laws and Customs of England"), and Fleta (c. 1290) is an epitome of Bracton. Samuel Puffendorf (1643–1694), whose life and career spanned several European states, is best known for his *De jure naturae et gentium* ("On the Law of Nature and Nations") and his attempt to establish by reason a law that should be applicable in all civilized nations. Dutch jurist Cornelius van Bynkershoek (1673–1743) wrote on a wide range of subjects, including the law of Holland. Jean Barbeyrac (1674–1744) is a leading figure in the development of international law and published an edition of Puffendorf with a commentary.

Why then are these works of these authors cited? A first part of the answer is that the judges had no useful cases they could rely on, not even English cases, far less American, not to mention any from New York.[13] A second part of the answer is the great importance attributed to these works. Justinian's restatement of Roman law[14] was—and still is—regarded as the foundation stone of subsequent Western law. Puffendorf, who was much admired in the United States at the time, was attempting to set up on rational principles rules that ought to be valid everywhere in the civilized world, hence including New York. Naturally in the circumstances of the time, these principles very much derived from the Roman law of Justinian. Fleta and Bracton give the English connection. Dukeminier and Krier do the student no service when they say the opinions "are peppered with references to a number of obscure legal works and legal scholars."[15] The works are assuredly not to be regarded as obscure, even though in all likelihood they would not have been cited by the court if there had been nearer authority in the shape of judicial precedent.

But something else is going on that is deeply significant for the nature of law: borrowing from a different system, from a different time. The law in the *Institutes* of the Byzantine emperor Justinian is very largely taken from a Roman jurist, Gaius, who was active near the middle of the second century. Fleta and Bracton took the Roman/Byzantine rule into medieval England, Puffendorf was making the Roman/Byzantine rule the law of all civilized nations in the Age of Reason, and Bynkershoek's work was more geared to showing it as law in the Dutch republic in the early eighteenth century. Now the majority of the court in *Pierson v. Post* was borrowing the rule for the state of New York at the beginning of the nineteenth century. That the rule was not inevitable appears from the dissenting judgment of Livingstone, J., and the reference to Barbeyrac. What I want to stress is not just that the casebook approach omits any treatment of this dimension for *Pierson v. Post* but even more that it ignores the significance of borrowing in general. As I have argued in previous chapters, at most times in most places, legal rules, structures, and institutions are borrowed—sometimes, but not always, out of respect for the time-tested accumulation of wisdom behind them.[16] This custom should perhaps make us wonder about the relationship between law and society.[17]

But we are not yet done with the significance of foreign law in *Pierson v. Post*. There are also wider implications. Judge Tompkins observes that Barbeyrac does not accept Puffendorf's definition, and Barbeyrac affirms that bodily seizure is not necessary in all cases for the acquisition of ownership. But there is a source that seems more direct. There is in Justinian's *Digest* 41.1.5.1 a text attributed to Gaius:

> The question has been raised whether a wild beast that has been so wounded that it can be captured is understood to be ours at once. Trebatius held it became ours at once and remains ours so long as we pursue it, that if we cease to pursue it it ceases to be ours and again becomes the property of one who takes it. And so, if during the time we were pursuing it another took it with the intention to make a gain he is regarded as

having committed a theft against us. The majority thought it did not become ours unless we captured it because much can happen that we do not capture it. This is the better opinion.

A question for us then becomes why the court does not refer to Trebatius (of the first century B.C.) when it does to Barbeyrac. The simplest answer is that, despite the lip service so often paid to Justinian's *Corpus iuris civilis*, the only part of this compilation usually consulted by U.S. courts was the *Institutes*, the elementary textbook, either through the American edition of Thomas Cooper (first published in 1812) or with one of the European commentaries intended for students, that of Heineccius (1681–1741) or that of Vinnius (1588–1657). The *Digest* was often simply not readily to hand or was thought overly difficult.[18] The contents of libraries have been surprisingly important for legal development.[19] As have been linguistic skills.[20]

Tompkins notes that use cannot be made of cases from England that have been "decided upon the principles of their positive statute regulations."[21] That statutory law does not apply outside of its own state is a proposition also of Grotius, who declares it precisely in the context of acquiring ownership of wild animals.[22] The proposition is reasonable enough, but it raises various issues concerning the strength of foreign authorities that are not discussed in the casebooks. Why should an outside juristic opinion or judicial decision have any weight if an outside statute does not? The issue would not arise today with regard to Roman law,[23] but it might with regard to a case or statute from another state. If a case arises in Georgia, why should a statute of North Carolina not be treated with the same regard as a case from North Carolina or an article by a North Carolinian law professor? Does a case from elsewhere represent a reasoned approach to an issue, while a statute does not? If we say that societies vary, hence an outside statute provides no guidance, why then does an outside case? Are students to presume that, in the absence of statute, law is somehow everywhere the same?

Livingstone's dissenting opinion also raises issues that really cannot be understood without some explanation drawn from outside the case. First, Livingstone expressly bases his opinion in large measure on social policy. To what extent is this allowable or standard practice? It should be noted that such an express basis was unusual at that time in the United States and even now in many legal systems is not common or is even forbidden. Livingstone's approach probably ought to be explained simply as the result of the absence of legal authority. Moreover, what gives U.S. judges the expertise to decide social policy? Are judges chosen because of their sensitivity to social issues? Livingstone believed that the greatest possible encouragement should be given to the destruction of foxes, an aim that would best be accomplished by favoring sportsmen. But would it? The experience from England at least is otherwise. Though foxes were indigenous to England, they had long been rare until they were imported in large numbers for the purpose of hunting.[24] The great increase of foxes in the nineteenth century was due to the sportsmen. Sportsmen wanted live foxes! Indeed, as is made plain time and again in Anthony Trollope's novels, the gentleman was expected "to preserve foxes," as the phrase went.[25] Woe—social woe—to the farmer who shot the fox devouring his chickens and did not preserve it for the hunt. Poisoning or shooting foxes could be described as "vulpicide" or "murder" by the hunting fraternity.[26] Should the law in Virginia, where in some parts riding to hounds is socially highly regarded, differ from that of a state where the sport is unknown?

Second, Livingstone wanted to rely on custom. This preference suggests that he had an instinctive theory about where law comes from. But how did Livingstone know what the custom was? I find that second-year students have had no exposure to the notion of custom as a source of law. Perhaps this lack is not too serious, given the very limited scope today of custom in making law, but in the absence of a theoretical treatment in the first-year classes, custom and social policy are apt to be linked together. Why is custom considered law? When does custom become law? How is custom, as law, discovered? Whose custom ought to be law? Why is custom, as a source of law, so little used today? What about its role in trade dealings between merchants? What about its place in alternative modes of resolving disputes?

Third, in the absence of further information, what is the student to make of Livingstone's argument to the effect that when times change, law changes (or should change)? And to what extent should the court be satisfied that the change, social or legal, is enduring rather than fashionable and transitory? I have already observed that one of the striking features of law is precisely its longevity. In this connection, I must stress that when a judge argues from the facts of history, the watchword is "beware." False history is probably as often adduced to support a proposition as is plausible or even accurate history. Of course, *pace* Livingstone, the Romans did keep and breed dogs for hunting, a pastime passionately pursued even by emperors.[27]

Fourth, how wide ought the rationale be for a decision? Livingstone bases his opinion about acquiring ownership of the fox in large measure on the destructiveness of that animal. Should the approach be different when the animal is largely innocuous, a rabbit or hare? Ought it to be relevant whether the animal was usually pursued for pleasure or profit? Ought there to be one basic approach to the acquisition of wild animals, or should the law vary from species to species? The casebook authors give no guidance.

Finally for this case, does it matter that Dukeminier and Krier omit the arguments of counsel for the parties and parts of the judgment?

Christopher Columbus Langdell, dean of the Harvard Law School, was mainly responsible for the success of the case method. He argued that law was a science and should be taught in a scientific manner, from cases.[28] But just imagine a college physics course where only a few isolated experiments are studied, where the relationship of one to the other is not set out, where the theoretical underpinnings are not stated, and where virtually all of the writings of scholars are ignored.[29]

Moreover, almost all substantive law courses are taught in the same way. It can be no surprise that third-year law students are widely perceived to be bored by law school.

In most law schools, though not in all, no first-year class is dedicated to the theoretical underpinnings of law. Since for the most part only first-year classes are required, this means there is no compulsory class in them. There is usually no such class as: (1) introduction to law, where the structure of the law is studied, where the interrelations of say, contract and tort, or contract and property, or tort and crime, are examined; (2) legal philosophy, where one might become acquainted with doctrines of natural law and might consider the relationship of justice to law or the functions of law; (3) sources of law, with their relative values, their strengths and weaknesses, their individual impact on how law develops; (4) comparative law, to emphasize that legal rules and structures are not inevitable, that different approaches are possible, that law is not set in stone, that no system—not even that of the United States—is the best in all respects; (5) legal history, which might indicate the extent to which the past governs the present. Legal education in the United States is geared to making legal plumbers, not legal scholars, nor reflective, philosophically and socially attuned practitioners. For example, second-year and third-year law students are unable to come to grips with the following issues:

1. They are unable to discuss the nature of the holding. They use the word *holding* glibly, but when asked to explain what it means or how to find it, they are at a loss.
2. They have never considered whether there might be a rational approach to statutory interpretation, whether any principles might be advanced. Is interpretation merely judicial politics?
3. They have never asked themselves what drives legal development. When asked, they will answer more or less vaguely, "society."
4. They have not wondered about the weight of precedents from another jurisdiction. Why are they cited? Which jurisdictions have weight?
5. They are quite unaware of the pressure of legal doctrine. Law seems to be about distinguishing one case from another "on the facts." Yet in the very subjects they have studied—contracts, torts, property—the great bulk of the law is settled.
6. For them, the relationship between one branch of law and another is quite obscure. They are daunted by such questions as "Why is employment not property?" Does it matter? Why may incorporeals be "things" in all of the states of the United States when in Germany they are not? Are foreign legal systems just so very different, not worth looking at for understanding our own legal assumptions?

To illustrate the extent of the unpreparedness of second-year students, I would like to stick to property law. I choose as my example the famous "Rule against Perpetuities," partly because like most legal doctrines it involves legal borrowing and legal history, partly because it remains important today.

George L. Haskins tells us with his usual insight, "The Rule against Perpetuities is among the oldest, most respected, and difficult to understand rules of the common law."[30] The classic statement of the Rule is by John Chipman Gray: "No interest is good unless it must vest, if at all, not later than twenty-one years after some life in being at the creation of the interest."[31] To those who are no longer cognoscenti, I give one simple example to illustrate the working of the Rule: "To *A* for life, remainder to his widow for life, remainder to the eldest of his brothers living at the widow's death." The remainder to the brother is void if *A*'s parents are alive. The rationale (I believe) is this. Even if *A* is now married, his wife may possibly predecease him, and possibly he may eventually marry someone who was not born at the time of the gift, and she may possibly outlive him by more than twenty-one years. Such a conjectural second wife would not be a life in being for the purpose of the Rule. Thus, a brother of *A* who might be born after the gift—not a life in being—could be the purported beneficiary more than twenty-one years after the death of *A*, the life in being. This is the position even if *A* is already very old. *A*'s mother, even if older than 100 at the time of the gift, could still give birth according to the Rule, which does not take physical impossibility into account. And any preexisting brothers of *A* may predecease his widow. The remainder to *A*'s widow is valid, even if she is yet unborn, because *A* is a life in being and obviously her interest must vest, if at all, within twenty-one years of his death. The Rule is fun.

The Rule Against Perpetuities is also notoriously difficult—"It gives me hives," said a colleague—a trap for students and for the practitioner, for wary and unwary alike.[32] But there are a few basic questions—ones that then should be generalized—to which I would expect no answer from second-year students who have studied property for a year.[33]

1. Why did the Rule not apply to the fee tail, the most obvious example of perpetuities?
2. What was the Rule's original purpose, since it did not cover fee tails? How well did it serve this purpose or purposes?
3. What useful function does it serve today?
4. What are its disadvantages? How, if at all—to justify its continued existence—do its advantages outweigh its disadvantages?
5. What input does today's society (other than lawyers) have into its application?
6. Why are the rules so rigid and so apparently removed from society?
7. What accounts for the Rule's longevity? Although it originated in a feudal or postfeudal landholding society, it flourishes in the capitalist, industrial world of England and the United States.[34]
8. If it emerged in seventeenth-century England in the conditions of the society of that time, how could the Rule be transported to the rather different North America?

9. Why is the Rule unknown outside of England and England's former colonies or other possessions? If it is as necessary and important as is often claimed, why is nothing like it found in such places as Germany[35] or Scotland?[36] Most strikingly, perhaps, there is in all of the vast surviving sources of ancient Roman law not the slightest trace of any of the problems that the Rule Against Perpetuities is supposedly needed to remedy.

Similar questions can be asked, and should be asked, for any legal doctrine. The answers are fundamental to an understanding of law, its course of development, and its relation to the society in which it operates. The questions are simple but are not posed to first-year students. The answers are fundamental but are not known to second-year students. Indeed, the questions, if asked, would throw light not just on legal doctrine but also on legal institutions and practice. Why in much of the United States, for example, are buyer and seller, mortgage holder, and attorneys all uselessly physically present at the settlement of a real estate transaction?[37]

Even the most superficial answers to the specific questions on the Rule Against Perpetuities—no more than superficiality need be attempted here—indicate that students have been left much uninformed about the nature of law.

1. *Why did the Rule not apply to the fee tail?* The statute *De donis conditionalibus* of 1285 placed the fee tail on a firm footing, though it did not create it.[38] Whatever the statute may originally have meant, by 1346 at the latest it was interpreted as continuing an entail in perpetuity.[39] The Rule Against Perpetuities, in contrast, was created by judicial precedent. Four formal sources of law have existed in the Western world: custom, statute, judicial precedent, and juristic opinion. But they are not all of equal authority. Thus, in general, precedent cannot overrule statute; hence the Rule Against Perpetuities, when it did eventually develop, did not apply to the fee tail, which was believed to have statutory support. Still, it should be noted that precedent can interpret, reinterpret, and misinterpret statute. Sources of law, their relative values, their interaction, are not subjects of explicit study in first-year classes.

2. *What, then, was the Rule's original purpose?* The Rule Against Perpetuities as it developed served no particular obvious useful purpose. It arose because of judicial hostility to the fee tail, resulting in a hatred of anything that smacked of

"perpetuities." Yet the fee tail was beyond the reach of the Rule. Not only that, but even before the Rule any "owner" in possession could by 1472[40] at the latest bar an entail by the device known as common recovery, and so in one sense there was no need for anything like the Rule with respect to the fee tail. (That is, the entail was valid—as it would not have been if the [future] Rule had applied to it—but it could have been ended at any time if the owner had wanted.) Other executory devises of terms that were not executed by the Statute of Uses (1535) and might have been thought to be objectionable[41] were for all practical purposes unaffected by the Rule as it emerged. To understand the complexities of the relationship between the development of law and society, the student would find it instructive to look at modern theories of the origins of the Rule. The theories vary according to the vision of the author, Marxist or otherwise, about the society of the time. Was seventeenth-century England a society changing from a feudal to a capitalist order? Was the dominant ethos that which prevailed in a landed class generally hostile to mercantile or capitalist ideas? Was the society fluid, so that a young lawyer of humble origins could amass an enormous fortune? The numerous theories of the origins of the Rule all fit the author's vision of the society. But not all of the theories can possibly fit the facts of the time; not all the visions can possibly fit the society of the time.[42]

Is it perhaps misleading, one must ask, to look for an explanation of legal development only in societal conditions?[43]

3. *Has the Rule a useful function today?* None that is obvious or significant.

4. *Has the Rule disadvantages?* The obvious disadvantage, apart from the discomfort of students and the threat of sanctions to legal draftsmen, is the thwarting of reasonable desires of owners for the future distribution of their property.[44] Owners do not often intend to tie up their property for centuries but usually have a relatively immediate goal. If I devise a piece of hunting land to my friend Don B "until the next human land on the moon, remainder to my oldest living direct descendant," I am not thinking of a situation that might arise in 2098. Nor am I trying to do anything that most people would find unreasonable. Yet the remainder is entirely void, even if at the time of the gift the United States is about to launch a man into space.[45] What is to be remembered is that because of the way the Rule developed—through cases, over time—the result is clumsy and arbitrary and thwarts reasonable intentions. Any danger that an interest would vest too far in the future could be avoided much more simply by rules akin to those in Germany.

5. *What is society's input?* None.

6. *Why is the Rule rigid and remote from society?* Law when developed by judges is largely dependent on the *legal* culture of that particular elite. Not all types of reasoning are culturally and legally acceptable.[46] In some systems, for example in France, judges may not refer to previous decisions; in England until 1992 judges were not allowed to refer to parliamentary debates for legislative history.[47] In particular, when the Rule was developing, judges did not (usually) regard it as appropriate to base express arguments on social realities.

7. *Why is the Rule so long-lived?* It is in the nature of law that once it is established it continues. Much of law—legal institutions, rules, modes of reasoning, theoretical structures—survives despite great changes in social, economic, political, and religious circumstances.

8. *How could it be transported to the English New World?* Transplanting or borrowing is the most fruitful source of legal development. Failure to accept the existence of the huge extent of borrowing, often mindless borrowing, is the greatest obstacle to understanding law and its relation to society.

9. *Why is the Rule known only to the common law world?* Borrowing, though often mindless, is usually selective in one sense: one foreign system comes to be regarded by another as *the* system to be raided. For the so-called civil law systems, this law to be borrowed was once Roman; in more modern times (for some systems), French law. English law was ignored. This emphasis on borrowing from one particular system again raises the issue of the appropriateness of law in its society.[48]

The answers given above are my own. I am not claiming that they are the only answers or that all scholars would find all of them the most plausible. Some, indeed, may be wrong. But my main point is that the questions invite answers that relate not only to the Rule Against Perpetuities but also to the fundamental understanding of law, and the questions are not put by law teachers to their first-year students. The origins, survival, rationale, scope, and utility of the Rule Against Perpetuities raise issues that prompt similar questions in very many other contexts.

It is in the highest degree revealing for the nature of law and law teaching that so soon into their studies students accept the Rule Against Perpetuities unthinkingly, without much questioning the wisdom of it, the need for it, at its beginnings or today. So of course do their elders and betters (or worsers) even though there has been tinkering with the Rule, above all in the famous wait-

and-see doctrine. Legal thinking, in the Western world at least, is authoritarian and essentially conservative.

One last question about the Rule. Is it necessary to know something of the history of the Rule to make its parameters explicable? If the answer is yes—as it certainly is—what are the implications of this for our understanding of the nature of law and of its relation to society?

My conclusions for this section may be set out in three propositions:

1. Students enter their second year unaware of fundamental elements and aspects of law and the broad sweeps of principle behind them. Questions of the utmost importance for understanding the nature of law and how it operates have never been put to them.
2. Teaching law through the study of a few (abridged) cases on each point, with no attempt to place them in a wider framework or to give any theoretical structure, presents a thoroughly misleading picture of the law.
3. Teaching law through the study of a few cases gives only a limited understanding even of these cases and their significance.

An introduction to law for second-year law students? By the beginning of the second year it is too late for students to learn to know better. First-year law students are misled because their teachers were themselves misled in their own first year.

As I pointed out in chapter 1, legal education elsewhere, for instance in Justinian's Byzantium, may also have been skewed: the sources of law may have been misrepresented, first-year law teaching may have given "official" but incorrect doctrine, the relationship of law to society—in this case, involving religion—may be very inaccurately presented, or, as in chapter 4, law may have been set forth without its living reality, or legal rhetoric may be offered without legal reality. But at least, through Justinian's *Institutes*, the attempt was made to present law simply, coherently, and as a system. Legal education, to that extent, was "student friendly." In contrast, American first-year teaching is "education by terror." I am not thinking specifically of those professors, a minority but not disapproved of by their colleagues, who deliberately humiliate insufficiently prepared students by asking them question after question that they cannot answer; students not infrequently burst into tears. Rather, I am thinking of the basic situation. The first-year curriculum is notoriously overloaded; the casebooks are not systematic, give at best insufficient information, and refer to cases that they do not print but that students are expected to read. In contrast, the professors are baby fed. The casebook authors provide a "teachers' manual" that gives the professors the questions that they ought to put, the answers to these questions, and a synopsis of the cases cited but not printed.

LAW REVIEW EDITOR

But if first-year law school is education by terror, the second year presents the best students with some opportunity for revenge on professors, as well as the chance to indulge in infinite boredom.

The "best" students—chosen by their first-year grades or sometimes by a "write-on" (that is, students whose grades were not high enough may be permitted to submit an essay)—are elected to serve on the school's law review. The electors are the existing board members, that is, students.

The law review is the most bizarre feature of American law schools and is, I believe, found in all schools. Indeed, many have more than one such journal, but one is always the lead journal, usually designated only as the *X Law Review*, not the *X Journal of Circus Law*. In almost all schools the editors are all students, though there is usually a faculty adviser. To begin with, virtually all editors are completely unfit for the task. It is not just that after only one year of law study they cannot have the expertise to judge the originality and quality of articles. It is also that their first-year education has left them woefully ignorant about law. How, then, do they evaluate the articles to be accepted or rejected? It is, I think, impossible to rank the reasons accurately in terms of importance, but the following seem to me the most powerful.

1. *Topicality.* Since editors can hold their post for two years at the most, it is of the utmost importance that an article appear to them to be of immediate relevance. That fashion will change in a year or two is of little significance for an article's acceptance. An eye-catching title is a great plus. Most law professors when they write an article submit it at the same time to a large number of law reviews, say, fifty. In the nature of things editors cannot give adequate attention to all the articles submitted to them. They focus on those that seize their attention. The reader must remember the woeful ignorance of the editors.

2. *The reputation of the author.*

3. *The reputation of the author's law school.* Factors 2 and 3 may be taken together and need not be further explained. The reader must remember the woeful ignorance of the editors.

4. *Timing of submission.* Since the election of editors is cyclical, and since once the total complement of articles has been accepted there can be no more, the time at which an article is sent to a law review is critical. Some professors devote considerable skill to the matter. When is the optimum time? Should the article be submitted to all reviews at once, or should it be sent out in waves, to the most distinguished first, to the least noteworthy last? The issue here is that editors may pressure the author to decide quickly whether to accept an offer or not. The author is in a quandary, because she wants the article to appear in the most prestigious journal possible. By delaying acceptance, she may receive a better offer or she may lose the one she has. The matter is of importance: a law professor's prestige is much dependent on the law review in which she publishes. In some schools the dean will send a memo around the faculty congratulating a professor whose article has been accepted by one of a handful of law reviews but not otherwise. As will be seen, it is not a prime function of a law review article to be read. The placing of an article is not rationally dependent on quality. The reader must remember the woeful ignorance of the editors.

5. *Pressure on editors by faculty members.* This is a subject much discussed in private by professors but not in public. The article by Professor X was turned down because of pressure from local Professor Y, who dislikes X or who thinks the article too favorable to Palestinians or too right wing. The article by Professor A was accepted because of pressure from local Professor B, who is Professor A's buddy. It will be remembered that where X or A publishes is to him or her a matter of supreme importance. That pressure is easily applied may at first sight seem surprising, but it is not. Law review editors are ambitious; if they were not, they would not accept what I will soon show to be an onerous, thankless, and unbelievably boring task. Their careers can be hindered by a professor who does not find the students' attitude to be "mature." She may fail to recommend the recalcitrant editors with sufficient enthusiasm for a position with a firm of attorneys or, more important, may decline to recommend them at all for a judicial clerkship. The reader must remember the woeful vulnerability of the editors. Besides, from the editors' point of view, the professor with her greater experience may be right. The reader must remember the woeful ignorance of the editors.

The problems for the editors multiply. They may read hundreds (literally) of articles only to find that the ones they want are snatched away by a more prestigious review. Despite what I said above, the editors may find themselves dealing with a task left behind by their predecessors; this is especially the case with symposia volumes, which may take more than a year for completion. Some authors contributing to such volumes may simply not submit their talks and certainly will often submit late. Some will not revise their talks. It is a known fact that articles in symposia volumes are accepted with less scrutiny than are others. A standard complaint among student editors is that other editors do not do their share of the work. It is prestigious to become an editor, and the fact of having been an editor enhances career prospects. But being an editor is boring, and prospective employers will not inquire as to how well the editor performed the tasks assigned. What matters most to many editors is simply to be able to put on their résumé that they have been editors. The quality of a volume of which they were editors will never be imputed to them as it would be in the case of journals edited by scholars.

But the problems in evaluating and choosing articles for publication in a law review are only the beginning of the tragedy of the role played by these articles.

An equally great disaster is the role that law reviews play in deciding the tenure and promotion of law professors. A standard requirement for tenure in law schools is two law review articles "or their equivalent" and for promotion to full professor a further two law review articles "or their equivalent." There are two issues: what is a law review article, and what is an equivalent?

A law review article is, first of all, an article published in a law review that is edited by students. This definition is generally understood. But if two law review articles are the standard for tenure and promotion, then there must be more to the issue. Can a law review article have two, three, or five pages? The answer is a resounding no. The length is standardized! It must be at least fifty pages.[49] And it must show signs of "careful" scholarship. So at least 100 footnotes are needed.

Law professors, like other scholars, may have brilliant ideas on a particular point that can be fully set out in two or twenty pages. But these ideas cannot be published as law review articles. Instead, the brilliant two pages are concealed in a sixty-page treatise on a more general topic. Fifty-eight pages have no worth, and it is hard to find the other two. Consequently, for the most part, once tenure or promotion has been granted, the article sinks almost without trace. This rapid demise may sound incredible, and it is, but the accuracy of the observation is easily proved. Law review articles play almost no role in legal education. They are seldom assigned to students for class preparation. To the best of my knowledge, no article has appeared in full in any casebook, the main educational tool. What is presented there are mere snippets. Thus to stay with Dukeminier and Krier. Their casebook runs to 1,270 pages of text. Of these only 18 are occupied with quotations from law review articles. The longest quotation is a fraction over 5 pages.

I have mentioned that each article has at least 100 footnotes. Every statement in the text must be supported by a note. You wish to give two examples in the text? Not allowed! One must be a note to support the example in the text. There are strict rules about the mode of citation. You are a legal historian and wish to refer to a book first published in 1652, which went into at least twenty editions in various places, at different times. The obvious mode of citation is by book, title, chapter, and paragraph, which allows any thoughtful reader the chance of looking up the passage and putting it in context. Not allowed! You must cite the edition you used and the page number. But most universities, if they have any copy of the book at all, have only one edition, and its pagination is unlikely to tally with that in yours. Still, this difficulty is treated as irrelevant. Careful editors will insist that you submit to them a photocopy of the title page and of the pages to which you refer. But unless the work is in English, they cannot read it. No matter, they have done their job. Again, the reader must remember the woeful ignorance of the editors.

The editors, though, are the students who have made it to the top. After the agonies and uncertainties of the first year, they are safe and arrogant. They are also faced with the unbelievably boring task of checking the accuracy of every footnote and so forth. To be creative, they edit. They believe their grammar is better than the author's; so is their style, and so is their understanding of the subject. They make changes, often with no comprehension. But often they are right. After all, the professors have had the same training.

What is the equivalent of a law review article? The answer is both that there is none and that there is one. What is treated as equivalent varies from law school to law school and varies even within a school. What is a constant in virtually all schools is that other publications are traditionally given much less weight: this is true of peer-edited journals, even the most prestigious,[50] foreign journals, and books including textbooks and scholarly investigations. More than once, and often, actually, I have heard expressed the view that law review articles are the "coin of the realm": with nothing else can one pay one's dues. The reason for this approach is not clear to me.[51] It may simply be tradition or a lack of interest in scholarship; as I have stressed before, law review articles are not meant to be read.[52] Whatever the reason,[53] the lowly regard of, say, scholarly monographs is easily demonstrated: law reviews seldom contain book reviews. The great majority of issues do not contain a review of a single book. This would not be the case if either the student editors were interested in having reviews of books or if professors were eager to write them.

A student law review editor who was previously a professor in the humanities wrote to me:

> I personally find the whole game utterly appalling, especially in comparison with academic scholarship in the humanities. As you know, a professor would never dream of sending off an article unless it was already virtually in publishable form. Editors are colleagues, and editors do not correct (or write) footnotes for authors. Multiple submission is absolute heresy. While there is much abuse of power in scholarly journals, it seems to me that legal scholarship needs to aim in the same direction—journals must refuse to even look at articles that do not immediately reveal a clear and necessary purpose. Multiple submissions should be frowned upon. I think that contributes enormously to the atmosphere where "finding a slot" is more important than contributing to legal scholarship. Certainly, you do a service by daring to expose the fraud.

PROFESSOR'S RESEARCH ASSISTANT

Another important milestone for an aspiring law student is to become a professor's research assistant. The financial rewards are meager, but the student's goal is to have a champion: a professor who knows the student personally, who approves of him, and who will accordingly further his career actively by enthusiastic letters of recommendation.[54] What the professor expects from the assistant varies. At one end of the scale she may expect the assistant only to bring up books from the library and to make copies of relevant material. Or the assistant may be asked to make computer searches. This work seems innocuous, but the reader must remember the woeful ignorance of students. A search by the non-expert for citations to a book or case may easily turn up only those in American law reviews, not even those in Canadian or English law journals. It may well not reveal citations in nonlaw journals and will not indicate those in books. But often the research assistant does much more. He or she will synthesize the case law and law review articles, and the professor will proceed on the basis of the syntheses.[55] The professor may write an article without full citation of sources and may then look for a research assistant to provide support from cases and law review articles. It is not unknown, even at the best schools, for a professor to advertise for a research assistant to write her footnotes, specifying the emotional and political proclivities that are desirable in the assistant.

To some extent the reliance of professors on research assistants can be readily documented. Many law review articles show the author at the outset expressing gratitude for the help of a number of student assistants. This gratitude is not, usually, just for fetching books from the law library. I quote from the letter I quoted above:

> In case you want to know what I did for Professor X last semester (as a "reward" for getting an "A" in his subject). I was paid to work for about 80 hours (and ended up working about twice that). My job was to "skim" 150 articles on his subject and write a 4–5 sentence summary of each, then categorize the articles, and assign each article a number corresponding to the number on a hard copy of the article. I did enjoy reading the articles, but all this work took place over the course of my busiest month (given the titles at the beginning of November, deadline December 4). Quite honestly, my grades did suffer; likewise, my sanity and my children. I do, however, feel sure that the Professor put in a very good word for me with the firm I eventually decided to join. A deal with the Devil, to say the least.[56]

THE JUDICIAL CLERK

The aspiring law student has graduated. Most second- and third-year classes were similar to those that he or she experienced in the first year except that they were less terrifying. They also were taught by the casebook method. This rule usually holds even for subjects remarkably unsuited to it, such as law and literature, jurisprudence, comparative law. As for the last, the method gives a very false impression of foreign legal systems in which cases are treated as less significant.[57] The student still has not been exposed to the theoretical—but vital—issues that were not discussed in the first year. But he or she has acquired quickness and glibness that convey a false sense of ability. With the considerable aid of the professors whose research assistant they were, stduents are appointed clerks to judges, usually for one year. This is their first full-time law job and is prestigious, an important determinant of the students' place in the pecking order at a law firm and a significant credential for those who want to become law professors. Judges typically have two or three clerks each year who work to assist the judge. What the clerk is expected to do varies from judge to judge. But, in general, they research the cases and literature for the judge. At the state court level, law clerks write memoranda to a pool of justices recommending that the court agree or decline to hear a particular case. The individual clerk, drawing on research, may suggest how the judge might wish to vote on the case or how the judge might wish to analyze a particular issue presented in the case. A clerk at the appellate level may suggest questions for the judge to ask of the attorneys at oral argument. The clerk helps the judge at the opinion-writing stage, sometimes through discussion, and sometimes even by drafting the opinion itself. A clerk, less than a year out of law school, may draft a Supreme Court judgment and have it accepted word for word. To grasp the impact of this procedure on the legal system, the reader should remember how inexperienced the law clerk is and the weakness of legal education (also that of the judges themselves). The reader should recall the casebook method in which the student was exposed to a tiny fraction of the cases on any subject; the opinions in them may have been influenced or even written by such an ill-equipped lawyer just out of law school.

LAW PROFESSOR

Let us assume that the aspiring lawyer wishes to become a law professor. After clerking, he/she will typically work in a law office for around four years. Then she is successful in her ambition. The qualifications that make her suitable for the university post are partly her grades in law school and mainly the recommendations of her professors and her judge. What she does not have is a rigor-ous training akin to a Ph.D. in law under a distinguished mentor. She has no publications, and she has nothing in course of publication. She has no scholarly record. Whether she is likely to become a scholar in the sense understood in the arts and sciences is not even usually under active consideration by the faculty that hires her.

So the cycle begins again. The assistant professor teaches first-year courses from casebooks, presenting the same false picture of law that she received. She writes her law review articles, making much use of student assistants. At this point it should be emphasized that, despite the battery of footnotes, professors often have not read the fundamental sources on which they rely.[58]

This chapter as a whole may make depressing reading for some. But I do not exaggerate. Law professors in the United States are not interested in law as an intellectual discipline. Most are not intellectually curious. They are not inter-ested in law. This contention is easily proved. It is enough to walk through the offices of law professors in any law school and to look at the books on the shelves. For the most part, the visitor will not find general treatises on law or even treatises on the specialty of the professor. What he or she will find on the average will be only casebooks on the professor's teaching areas and the accom-panying teachers' manuals. These are gifts from the publishers to persuade the professor to adopt the book. Law professors do not buy law books. Out-of-date editions of casebooks are kept with the new. They help to fill up the shelves.

Still, I should not leave the reader with a wrong impression. Law professors are, in general, very smart. Most are dedicated teachers. They do a very good job of imparting what they want to impart. Many produce very sophisticated pub-lications on very technical issues (though for the most part they neglect funda-mentals). Some few write pathbreaking scholarship.

CHAPTER SEVEN

SITZ IN LEBEN

Law often out of context? A fact that is often unremarked? The most important trial in history is recorded in the Gospels in four different ways, all from one partisan standpoint, but the fact that the versions of it differ is scarcely noticed by legal scholars. The greatest Western compilation of law presents its own obsessively Christian Byzantium as godless. The most influential legal textbook of all time sets forth law with elementary mistakes. Subsequent commentators are not much concerned. Traditional law teaching in today's United States misstates law from the outset. Delictal liability in South Africa rests theoretically on legal history: this legal history is largely false, yet it still has an impact. Roman jurists present law remote from real life; Roman rhetoricians present legal argument remote from real law. How can this be? The examples should be set in context.

The relationship between law and society is very complex and more chaotic than is usually believed. Scholars try to impose an order that is not there. Thomas R. R. Cobb correctly claimed that philosophy is the handmaid of law and that history is the groundwork and only sure basis of philosophy. But this comparative legal history that he insisted on for understanding law in society is neglected.

Yet for the Western world the lessons of comparative legal history are very obvious and would not be denied, I believe, by any competent legal scholar.[1] In general, governments are not much interested in lawmaking, provided the tax money rolls in and the public peace is kept. But law is needed. If it is not made by governments, it will be made by subordinate lawmakers: judges, jurists, or law professors. But they are not usually appointed to make law or given the power to do so. Rather, the government acquiesces in their lawmaking. To justify their decisions or opinions, they have to seek legal authority. Hence, they will always be looking back, at their own past or at someone else's. These subordinate lawmakers are self-selecting and self-sustaining. They manufacture their own legal culture.[2] They find legal authority by borrowing.[3] They choose one system as their prime quarry, and they take even when the law is inappropriate.[4] When they can find no authority there, they will invent it and mislabel it.[5] It is hard for law not to be out of context. Even when great legislators emerge, they do not insert any precise social, political, or economic message into the law. This is true, for example, of Justinian, Frederick the Great, Napoleon, and Atatürk.[6]

The making of law is much misrepresented. I tend to suspect that legal scholars are willing self-deceivers who do not want to recognize the truth. The notion of customary law is a simple case in point. The general theory is that custom becomes law when people in a particular society follow it in the belief that it is law. This theory looks right to common sense, but the notion is badly flawed, as even a cursory look at any one customary system shows. Very frequently, there is no custom, or it cannot be found. Judges faced with the necessity of making a decision in a particular case cannot say that there is no answer.[7] So they invent a custom or borrow it from elsewhere. Jurists, writing down their own customs, do the same. Thereafter this expression of false custom becomes the law as custom.[8] Frequently, jurists writing down their customs give as reasons that the old customs are much destroyed and liable to be forgotten.[9] How can this be the case if they are the custom by which the people live?

Society is complex. To deal with this fact, developing law oversimplifies. Multifaceted social relationships, between neighbors, for instance, are divided into manageable legal units. The oldest Roman contract, the *stipulatio*, is a prime example. It was unilateral, only one party being bound. The promisee asked, "Do you promise?" and the other responded, "I promise," using the same verb. The promisor was bound strictly by the words used. Little else was taken into account, not even fraud. But why would one ever make a binding unilateral promise? The answer must be either that it was met by a return promise or a performance or that there was an ongoing relationship between the parties. For law to cope, the relationship was broken down into separate, distinct transactions.[10] When a legal issue arose on one of these, the connected transactions were ignored. Another example may be chosen from divorce in those countries in which it was granted for a "matrimonial fault," not a "breakdown of the marriage." Thus in England until the Divorce Reform Act of 1969, divorce was based on fault. There had to be a guilty party. One spouse had to be guilty of a matrimonial offense, such as adultery. But a fault on both sides blocked the divorce.[11] And behavior by a spouse that contributed to the other's committing the matrimonial fault but did not amount legally to a matrimonial fault was irrelevant for the granting of a divorce decree against the latter. In Scotland when divorce was based on fault, adultery involved the insertion of a penis into a vagina. There was no adultery, and thus no divorce, when a spouse performed an act of oral sex or masturbation with someone not a party to the marriage.[12] Although either of these two acts could be as gross an act of infidelity to the spouse as adultery, practical reality was ignored if the precise technical rule was not violated. Causes, including extreme neglect, that precipitated adultery were not relevant.

Law is also a distorting mirror. When it is treated with any degree of abstraction, it presents a very false picture. Again, stipulatio is a contract of strict law, the promisor being bound by what he said. In "early" times, most arrangements have vague terms and could not amount to contracts. The point of the stipulation was to create an enforceable promise. Hence the wording was strictly construed. But the real purpose was to give effect to the intention of the parties, a matter of everyday good faith.[13] On the other hand sale, *emptio venditio*, was a contract of good faith, and modern scholars stress the contrast between the stipulatio and sale. But the notion of good faith in sale was of limited extent. It did not cover disparity between the price and the value of what was bought. It did not for centuries involve a guarantee of good title or a guarantee against hidden defects.[14] Sale was recognized as a contract by the late third century B.C.; barter, *permutatio*, as a contract scarcely at all even four centuries later. Yet barter must have been prominent in an early society. Why the difference? Part of the answer is that in a sale one party is typically in the business and will make a profit, whereas in barter typically the parties are on the same plane. "Good faith" is needed in sale to protect the weaker party.[15]

The relationship between law and society is so complex[16] that even distinguished scholars distort by oversimplification. I choose one example because it is relevant for both Aquilian liability and contemporary American legal education. Lawrence M. Friedman in his celebrated *History of American Law* writes: "For the 19th century, it is hard to think of a body of new judge-made law more striking than tort laws. As we have seen, the law of torts was totally insignificant before 1900 [*sic*: but perhaps it should read '1800'], a twig on the great tree of law. The common law had little to say about personal injuries brought about by carelessness—the area of law and life that underwent most rapid growth in the century. The modern law of torts must be laid at the door of the industrial revolution, whose machines had a marvelous capacity for smashing the human body."[17] And most of this paragraph is quoted with obvious approval by

Mark A. Franklin and Robert L. Rabin at the very beginning of what is probably the most favored casebook on torts in America.[18] Friedman also stated:
"The explosion of tort law, and negligence in particular, has to be attributed
to the industrial revolution—to the age of engines and machines. Mainly, this
branch of law is about personal injuries. In preindustrial society, there are few
personal injuries, except as a result of assault and battery. Modern tools and
machines, however, have a marvelous capacity to cripple and maim their servants."[19] Certainly one cannot reasonably doubt that as a result of the Industrial
Revolution the number of injuries resulting from negligence greatly increased.
But one cannot simply jump from the number of injuries to an explosion in torts
law in England and America. And Friedman's statements have the appearance of
generalizations: societal conditions create appropriate law. Indeed, in his pro-
logue Friedman had already set out his belief:

> In one sense, law is always up-to-date. The legal system always "works";
> it always functions. Every society governs itself and settles disputes. Every
> society, then, has a working system of law. If the courts, for example, are
> hidebound and ineffective, that merely means some other agency has taken
> over what courts might otherwise do. The system works like a blind, in-
> sensate machine. It does the bidding of those whose hands are on the con-
> trols. The laws of China, the United States, Nazi Germany, France, and
> the Union of South Africa reflect the goals and policies of those who call
> the tune in those societies. Often, when we call law "archaic," we mean
> that the power system of its society is morally out of tune. But change the
> power system and the law too will change. The basic premise of this book
> is that, despite a strong dash of history and idiosyncrasy, the strongest in-
> gredient in American law, at any given time, is the present: current emo-
> tions, real economic interests, concrete political groups. It may seem a cu-
> rious beginning to a book of history to downgrade the historical element
> of law. But this is not really a paradox. The history of law has meaning
> only if we assume that at any given time the vital portion is new and chang-
> ing, form following function, not function following form. History of law
> is not—or should not be—a search for fossils, but a study of social de-
> velopment, unfolding through time.[20]

But no explanation of English and American tort law can be so very simple.
Comparative legal history indicates otherwise. As we have seen, in classical Ro-

man law recorded in the *Digest*[21] the notion of negligence as a basis of liability
for injury was already highly developed. And most of the South African cases
on tortuous liability that I have discussed in chapter 5 do not result from the
marvelous capacity of modern tools and machinery "to cripple and maim their
servants." An American (or English) legal historian who seeks not only to describe but also to explain legal change should ask himself why ancient Rome
and seventeenth-century Holland[22] had what appears to be a much more "modern" law of negligence than had England or America in the mid–nineteenth
century. No industrial revolution had occurred.

The development of law is enormously complicated. The equivalent of torts
law, that of *délit* and *quasi-délit* in French law is a case in point. It developed very
much under the influence of Domat and Pothier in response to Roman law that,
in this area, was rejected to a great extent. The *code civil*, articles 1382–1386, was
the result.[23] They provided a very simple-seeming framework, and they were
very much adopted in the civil codes of other countries. Article 1384 covered,
inter alia, liability for damage caused by a thing "under one's guard." This part
of the article was not much used, and was understood narrowly, until 1870.[24]
The Industrial Revolution had not occurred when the code was promulgated.
But after 1870, article 1384 was very much used, even abused, with consequent
problems, and is the basis of modern products liability law.[25] The cases and professional discussion show the enormous growth and changes that must be primarily the result of the Industrial Revolution. My point is that, despite all of
these developments, the relevant law was actually already in place, in article 1384.
And this part of the law is unchanged and is still the law in France. Case decisions do not in theory make law for subsequent decisions and cannot be cited.[26]

I stress Franklin and Rabin's reliance on Friedman because of the important
role of their book in legal education. The point I want to make is that by its
very nature the casebook method is antithetical to legal history and hence to any
understanding of the relationship between law and society.[27]

My concern in this book has not been the notion that I have developed elsewhere, that law is out of step with the society in which it operates.[28] It may be
that law functioned well in Justinian's Byzantium, but if so, it was not altogether
the law set out in the *Corpus iuris civilis*. Law in action in the Roman empire, whatever its qualities, was not the same as that in juristic writings or in professional
rhetorical exercises. Aquilian liability in South Africa does not really equate with
the supposed historical roots and judicial examination of them. American legal

education misrepresents law as it is and misrepresents as well how it develops. My argument is that the expression of law and of law as it is are often more different than is usually realized.[29]

I would like to finish by adducing another example on which I will not elaborate. There is no need. It is the treatment of slavery in the U.S. Constitution. There is none. Slavery was a prime issue, but it is not mentioned.[30]

ABBREVIATIONS

A.D.	Appellate Division
Am. J. Comp. L.	*American Journal of Comparative Law*
Buckland, *Textbook*	W. W. Buckland, *Textbook of Roman Law*, 3d ed., ed. P. Stein (Cambridge, 1963)
C.	*Code of Justinian*
Collatio iuris Romani	*Collatio iuris Romani*, ed. R. Feenstra et al. (Amsterdam, 1995)
C.P.D.	Cape Provincial Division
C.Th.	*Theodosian Code*
D.	*Digest of Justinian*
D.L.R.	Dominion Law Reports
E.D.C.	Eastern Districts Court
E.D.L.D.	Eastern Districts Local Division
G.	*Institutes of Gaius*
h.t.	*huius tituli* (meaning that the text belongs to the same *Digest* or *Code* title as the text just cited)
J.	*Institutes of Justinian*
LQR	*Law Quarterly Review*
N.L.R.	Natal Law Reports

N.P.D.	Natal Provincial Division
New Jerome	*The New Jerome Biblical Commentary*, ed. Raymond E. Brown and others (Englewood Cliffs, N.J., 1990)
O.P.D.	Orange Free State Provincial Division
pr.	*principio* (meaning that the fragment is the first in a text of the *Digest, Institutes,* or *Code*)
S.A.	South African Law Reports
S.C.	Cape Supreme Court Reports
S.W.A.	South West Africa
Thomas, *Textbook*	J. A. C. Thomas, *A Textbook of Roman Law* (Amsterdam, 1976)
T.P.D.	Transvaal Provincial Division
T.v.R.	*Tijdschrift voor Rechtsgeschiedenis*
T.S.	Transvaal Supreme Court
Watson, *Ancient Law*	Alan Watson, *Ancient Law and Modern Understanding: At the Edges* (Athens, Ga., 1998)
Watson, *Evolution*	Alan Watson, *The Evolution of Law* (Baltimore, 1985)
Watson, *Law Making*	Alan Watson, *Law Making in the Later Roman Republic* (Oxford, 1974)
Watson, *Roman Law and Comparative Law*	Alan Watson, *Roman Law and Comparative Law* (Athens, Ga., 1991)
Watson, *Society and Legal Change*	Alan Watson, *Society and Legal Change* (Edinburgh, 1977)
Watson, *Spirit*	Alan Watson, *The Spirit of Roman Law* (Athens, Ga., 1995)

Watson, *Studies*	Alan Watson, *Studies in Roman Private Law* (London, 1991)
Watson, *Transplants*	Alan Watson, *Legal Transplants: An Introduction to Comparative Law*, 2d ed. (Athens, Ga., 1993)
W.L.D.	Witwatersrand Local Division
ZSS	*Zeitschrift der Savigny Stiftung (romanistische Abteilung)*

NOTES

INTRODUCTION

1. The extent to which law, though not noticed, intrudes into everyday life is well brought out in Rudolf von Jhering, *Law in Daily Life*, trans. Henry Goudy (Oxford, 1904).

CHAPTER ONE. THE FIRST RECEPTION OF ROMAN LAW

1. "Reflections on the First 'F.e 'eption' of Roman Law in Germanic States," now in Ernst Levy, *Gesammelte Schriften*, vol. 1 (Cologne, 1963), 201ff.

2. Custom was never important and may be ignored here.

3. See, e.g., G. Rotondi, *Leges publicae populi romani* (Hildesheim, 1966).

4. See, e.g., Watson, *Law Making*, 14ff.

5. *Vita Probi* 13.1; cf. Buckland, *Textbook*, 12ff.

6. Cf., e.g., Buckland, *Textbook*, 9ff.; Thomas, *Textbook*, 35ff.

7. For the Edict, see above all Otto Lenel, *Das edictum perpetuum*, 3d ed. (Leipzig, 1927).

8. See Alan Watson, "The End of Roman Juristic Writing," 29 *Israel Law Review* (1995), 228ff.

9. See, e.g., Max Kaser, *Das römische Privatrecht*, vol. 2, 2d ed. (Munich, 1971), 3.

10. For the argument, see my papers "The Rescripts of the Emperor Probus (272–282 A.D.)" and "Private Law in the Rescripts of Carus, Carinus, and Numerianus," now in Alan Watson, *Legal Origins and Legal Change* (London, 1991), 61ff. and 45ff., respectively.

11. The translation is that of Clyde Pharr, *The Theodosian Code* (Princeton, 1952), 15.

12. Even before this these five had come to occupy a preeminent place. See Jean Gaudemet, *La formation du droit séculier et du droit de l'église aux quatrième et cinquième siècles* (Paris, 1975), 75.

13. Cf. the schema in Franz Wieacker, *Textstufen klassischer Juristen* (Göttingen, 1960), 153f.; and Gaudemet, *La formation*, 75.

14. "Interpolationen im Theodosianus?" 34 *ZSS* (1913), 274ff. This view is widely

accepted: cf. the literature cited by Kaser, *Privatrecht*, 2, 19 n.3. Recently, Wieacker has tended to the view that the original constitution was the text as we have it; see *Textstufen*, 156 n.153.

15. See, e.g., Josephus *Jewish Antiquities* 19.291.

16. See, e.g., Gaudemet, *La formation*, 15. Where the petition had been forwarded to the emperor by a provincial governor, the *subscriptio* would be put up in the province.

17. See, e.g., H. F. Jolowicz and B. Nicholas, *Historical Introduction to Roman Law*, 2d ed. (Cambridge, 1972), 371f.; also, with full citation of sources and literature, N. Palazzolo, "Le modalità di trasmissione dei provvedimenti imperiali nelle province," 28 *IURA* (1977), 40ff.

18. Olivia Robinson not unreasonably thinks they were official, authorized by Diocletian; see *The Sources of Roman Law* (London, 1997), 19, 61.

19. The translation is mainly that of Pharr, *Theodosian Code*, 11f.

20. *Minutes* §4; *C.Th.* 1.1.5.

21. The final section, §3, adds nothing for present purposes.

22. The contrary, wrong view, "alterations could be made in the rescripts to bring them up-to-date," will be found, e.g., in Watson, *Roman Law and Comparative Law*, 84.

23. *P. Oxy.* 1814.

24. For these and other arguments, see above all Fritz Pringsheim, "Die Entstehungszeit des Digestenplans und die Rechtschulen," *Gesammelte Abhandlungen*, vol. 2 (Heidelberg, 1961), 41ff.

25. For the other two very special cases where substantive interpolation occurred, see Alan Watson, "Prolegomena to Establishing pre-Justinianic Texts," 62 *Tijdschrift voor Rechtsgeschiedenis* (1994), 113ff. at 120ff. (1) These are texts that had to be retained because of their relevance but that referred to an institution now obsolete and replaced. Thus texts concerning slaves that mention delivery by *traditio* would originally have referred to delivery by the obsolete *mancipatio*. (2) Where a text relates to a basic proposition that had to be set out, then an innovation by Justinian might be inserted into it. See also J. H. A. Lokin, "The End of an Era: Epilegomena to a Century of Interpolation Criticism," in *Collatio iuris Romani*, vol. 1, 261ff.

26. This approach ignores any pre-Justinianic alteration of the juristic texts, but see above.

27. See, e.g., Wolfgang Kunkel, *Herkunft und soziale Stellung der römischen Juristen*, 2d ed. (Graz, 1967), 170f.

28. The question of the extent of interpolation of substance is vexed, but see my arguments earlier in this chapter against interpolation except in very limited circumstances.

29. See, e.g., Watson, *Spirit*, especially 205ff.

30. See Watson, *Spirit*, 49f.

31. See, e.g., Alan Watson, "The Origins of the *Code noir* Revisited," 71 *Tulane Law Review* (1997), 1041ff. at 1045ff.

32. Thus it is no surprise that in O. F. Robinson's book on the administration of Rome, the great majority of sources cited are not from the *Digest: Ancient Rome: City Planning and Administration* (London, 1992), 232ff.

33. See, e.g., *Cristianesimo e istituzioni politiche da Constantino a Giustiniano*, ed. Enrico dal Covolo and Renato Uglione (Rome, 1997).

34. References to a deity could be cut out. Often they would not exist in the original because they would be understood.

35. *D.*12.2.13.6.

36. The other text in the title that uses the word *deus*, *D.*12.2.3.4, also concerns this issue.

37. The remaining texts that contain the word *deus* are: *D.*1.1.2; 4.8.32.4; 34.2.38.2; 49.14.3*pr.*

38. For general accounts, see Buckland, *Textbook*, 117f.; Percy E. Corbett, *The Roman Law of Marriage* (Oxford, 1930), 218ff.; Susan Treggiari, *Roman Marriage* (Oxford, 1991), 435ff.

39. Nor was it in Gaius's *Institutes.*

40. *Novellae* 117.10.

41. This influence is clear despite the rescinding of the rule by Justinian's successor, Justin II, in 566; *Novellae* 140.

42. *C.Th.* 3.16.1 (A.D. 331).

43. *C.Th.* 3.16.2 (Honorius, Theodosius, and Constantius, A.D. 421); 5.17.8 (Theodosius and Valentinian, A.D. 449): cf. Corbett, *Marriage*, 244f.

44. *C.*5.17.10.

45. *Novellae* 22.6.

46. *C.* 5.17.2.

47. The treatment of divorce in the *Digest* is itself a strong argument against substantive interpolation.

48. See, e.g., Wieacker, *A History of Private Law in Europe* (Oxford, 1995), 183; Tony Honoré, "Conveyances of Land and Professional Standards in the Later Empire," in *New Perspectives in the Roman Law of Property*, ed. P. Birks (Oxford, 1989), 137ff.

49. See, e.g., Wieacker, *Private Law*, p. 185.

50. For an account, see Alan Watson, "The Importance of Nutshells," 42 *Am. J. Comp. L.* (1994), 1ff. at 9ff.

51. I.e., in Justinian's *Codex.*

52. For law misleading the U.S. student from the very start, see the beginning of chapter 6.

53. For a skilled attempt at reconstructing the precise sources used for each text, see above all Contardo Ferrini, *Opere*, vol. 2 (Milan, 1929), 307ff.

54. *D*.20.1.5.1.

55. See, e.g., *D*.20.1.1.2.

56. See, e.g., *D*.20.1.3.

57. *D*.43.33.

58. Cf. the absence of any attributed source in Ferrini, *Opere*, vol. 2, 410.

59. Such, indeed, is the translation of J. A. C. Thomas, *The Institutes of Justinian* (Cape Town, 1975), 307.

60. See, e.g., Thomas, *Textbook*, 383; Max Kaser, *Das römische Privatrecht*, vol. 1, 2d ed. (Munich, 1971), 634.

61. Indeed, Kaser goes so far as to regard *Institutes 4.9pr.* as giving genuinely classical law, whereas *D*.9.1.1.7 has been subject to later alteration. *Privatrecht*, vol. 1, 634 n.34.

62. *D*.9.1.1.9.

63. For present purposes I leave aside the controversial issue, which is rather different, as to whether an animal's owner is liable if an animal that is wild by nature, such as a bear, causes harm; cf. *D*.9.1.1.10.

64. See, e.g., Francis de Zulueta, *Institutes of Gaius*, vol. 2 (Oxford, 1953), 273.

65. For an introduction to the subject, see *The Law of South Africa*, vol. 1, ed. W. A. Joubert (Durban, 1976), 372ff.

66. See, e.g., J. A. C. Thomas, "Arra in Sale in Justinian Law," 24 *T.v.R.* (1956), 253ff. (and the references given therein); "Arra Reagitata," *Butterworths South African Law Review* (1956), 60ff.; "A Postscript on Arra," 10 *IURA* (1959), 109ff.; *Institutes*, 231; A. D'Ors, "Las Arras en la Compraventa Justinianea," 6 *IURA* (1955), 149ff.; "'Arra Reagitata' sive in scriptis sive sine scriptis," 9 *IURA* (1958), 78ff.; Werner Schuster, "Die Funktion der 'Arrha' bei Justinian," 5 *Labeo* (1959), 26ff.; T. H. Tylor, "Writing and Arra in Sale under the *Corpus Juris*," 77 *LQR* (1961), 77ff.; A. M. Honoré, "Arra as You Were," 77 *LQR* (1961), 172ff.; J. M. Thomson, "Arra in Sale in Justinian's Law," 5 *Irish Jurist* (1970), 180ff. What follows is in large measure a shortened version of my "*Arra* in the Law of Justinian," now in Alan Watson, *Studies*, 179ff.

67. Contra D'Ors, "Las Arras," 149ff.

68. Francis de Zulueta is surely wrong when he says that this constitution laid down that subscription is required of documents made *per alium* but not of autographs of the parties; see *The Roman Law of Sale* (Oxford, 1945), 22. Possibly *J*.3.23pr. relaxed the provision where the writing was the autograph of the parties, but this does not necessarily follow from the wording of the text.

69. Cf. Thomas, "*Arra in Sale*," 263ff.

70. Cf. Thomas, "*Arra in Sale*," 263ff.

71. Nothing in Theophilus *Paraphrasis* or the *Basilica* militates against this solution.

72. *Textbook*, 662ff. The reference is to *J*.4.6.24 at 665 n.7.

73. *Imperatoris Iustiniani Institutiones*, 5th ed. (Oxford, 1912), 542ff.

74. *Textbook*, 662ff.

75. *Institutes*, 282ff.

76. *Institutionum libri*, 543f.

77. *Institutes*, 293.

78. The distinction surfaces again at *J*.4.6.13.

79. *Institutionum libri*, 551. It is worth noticing that *J*.4.6.15 does make clear a distinction between the old and contemporary law.

80. *Institutionum libri*, 553.

81. *Institutes*, 296.

82. *Institutes*, 296.

83. *Textbook*, 666f.

84. Especially in the pseudo-Platonic dialogue *Minos*.

85. On the text, see, e.g., Joseph A. Fitzmyer in *New Jerome*, 837.

86. *De legibus* 1.7.22ff.; 1.11.32ff.

87. *Contra Faustum* 22.27. Johann Sauter presents us with an intriguing text: "lex aeterna et ratio in mente Dei existens, quae res omnes per consentanea media in suos fines diriguntur," "The external law and reason existing in the mind of God, which directs all things in their proper boundaries according to fit means"; *Die philosophischen Grundlagen des Naturrechts* (Vienna, 1932), 59. He attributes this to Augustine, *De libero arbitrio* 1.5. Unfortunately I cannot find it there, nor does it seem to be by Augustine or to be Roman or even medieval. I am grateful to Tom Burns for help in trying to trace the text.

88. *Enarratio in Psalmos XXXI*, 3.5.

89. See, e.g., Rogerius (active in 1158) *Quaestiones in Institutiones* 1.2.1.

90. See already Alan Watson, "Some Notes on Mackenzie's *Institutions* and the European Legal Tradition," 16 *Ius Commune* (1989), 303ff.

91. See Watson, *Roman Law and Comparative Law*, 217ff.

92. *Ulpian* (Oxford, 1982), 31.

93. G.1.1.

94. To this text we will return in chapter 3.

95. But it could later be given one; see chapter 3.

96. See already Watson, *Roman Law and Comparative Law*, 214ff.

97. Cf., e.g., Ferrini, *Opere*, vol. 2, 334.

98. But it could, e.g., for Thomas R. R. Cobb; see chapter 3.

99. See above all Paul Collinet, *Histoire de l'Ecole de Droit de Beyrouth* (Paris, 1925), 207ff., especially 234ff.

100. 2.8.20; 3.1.5; 3.7.2; 8.8.1, 3; 9.7.5; 9.17.6, 7; 9.35.4, 5; 9.38.3, 4, 6, 7, 8; 9.40.8; 9.45.1; 11.7.10, 13; 11.30.57; 11.36.20, 31; 11.39.8, 10, 11; 12.1.59, 60, 63, 75, 77, 103, 104, 112, 115, 121, 123; 12.12.12; 13.1.5, 6, 11; 13.10.4, 6; 14.3.11; 15.7.1, 3, 4, 8, 9, 10, 12; 16.1.1, 2, 3, 4; 16.2.17, 18, 19, 20, 21, 22, 23, 24, 25, 26, 27, 28; 16.3.1, 2; 16.4.1, 2, 3; 16.5.3, 4, 5, 6, 7, 8, 9, 10, 11, 12, 13, 14, 15, 16, 17, 18, 19, 20, 21, 22, 23, 24; 16.6.1, 2; 16.7.1, 2, 3, 4, 5; 16.8.11, 13, 14, 15; 16.10.7, 8, 9, 10, 11, 12.

101. 1.1.1, 2; 1.2.2, 3; 1.3.6, 7, 8, 9; 1.4.1, 2, 3, 4; 1.5.2; 1.6.1, 2; 1.11.2; 3.12.5(6), 6(7), 7(8); 7.65.4a; 10.23.1; 11.66(65).4; 11.71(70).1.

102. 3.1.5; 3.7.2; 7.8.2; 9.7.5; 12.1.99; 13.5.18; 16.7.3; 16.8.8, 9, 10, 12, 13, 14, 16, 17.

103. 1.6.2; 1.8.4, 5, 6, 7; 11.51(50).1.

104. 1.6.9; 1.15.8; 2.4.5; 6.9.1; 9.38.3, 6, 7, 8; 10.10.16; 12.12.8; 13.11.1.

105. 1.6.2; 1.23.5; 9.29.1, 2, 3; 11.9(8).3.

106. 3.1.4, 5, 6, 7; 3.4.1; 11.15.2 (a sale to the state); 12.3.1; 13.6.6, 7.

107. 4.38.14; 4.40.15.1, 2; 4.41.1; 4.44.15, 16; 4.58.4; 4.60.1; 10.3.5, 6; 10.34(33).1.

108. 2.4.5; 4.18.1; 4.20.1; 11.37.1; 11.38.1.

109. 3.16.1; 7.69.1; 8.4.6, 7; 8.10.8; 8.11(12).3, 4, 5, 6; 9.31.1; 11.59(58).8; 11.62(61).3, 4, 5, 6, 8.

110. For this procedure, see, e.g., Max Kaser, *Das römische Zivilprozessrecht* (Munich, 1966), 339ff.

111. See above all Reuven Yaron, "The Competitive Coexistence of Latin and Greek in the Roman Empire," *Collatio iuris Romani*, vol. 2, 657ff.

CHAPTER TWO. LAW IN LITERATURE: THE GOSPELS

1. See chapter 6.

2. Now in David Daube, *Collected Studies in Roman Law*, vol. 2 (Frankfurt am Main, 1991), 1379ff.

3. Two examples that will not be examined here where law is not the main focus but is pivotal and is misrepresented are the thirteenth-century Icelandic saga of burnt Njal, *Brennu-Njals Saga*; and Anthony Trollope, *The Eustace Diamonds* (1871 to 1873).

A truly remarkable, outstanding example of law in literature appears in Rabelais, *Le tiers livre*, chapters 39–44. To develop law, medieval and later jurists had to resort to taking Roman legal texts out of context so that they could be understood as saying something that had never been intended. (For examples on the non-Roman subject of conflict of laws from Bartolus, 1314–1357, and Huber, 1635–1695, see Alan Watson, *Joseph Story and the Comity of Errors* [Athens, Ga.; 1992], 1ff.) To comic effect Rabelais has Judge Bridoye ("Bridlegoose") do the same, citing Roman and canon law, and the commentators, in exactly the way the commentators themselves did. For example, at the beginning of chapter 39, Bridoye explains that he uses large dice, not small ones, in deciding cases because of failing eyesight: "And also by legal prescription imperfections of nature must not be imputed as crime as appears *ff. de re milit. l. qui cum uno, ff. de reg. jur. l. fere, ff. de edil. ed. per totum, de term. mo. l. Divus Adrianus resolu. per Lud. Ro. in l. si vero, ff. solu. matri.*" (my translation). The first reference (of these five) is to the *Digest* title on military law, *49.16.4pr.*, which may be translated: "A man who is born with one testicle or who has lost one can lawfully serve as a soldier in accordance with the rescript of the deified Trajan: for the generals Sulla and Cotta are reported to have been in that condition by nature."

4. Cf. Frans Neirynek in *New Jerome*, 587ff.

5. But all the verses cited could easily be later explanatory insertions. But certainly Mark wrote for a readership that could read Greek.

6. Despite, e.g., C. Clifton Black in *The Harper Collins Study Bible* (New York, 1993), 1915.

7. By "ordinary believing Jews," I mean those who would not be classified as Pharisees, Sadducees, Zealots or Essenes, or agitated followers of a prophet like Isaiah. They would be content with moderate religious observance except in extreme circumstances. Readers will easily think of modern parallels.

8. I have argued elsewhere that the evangelists had no firm knowledge of Jesus before his ministry: the traditions had been invented, reasonably enough, because there was great curiosity; *Jesus: A Profile* (Athens, Ga., 1998), 33ff. Such invention was not to be avoided.

9. The chaptering is not original.

10. The laying on of hands was not as a blessing, which would not have counted as work.

11. I mention this point to indicate that to some extent Mark's structuring is aesthetically contrived.

12. See, e.g., David Flusser, *Jesus* (Jerusalem, 1997), 58f.

13. For an explanation of the hostility of the Herodians to Jesus, see Watson, *Jesus: A Profile*, 23ff.

14. Luke 13.14.

15. Cf. Catullus, 41.5ff.

16. For handwashing, see Flusser, *Jesus*, 59ff. Again it must be remembered that Jesus was to be regarded as somebody special, and the behavior of his disciples would be worthy of note.

17. For this see, too, Flusser, *Jesus*, 60ff.

18. For Corban, see Mishnah Nedarim.

19. For the argument, see Watson, *Jesus: A Profile*, 56ff.

20. See Mishnah Shekalim.

21. Still, Jesus can be interpreted as not minding if the Gentiles eat the scraps.

22. The amount of law in Mark appears even more striking when we look at the Gospels of Thomas and Peter. In them law does not appear.

23. See Watson, *Jesus and the Jews: The Pharisaic Tradition in John* (Athens, Ga., 1995).

24. I am only too well aware that readers unfamiliar with or in disagreement with my views on *S* will find much of this section unacceptable. As far as I can I will relegate *S* to the background. Geoffrey P. Miller, a friendly critic, has suggested that perhaps *S* should be seen as a Christian source: Jesus from the outset is shown as hostile to pharisaic values: 1 *Edinburgh Law Review* (1997), 273ff. at 274. This approach would not affect my exposition here. I do not accept it primarily because Nicodemus, who appears in John as the one person without fault, is represented as a leading Pharisee and not a Christian.

25. See already Watson, *Jesus and the Jews*, 23.

26. For the argument, see Watson, *Jesus and the Jews*, 29ff.

27. See Watson, *Jesus and the Jews*, 87.

28. The Greek does not have "he was blind" in Jesus' reply.

29. For more detail, see Watson, *Jesus and the Jews*, 44ff.

30. Pheme Perkins in *New Jerome*, 971.

31. Dennis C. Dulling in *Harper Collins Study Bible*, 1866.

32. *The New Testament and Rabbinic Judaism* (London, 1956), 55ff.; cf. already Alan Watson, *Jesus and the Law* (Athens, Ga., 1996), 74ff.

33. See already, also for Luke, Watson, *Jesus and the Law*, 26ff.

34. But here female uncleanliness is more in the background than in Mark; Watson, *Jesus and the Law*, 52ff.

35. *The Trial of Jesus* (Athens, Ga., 1995), 98ff.

36. Josephus *Jewish War* 2.169ff., 175; *Jewish Antiquities* 4.72f.; 18.55ff., 85ff.; Philo *Embassy to Gaius* 301.

37. Mishnah Sanhedrin 4.1.

38. Mishnah Sanhedrin 5.1ff.

39. On this see David Daube, "Judas," 13 *Rechtshistorisches Journal* (1994), 21ff. at 21.

40. I say so despite Mishnah Sanhedrin 7.5. For my argument, see Watson, *The Trial of Jesus*, 115ff.

41. Cf. Leviticus 10.6f.

42. Cf. Raymond E. Brown, *The Death of the Messiah*, vol. 1 (New York, 1994), 679ff.

43. It is, of course, possible that Simon acquired the nickname before he became a disciple of Jesus. Then at the least the nickname would tell us nothing about Jesus' attitude to Zealots, but its very retention would still suggest that Jesus' group were no revolutionaries.

44. Cf., e.g., D. Cohen and C. Paulus, "Einige Bemerkungen zum Prozess Jesu bei den Synoptikern," 102 *ZSS* (1985), 437ff. at 445f.

45. I do not think it necessary to discuss here the trial as set out in Matthew and Luke, but see Watson, *Trial of Jesus*, 53ff.

CHAPTER THREE. LITERATURE IN LAW: THOMAS R. R. COBB

1. Still, slavery is becoming almost a fashionable subject, thanks in large measure to Paul Finkelman. Among the many books on the subject, see Paul Finkelman, *An Imperfect Union: Slavery, Federalism, and Comity* (Chapel Hill, 1981); Paul Finkelman, *Slavery in the Courtroom* (Washington, D.C., 1984); Paul Finkelman, *Slavery and the Founders: Race and Liberty in the Age of Jefferson* (Armonk, N.Y., 1996); *Slavery and the Law*, ed. Paul Finkelman (Madison, 1997); Thomas D. Morris, *Free Men All: The Personal Liberty Laws of the North, 1780–1861* (Baltimore, 1996); Thomas D. Morris, *Southern Slave Law* (Chapel Hill, 1996); William E. Wiethoff, *A Peculiar Humanism: The Judicial Advocacy of Slavery in High Courts of the Old South, 1820–1850* (Athens, Ga., 1996); Mark Tushnet, *The American Law of Slavery* (Princeton, 1981); A. Leon Higginbotham, Jr., *In the Matter of Color* (New York, 1978); Philip J. Schwarz, *Slave Laws in Virginia* (Athens, Ga., 1996); Judith K. Schafer, *Slavery, the Civil Law, and the Supreme Court of Louisiana* (Baton Rouge, 1994); *Historical Guide to World Slavery*, ed. Seymour Drescher and Stanley L. Engermann (New York, 1998); and Alan Watson, *Slave Law in the Americas* (Athens, Ga., 1989).

2. The title page of the *Inquiry*, which is unadorned, does not claim to be volume 2.

3. P. xxxvi.

4. Since my concern is Cobb's art, I relegate to a footnote my conviction that on this issue he is 100 percent correct. Abstract philosophies of positive law, such as those of John Austin (1790–1859) or Herbert Hart (1907–1992), that ignore what happens and contain no history are fundamentally sterile. I accept that comparative legal history, on which Cobb is about to embark, is the only way to understand law in society; see, e.g., Watson, *Roman Law and Comparative Law; Transplants.*

5. Genesis 9.22ff.

6. Genesis 6.8.

7. P. xli.

8. Pp. ccixff.

9. Pp. ccxiff.

10. Pp. ccxiiiff.

11. Surprisingly, perhaps, Ruth M. Karras, writing about slavery in medieval Scandinavia, downplays an economic role for slaves there and claims that the society had a need to categorize a group of people as outsiders: "The existence of slaves . . . allowed even the most dependent nonslave to participate in the dominant culture in a way, to be a member of society. It allowed the theory, the pretense, that all nonslaves were equal at

least in rights if not in wealth or power" (*Slavery and Society in Medieval Scandinavia* [New Haven, 1988], 165f.).

12. To some extent in these quotations I am doing Cobb an injustice for the sake of brevity. I have omitted some of his arguments and examples, and I have cut out his foot-notes. But I hope to have given enough of the flavor of Cobb's exposition.

13. J.1.3.2. Cobb is exact. The most recent translation of the *Institutes* into English, which takes *contra naturam*, "contrary to nature," as "contrary to the law of nature," is simply wrong; *Justinian's Institutes*, trans. Peter Birks and Grant Mcleod (Ithaca, N.Y., 1987), 39. Their mistake is disastrous.

14. P. 5.

15. The quotation from Potgiesser might be translated: "Either that all and individual men are held to live in natural liberty subject to the rule of no one; or that they are understood to have entered into civil society only with some, to be joined with others by no bond, unless that of common humanity."

16. The Scottish jurist is Andrew McDouall (Lord Bankton), *An Institute of the Law of Scotland*, 3 vols. (1751–1753). Cobb's reference is to 1.2.77.

17. The same distinction is probably found in J.1.2.2, despite the wording "But the *ius gentium* is common to all mankind. For human peoples established it for them-selves under the compulsion of need and human necessity: the fact is that wars arose and captivities and enslavements followed which are contrary to the law of nature. For by the law of nature from the beginning all men were born free. From this same *ius gentium* . . ." Thus, here slavery is part of the ius gentium, and enslavement, found everywhere, was not part of the original state of affairs. Justinian says that slavery is contrary to the law of nature, but in the context he is referring to the original human situation.

18. See above all Michael Hoeflich, *Roman and Civil Law and the Development of Anglo-American Jurisprudence in the Nineteenth Century* (Athens, Ga., 1997), 54, 72.

19. See, e.g., Alan Watson, *Joseph Story and the Comity of Errors* (Athens, Ga., 1992).

20. See, e.g., Richard J. Purcell in *Dictionary of American Biography*, vol. 3, ed. Allen Johnson and Dumas Malone (1931), 162.

21. §48; 49.

22. §51; 53.

23. §52: 51.

24. I assume that no command was necessary.

25. 5 Sandford 681 (1852).

26. Quoted in William B. McCash, *Thomas R. R. Cobb (1823–1862): The Making of a Southern Nationalist* (Macon, Ga., 1983), 166.

27. *Dred Scott v. Sandford* 19 Howard 393.

28. P. 317.

29. Still, it should be remembered that Cobb was killed at the battle of Fredericksburg in 1862.

30. See McCash, *Cobb*, 172ff.

31. Slave law is a fruitful field for rhetoric in law. For Lord Mansfield's rhetoric in *Somerset v. Stewart* Lofft 1, see, e.g., Watson, *Joseph Story*, 67ff.

32. See, e.g., E. N. Elliott, *Cotton is King, and Pro-Slavery Arguments* (Augusta, Ga., 1860). The many primary sources on the proslavery argument are too voluminous to detail here. The best short introduction to the proslavery arguments is Eric McKitrick, ed., *Slavery Defended: The Views of the Old South* (Englewood Cliffs, N.J., 1963).

33. See already Watson, *Joseph Story*, 42.

34. For his passions and convictions, see, e.g., McCash, *Cobb*.

CHAPTER FOUR. LAW AS LITERATURE, LITERATURE AS LAW

1. See above all the discussion of factual situations in A. W. Brian Simpson, *Leading Cases in the Common Law* (Oxford, 1995).

2. See, e.g., D.16.3.27; cf. Watson, *Ancient Law*, pp. 25ff.

3. Although the point is irrelevant to the present discussion, Ulpian's final statement is unpersuasive. The contractual remedy is made to depend on the owner's representing an inexperienced slave as experienced. The actio legis Aquiliae turns purely on the slave's negligence.

4. The Roman juristic texts are in some ways similar to some law teaching I came across in Oxford in the 1950s and 1960s. (I am not suggesting a historical dependence despite the importance of Roman law in the syllabus of the time.) The tutor would make up problems with (usually) simple but striking facts. The student was expected to respond solely on the legal points with a very legalistic argument. This is very different from the norm in American legal education.

5. Act 3, scene 2, lines 77ff.

6. *Spirit*, 34ff.

7. My full understanding of the attitude of the jurists is not relevant in this limited context. I believe they also were not much interested in law reform, systematization of law, or giving opinions that were decidedly result-oriented; see *Spirit*. For a vigorous attack on my position, see Kenneth Pennington, "The Spirit of Legal History," 64 *University of Chicago Law Review* (1997), 1097ff. Unfortunately, he produces no contrary evidence from the Roman materials. Pennington writes from gut reaction, "what must have been," rather than from a consideration of the evidence, which he does not present or discuss. A prime purpose of "The Spirit of the Laws" series (University of Georgia

Press) is precisely to show that the underlying approaches to law and legal values vary from society to society.

8. See, e.g., the discussion in Watson, *Spirit*, 195ff. J. W. Tellegen argues that there was no sharp distinction between orators and jurists: "*Oratores, Jurisprudentes,* and the *Causa Curiana,*" 30 *Revue Internationale des Droits de l'Antiquité* (1983), 293ff.; "Parva Quaestio sed tamen Quaestio," 195 *Juridical Review* (1987), 195ff.

9. See above all S. F. Bonner, *Roman Declamation in the Late Republic and Early Empire* (Liverpool, 1949). J. A. Crook disagrees with Bonner in much the way that I do; see *Legal Advocacy in the Roman World* (Ithaca, N.Y., 1995), 163ff.

10. *Declamation*, 36.

11. The high quality of Bonner's book is also rightly stressed by M. Winterbottom, *The Elder Seneca*, vol. 1 (Cambridge, Mass., 1974), p. xxv.

12. *Declamation*, 84ff.

13. The translation is that of Winterbottom, *Seneca*, vol. 1, 409f.

14. *Declamation*, 116f.

15. *D.9.2.49.1.*

16. *Declamation*, 115f.

17. See, e.g., pro *Murena* 10.23ff.; 14.30; *De legibus* 1.4.14; *De oratore* 1.45.199.

18. I stress "secular." Religious law is often the search for "law as truth" and accordingly may well appear to outsiders almost absurdly legalistic.

CHAPTER FIVE. THE LEX AQUILIA IN SOUTH AFRICA

1. In this chapter I use the standard abbreviations for referring to South African cases (see my list of abbreviations). For more detail on South African law reports, see, e.g., H. R. Hahlo and Ellison Kahn, *The South African Legal System and Its Background* (Cape Town, 1968), 293ff.

2. See, e.g., Hahlo and Kahn, *South African Legal System*, 571.

3. E.g., Van den Heever, J.A., in *Director of Food Supplies and Distribution* 1949 (3) S.A. 695; cf. Watson, *Society and Legal Change*, 100ff.

4. For an extreme example, see, e.g., *R. v. Mtaung* 1948 (4) S.A. 120 (O.P.D.), where the citations include Cujas (French, sixteenth century), Pothier (French, eighteenth century), Gluck, Sohm, Puchta, Mommsen, Muhlenbruch (German, all nineteenth century), and Moyle (English, active well into this century).

5. The precise meaning of "quod usserit ruperit fregerit" in the statute is disputed, but see Watson, *Studies*, 253ff. It is likely that at the outset the action was confined to injuries less than death to slaves and herd animals; see David Daube, "On the Third Chapter of the Lex Aquilia" 52 *LQR* (1936), 253ff.; Watson, *Studies*, 254ff.

6. "Third Chapter," 253ff.

7. At times when case law is deficient or scholars disagree, I have given myself the liberty of arguing a position in the way that I think a South African scholar might do. No doubt this indulgence is presumptuous. To avoid second-guessing myself I have refrained from looking at cases or juristic writings after 1961. But the reader should note the different treatments by Annél van Aswegen, "Aquilian Liability 1 (Nineteenth Century)," in *Southern Cross: Civil Law and Common Law in South Africa*, ed. Reinhard Zimmerman and Daniel Visser (Oxford, 1996), 559ff.; and Dale Hutchison, "Aquilian Liability II (Twentieth Century)," in the same volume, 595ff.

8. The concept of the reception of Roman law is extremely complex. For an introduction, see Franz Wieacker, *A History of Private Law in Europe*, trans. Tony Weir (Oxford, 1995), 91ff.

9. *Ad legem Aquiliam:* cf. G. C. J. J. Van der Bergh, *The Life and Work of Gerard Noodt (1647–1725)* (Oxford, 1988), 173ff.

10. *Commentarius ad Pandectas,* 9.2.

11. Thomasius was born in Leipsig in 1655, studied at Frankfurt am Oder, was professor at Leipsig and Halle, and died in 1728. The present work was first published at Halle in 1703.

12. In his *Recitationes in elementa iuris civilis* 4.3.§MXCV. iiii. "Quarto superest, ut de usu huius tituli hodierno disquiramus. Et hic quidem doctores vulgo mirifice celebrant huius actionis usum. Sed si calculum recte ponas, nullum fere in foro deprehendes. Agitur quidem apud nos de damno dato: agitur ad damnum resarciendum, poenamque persolvendam. Sed id etiam apud Turcas et Sinenses fit, qui numquam ex iure Romano quidquam receperunt. Sed, quaeso, an et nos hodie distinguimus servos et pecudes quadrupedes a reliquis rebus? An et nos aestimemus res, quanti integra annum vel 30 dies plurimi fuere? An et apud nos quaeritur subtiliter, fitne damnum corpore corpori, an corpore sed non corpori, an nec corpore nec corpori datum? An denique et apud nos lis infitiando crescit? Nemo sane hoc dixerit. Et qui dici ergo potest, actionem ex L. Aquillia esse receptam? Est ergo hodierna actio de damno dato vere ex iure naturali et statutis patriis, non ex L. Aquillia."

13. *De criminibus* (Utrecht, 1644) 47.3.3.

14. *Aquilian Damages in South African Law*, vol. 1 (Capetown, 1941), 30.

15. For the reception of the lex Aquilia in Germany, see the excellent account by H. Kaufmann, *Rezeption und Usus modernus der Actio Legis Aquiliae* (Cologne, 1958).

16. There is a full discussion (concluding in the negative) of whether an actio legis Aquiliae lies to one having an interest if a tomb (i.e., a *res nullius*, belonging to no one) is damaged iniuria; see Suarez de Mendoza *Ad legem Aquiliam* (Salamanca, 1640) 2.2.6. This solution would not apply today, since what was in Roman times (and later) res

nullius normally now belongs to the state, so there is a possible plaintiff. Cf. R. W. Lee, *An Introduction to Roman-Dutch Law*, 5th ed. (Oxford, 1953), 126. Indeed, it was forcefully argued in *Gillespie v. Toplis and Another* 1951 (1) S.A. 290 (C) that an action under the lex Aquilia would lie for damage to a tomb to the owner, possessor, or holder of a *right in rem*, and this seems correct.

17. *D.*9.2.27.21; *G.*3.202.

18. *D.*19.5.14.2.

19. *D.*4.3.7.7.

20. See R. G. McKerron, "Liability for Non-defamatory Statements," 47 *South African Law Journal* (1930), 359ff.

21. 1934 C.P.D. 151, 328.

22. *The Law of Delict*, 5th ed. (Cape Town, 1959), 191.

23. Pp. 194f.

24. See now R. G. McKerron, *The Law of Delict*, 7th ed. (Cape Town, 1971), 218ff.

25. 4th ed. (Cape Town, 1952), 257.

26. The duty of care is discussed later in this chapter.

27. *Negligence in the Civil Law* (Oxford, 1955), 104f.

28. For the survival of the former sense of iniuria in classical law, see Ben Beinart, "The Relationship of *iniuria* and *culpa* in the *lex Aquilia*," *Studi Arangio-Ruiz*, vol. 1 (Naples, 1953), 279ff.

29. *Negligence*, 149.

30. For a very different understanding of the text, see P. Birks, "Cooking the Meat: Aquilian Liability for Hearths and Ovens," 20 *Irish Jurist* (1985), 352ff.

31. "Aquilian Liability for Negligent Statements," 67 *South African Law Journal* (1951), 78.

32. *D.*9.2.37pr.; 50.17.157pr., 169; 44.7.20.

33. E.g., Zoesius *Commentarius ad Digestorum libros L.*, on *D.*9.2.19, 20; Brunnemannus *Commentarius ad Pandectas* 9.2.37; Molinaeus *In Codicem* III 35.c.; Iulius Clarus *Practica criminalis* lib. V quest. 89.

34. *D.*9.2.13pr. and perhaps also *h.t.*52.1.

35. Grotius *Inleidinge tot de hollandsche rechtsgeleertheyd* 3.34.2; Voet *Ad Pandectas* 9.2.11.

36. *Coetze v. South African Railways and Harbours* 1934 C.P.D. 22a; *Pauw v. African Guarantee & Indemnity Co. Ltd.* 1950 (2) S.A. 132 (S.W.A.).

37. For a fuller account, see infra.

38. *D.*9.2.5.3; *h.t.*7pr., 4. It is not clear when the action was introduced or whether it was originally direct or merely utilis or in factum. Cf. Lawson, *Negligence*, 21.

39. Otherwise, since an actio utilis was given to a freeman who was wounded, it is difficult to see why when a freeman was killed his filius had no actio utilis on the score of loss of support.

40. Grotius *Inleidinge* 3.34.3; Voet *Ad Pandectas* 9.2.11.

41. Except, in classical law, for religious purposes.

42. But the basis is not the same as in the action by indigent parents, etc., discussed infra.

43. Grotius *Inleidinge* 3.34.3; Voet *Ad Pandectas* 9.2.10; van der Kessel (1738–1816) *Dictata ad Justiniani Institutionum libros quattuor* 3.34.3.

44. *Union Govt. v. Ocean Accident and Guarantee Corp., Ltd.* 1956 (1) S.A. 577 (A.D.).

45. *Union Govt. (Minister of Railways) v. Lee* 1927 A.D. 202.

46. *De Vaal, N.O. v. Messing* 1938 T.P.D. 34.

47. *D.9.3.7.*

48. E.g., Grotius *Inleidinge* 3.34.2; Voet *Ad Pandectas* 9.2.11.

49. Matthaeus *De criminibus* 47.3.4; Voet *Ad Pandectas* 9.2.11; Groenewegen *Tractatus de legibus abrogatis et inusitatis, D.9.3.7.*

50. In his *Commentarii variique resolutiones juris civilis communis et regii* 3.6.12.

51. *Praxis et theoria criminalium rerum quaestiones* 119.116.

52. Matthaeus *De criminibus* 47.3.4.

53. Groenewegen *Tractatus de legibus abrogatis et inusitatis, D.9.3.7.*

54. Lee's translation.

55. Grotius *Inleidinge* 3.34.2.

56. *Pauw v. African Guarantee & Indemnity Co. Ltd.* 1950 (2) S.A. 132 (S.W.A.); *Clair v. Port Elizabeth Harbour Board* 5 E.D.L.D. 311.

57. *Union Govt. (Minister of Railways and Harbours) v. Warneke* 1911 A.D. 657; *Brown v. Bloemfontein Municipality* 1924 O.P.D. 226.

58. E.g., Lawson, *Negligence*, 6f.

59. H. Lévy-Bruhl, "Le deuxième chapitre de la loi Aquilia," 6 *Revue Internationale des Droits de l'Antiquité* (1958), 507ff.

60. A selection is given by Voet *Ad Pandectas* 9.2.5.

61. *Ad legem Aquiliam* cap.1.

62. *Ad legem Aquiliam* cap.13.

63. Voet *Ad Pandectas* 9.2.5.

64. "Tum quia caput secundum non abrogatum, sed desuetudine inumbratum fuit; . . . quam tamen volenti accomodari et utilem quandoque esse posse, dicam. . . . Neque haec de capitis secundi sententia disseruisse piget, cum illud ita explanatum sua etiam nunc non careat utilitate, si exemplo actionis de servo corrupto, quin et eius, quae ex primo et tertio hujus legis capite data est, ad corruptos filiorum-familias, monachorum, subjectorum, vasallorum, similiumque mores cum Jurisconsultis et Interpretibus porrigatur."

65. E.g., *D.9.2.2pr.; h.t.21pr.*

66. *Aquilian Damages in South African Law* (Cape Town, 1944), 9.

67. E.g., G.3.212.

68. G.3.212; J.4.3.10; D.9.2.23pr.; *h.t.*51.

69. David Daube, "Third Chapter," 267ff.

70. Daube's view is contrary to the previously standard view that held that in classical law the measure of damages was the value of the whole object even where there was only partial injury of it: cf., e.g., Fritz Schultz, *Classical Roman Law* (Oxford, 1954), 590. This view cannot be accepted, since, as Daube argues, it would mean the complete overthrow of the Roman economic system: *Roman Law, Linguistic, Social, and Philosophical Aspects* (Edinburgh, 1969), 66ff. For instance, if a brick of a building were negligently chipped, the damages would be the value of the complete building. If I walk through your field of growing corn, you could recover from me the value of the whole field. Moreover, the old view does not take into account D.9.2.24, which shows that only *interesse* is given. This tiny text cannot be interpolated, because if it were, it would have to be a complete fabrication, and the obvious course of the compilers would have been, not to make a fresh text ascribing it to a particular work of a particular jurist, but to add it to the previous text with which it is intimately connected. Furthermore, the text cannot have represented anything other than at least a majority opinion, or the rhetorical question would be absurd.

71. E.g., Noodt *Ad legem Aquiliam* cap. 21; Voet *Ad Pandectas* 9.2.6. Their interpretation was the same as that accepted into modern times but shown by Daube to be erroneous.

72. Cf. Matthaeus *De criminibus* 47.3.3.4 and the references he cites.

73. *G & M Builders Suppliers (Pty) Ltd. v. South African Railways and Harbours* 1942 T.P.D. 120.

74. *G & M Builders Suppliers (Pty) Ltd. v. South African Railways and Harbours.*

75. *McKenzie v. S.A. Taxi-Cab Co.* 1910 W.L.D. 232.

76. Greenberg, P. (obiter), in *G & M Builders Suppliers (Pty) Ltd. v. South African Railways and Harbours.*

77. *Klingman v. Lowell* 1913 W.L.D. 186 followed; *Hulley v. Cox* 1923 A.D. 234 distinguished.

78. *Page v. Malcomess & Co.* 1922 E.D.L.D. 284.

79. *Ward v. Steenberg* 1951 (1) S.A. 395 (W); *Modern Engineering Works v. Jacobs* 1949 (3) S.A. 191 (T).

80. *Sandler v. Wholesale Cool Suppliers Ltd.* 1941 A.D. 194.

81. *Reid v. The Town Council of Port Elizabeth* 1905 Buch. A.C. 208, per De Villiers C.J. (obiter) 219, relying on Voet *Ad Pandectas* 9.2.6.

82. On the question of prospective loss, see also *Jacobs v. Cape Town Municipality*, 1935 C.P.D. 474.

83. Cf. McKerron, *Delict*, 109ff.

84. *Radebe v. Hough* 1949 (1) S.A. 380 (A.D.).

85. *Pauw v. African Guarantee & Indemnity Co. Ltd.* 1950 (2) S.A. 132 (S.W.A.).

86. 68 *South African Law Journal* (1951), 372f.

87. *Per* de Villiers, J.P., in *Brown v. Bloemfontein Municipality* 1924 O.P.D. 226.

88. *Clair v. Port Elizabeth Harbour Board* 5 E.D.L.D. 311.

89. *Goldie v. City Council of Johannesburg* supra.

90. Cf. infra.

91. *Waterson v. Maybery* 1934 T.P.D. 210; *Jacobs v. Cape Town Municipality* 1935 C.P.D. 474.

92. *D.*9.2.2; *h.t.*27.5, 6.

93. *D.*9.2.5.3; *h.t.*7pr.4.

94. *D.*25.3.5.2.

95. Grotius *Inleidinge* 3.34.3.

96. Grotius *Inleidinge* 3.34.3; Voet *Ad Pandectas* 9.2.11.

97. Voet *Ad Pandectas* 9.2.11; Matthaeus *De criminibus* 48.5.7.11; Van Leeuwen *Het Roomsch Hollandsch recht* 4.34.14; Vinnius in *Institutiones* 4.3.1.

98. *Union Govt. v. Ocean Accident and Guarantee Corp. Ltd.* 1956 (1) S.A. 577 (A.D.).

99. *Waterson v. Maybery* 1934 T.P.D. 210; *Jacobs v. Cape Town Municipality* 1935 C.P.D. 474; *in re Koop* 10 S.C. 198; *Ford v. Allen and others* 1925 T.P.D. 5.

100. *Graaff v. Speedy Transport* 1944 T.P.D. 236. Marital community property did not exist at Rome.

101. *Ad Pandectas* 9.2.11.

102. *Gildenhuys.*

103. *Abbott v. Bergmann* 1922 A.D. 53.

104. *Plotkin v. Western Assurance Co. Ltd.* 1955 (2) S.A. 385 (W).

105. *Suid-Afrikaanse Nasionale Trust en Assuransie Maatskappy Bpk v. Fondo* 1960 (2) S.A. 467.

106. Cf. the authorities cited above.

107. *Union Govt. (Minister of Railways) v. Lee* 1927 A.D. 202.

108. *Jameson's Minors v. C.S.A.R.* 1908 T.S. 575.

109. *Ex Parte Oliphant* 1940 C.P.D. 537.

110. *Ad Pandectas* 9.2.12; cf. Noodt *Ad legem Aquiliam* cap. 15; Matthaeus *Verhandeling over de Misdaden* 1.1.12.

111. See, generally, T. B. Barlow, "The Rights of a Husband or Wife Against Whom a Delict Is Committed by the Other Party to the Marriage," 55 *South African Law Journal* (1938), 137.

112. Barlow, "Rights of a Husband or Wife," 137; McKerron, *Delict*, 79.

113. The case is an excellent source for material on the subject.

114. Cf. Watson, *Roman Law and Comparative Law*, 232ff.

115. *D.*9.2.11.8; *h.t.*17; cf. Lawson, *Negligence*, 65f.

116. *D.*9.2.11.10; 7.1.17.3.

117. *D.*9.2.30.1.

118. *D.*9.2.27.14.

119. *D.*9.2.11.9; 19.2.41.

120. *D.*19.1.13.12.

121. Grotius *Inleidinge* 3.37.5.

122. Cf. the Canadian case *Nova Mink Ltd. v. T.C.A.* 1951 (2) D.L.R. 241.

123. Compare the analogous case of trade competition.

124. See, e.g., *Salmond & Heuston on the Law of Torts*, 20th ed. by R. F. V. Heuston and R. A. Buckley (London, 1992), 204ff.

125. *D.*9.2.11.3; *h.t.*15.1; *h.t.*51.

126. *Negligence*, 41.

127. Which cannot possibly be technical and which occurs only in *D.*9.2.44*pr.* On *culpa levissima,* see, above all, O. T. Tellegen-Couperus, "Culpa levissima en de onrechtmatige daad," *Tertium datur* (Tilburg, 1995), 89ff.

128. As does Zoesius *ad Pandectas* on *D.*9.2.9; Lawson, *Negligence*, 40; *cf. Hume v. The Divisional Council of Craddock,* 1 E.D.L.D. 104 at 122–125.

129. In that case, Kotzé, J.P., disapproved on the facts the decision in the earlier case of *Brink v. Choete* Buch. 1869, 215, on the ground that it was foreseeable that the prevailing wind that was then blowing would freshen.

130. *Hendy v. Oomkens and Shallies* 1924 T.P.D. 165.

131. *Cambridge Municipality v. Millard* 1916 C.P.D. 724. Obiter dicta in that case come close to an acceptance of the English case of *Rylands v. Fletcher* (1866) L.R. 3 H.L. 330.

132. *Ad Pandectas* 9.2.18.

133. P. 28.

134. As the quotation from Innes, C.J., in *Fleming v. Rietfontein Deep Gold Mining Co.* 1905 T.S. 111 at 117 clearly shows.

135. *D.*19.2.9.5; 9.2.8.1; 1.18.6.7; *J.*4.3.7; Voet *Ad Pandectas* 9.2.23; Van Leeuwen *Censura forensis* 4.39; *Coppen v. Impey* 1916 C.P.D. 309.

136. P. 444.

137. *D.*9.2.8*pr; J.*4.3.6.

138. *D.*9.2.30.3. For perhaps another example, see *h.t.*27.33.

139. *Ad Pandectas* 9.2.3. *in fin.*

140. *De criminibus* 48.5.6.5.

141. The opposite had been held, De Villiers, J.P., dissenting, before the Transvaal Provincial Division, 1912 T.P.D. 593.

142. P. 672.

143. *D.*9.2.27.9.

144. His dispute with Matthaeus is almost completely verbal, since they used omissions in different senses; Voet *Ad Pandectas* 9.2.3, Matthaeus *De criminibus* 48.5.6.5.

145. *D.7.1.13.2*. Van der Heever *Aquilian Liability* 112, errs in his criticism of Voet here. There is no Aquilian liability where loss follows on a failure to cultivate.

146. Perhaps some indirect evidence is found in *D.45.1.91pr*.

147. *Ad Pandectas* 9.2.3.

148. *Van Reenen v. Glenlily, Fairfield, and Parow Village Management Board* 1936 C.P.D. 315. Discussed above.

149. "Aquilian Liability and the 'Duty of Care': A Return to the Charge," 1959 *Acta Juridica* 120ff. at 179–182.

150. Pp. 584–585.

151. That was a case where "duty of care" in the nontechnical sense was used and the use was unfortunate in reaching the decision.

152. *Delict*, 114–115.

153. For other cases that may be relevant, see McKerron, *Delict*, 115 n.13.

154. Subrogation or a contractual clause is needed.

155. *Negligence*, 15.

156. *Inleidinge* 3.4.4.

157. Cf. Voet *Ad Pandectas* 9.2.15.

158. *Roman Law and Common Law*, 2d ed., ed. F. H. Lawson (Cambridge, 1952), 96.

159. Cf. Buckland and McNair, *Roman Law and Common Law*, 97f.; P. Bonfante, *Corso di diritto Romano* II.i (Rome, 1926), 290ff.

160. E.g., *D.39.2.24.12; 8.2.9; 50.17.55, 151, 154.1*.

161. *D.39.3.1.11, 12; h.t.2.5, 9*.

162. For this reason the restrictions on the use of servitudes have not been regarded as cases illustrating prohibition of the use of rights.

163. *Ad Pandectas* 39.3.4.

164. See the full citation of authority by J. E. Scholtens, "Abuse of Rights," 75 *South African Law Journal* (1958), 39ff.

165. *E.g. van Eck and Another v. Etna Stores* 1947 (2) S.A. 984 (A.D.) at 999; *Kirsch v. Pincus* 1927 T.P.D. 206.

166. *D.9.2.51.1*.

167. For a summary of the possible views, see Matthaeus *De criminibus* 48.5.3.19.

168. 1922 T.P.D. 56.

169. *Esterhuizen v. Brandfort Munisipaliteit* 1957 (3) S.A. 768 (A.D.).

170. See also *Van Heerden v. African Guarantee & Indemnity Co. Ltd.* 1951 (3) S.A. 730 (C); *Richards v. Richardson* 1929 E.D.L.D. 146; *Mulder v. South British Insurance Co. Ltd.* 1957 (2) S.A. 444 (W); and *Cardoso and Another v. South African Railways and Harbours* 1950 (1) S.A. 773 (W).

171. Cf. McKerron, *Delict*, 54ff.

172. See, e.g., Watson, *Transplants*, 57ff., 88ff.; "Aspects of Reception of Law," 44 *Am. J. Comp. L.* (1996), 335ff. at 345ff.; *Ancient Law*, 84ff.

CHAPTER SIX. THE ASPIRING LAWYER IN THE UNITED STATES

1. *Property*, 4th ed. (New York, 1998), 99. In no sense do I concentrate on this book because I regard it as the worst among the casebooks. On the contrary, it is the one I use most when I teach property. The approach does not differ much from casebook to casebook, nor from property to contract to torts. Moreover, according to a flier from the publisher, Dukeminier and Krier's book is "Universally Admired for its Teachable and Engaging Presentation of Property Law" and is adopted at more than 150 law schools.

For a rather similar critical approach to the casebook method but with regard to the very special issue of casebooks on comparative law, see William Ewald, "Comparative Jurisprudence (1): What Was It Like to Try a Rat?" 143 *University of Pennsylvania Law Review* (1995) 1889ff. at 1966ff., 1985. I agree completely with him (and have long held the opinion) that these books desperately misrepresent the spirit of continental European law.

2. 3d ed., ed. Walter B. Rauschenbush (Chicago, 1975), 19ff.

3. On the place of theory in casebooks, Dennis Patterson writes: "It is almost impossible in the modern American law school to encounter any subject matter that does not carry with it a heavy theoretical orientation. For example, in their first semester of law school, students are virtually barraged with all matter of theoretical perspective. Subjects ranging from philosophy to economics to critical theory are all very much a part of American casebooks and the teaching styles of American law professors." *A Companion to Philosophy of Law and Legal Theory* (Cambridge, Mass., 1996), p. xii. In my experience this is a gross exaggeration.

4. 1 Strange 505, 93 Eng. Rep. 664 (K.B. 1722), in Dukeminier and Krier, *Property* 100ff.

5. [1945] K.B. 509, in Dukeminier and Krier, *Property*, 103ff.

6. *McAvoy v. Medina* 93 Mass. (11 Allen) 548 (1866), is discussed by Dukeminier and Krier, *Property*, 110ff., but it need not be treated in this chapter.

7. It does, as a matter of fact.

8. The Byzantine emperor Justinian, as we have seen in chapter 1, would strongly disagree with such an opinion. His *Institutes* was at the same time statute law and a textbook for first-year students. It was expressly designed to make the approach to law easy for beginners: *J.1.1.2*. Has this purpose anything to do with the success of the *Institutes* as a teaching tool over many centuries and in many lands? For the view that, without the *In-*

stitutes, the shape of modern law would be very different in the United States as well as in continental Europe and Latin America, see Alan Watson, "The Importance of 'Nut-shells,'" 42 *Am. J. Comp. L.* (1994), 1ff.

9. *Ashby v. White* 2 Ld Raymond 938.

10. *Rust v. Cooper* 98 Eng. Rep. 1279.

11. 3 Cai. R. 175, 2 Am. Dec. 264 (N.Y. Sup. Ct. 1805).

12. Even if the previous cases then have to be reinterpreted.

13. It should be remembered how few American law reports there then were.

14. Now known as the *Corpus iuris civilis*.

15. Dukeminier and Krier, *Property*, 23. Interestingly, the casebook authors have increased the obscurity of the works cited in the case from their treatment in the second edition. See *Property*, 2d ed. (Boston, 1988), 19.

16. See generally Ewald, "Comparative Jurisprudence (1)."

17. For another property case that is just as instructive for the use of authority and for legal transplants, see *Nebraska v. Iowa*, 143 U.S. 359 (1891). In its turn, this case is cited with approval in the Scottish case of *Stirling v. Bartlett*, 1993 S.L.T. 763.

18. Cf. Michael H. Hoeflich, *Roman and Civil Law and the Development of Anglo-American Jurisprudence in the Nineteenth Century* (Athens, Ga., 1997), 13f., 56f.

19. See Alan Watson, "Aspects of Reception of Law," 335ff.

20. For example, the great Chancellor Kent (1763–1847) is celebrated for the use he made for American law of Roman and French law. But he cites no works in German, a language he did not know; see, e.g., Alan Watson, "Chancellor Kent's Use of Foreign Law," in *The Reception of Continental Ideas in the Common Law World*, ed. Mathias Reimann (Berlin, 1993), 45ff.

21. 2 Am. Dec. at 265. And other cases were irrelevant because they arose between huntsmen and the owners of the land they hunted.

22. *De jure belli ac pacis* 2.2.5. The proposition was, of course, a commonplace even long before. See Bartolus, on Justinian's *Code* 1.4, *De summa trinitati*, gloss *Quod si Bononiensis*, §19.

23. The use of Roman law gives rise to particular questions in this context. The *Corpus iuris civilis* was statute law of the Byzantine empire but was widely regarded elsewhere as authoritative or influential. And Justinian's *Code* contained the legal replies of previous emperors.

24. See Brian Seymour Vesey-Fitzgerald, *Town Fox, Country Fox* (London, 1973).

25. Perhaps nowhere more clearly than in chapter 9 of *The Landleaguers*, of which publication began in 1882.

26. See, e.g., Anthony Trollope, *The American Senator* (publication began in 1876), chaps. 3–4.

27. See J. K. Anderson, *Hunting in the Ancient World* (Berkeley, 1985), 83ff. The emperor

Hadrian's (117–138) passion for hunting made the activity even more fashionable: Anderson, *Hunting*, 101ff. Later, Nemesianus dedicated his *Cynegetica*, a treatise on breeding and training dogs, to the emperors Carinus (283–285) and Numerianus (283–284); Anderson, *Hunting*, 139ff. A mosaic of circa A.D. 200 from Roman North Africa shows hounds coursing after hare and fox; Anderson, *Hunting*, 98. I have a Roman oil lamp whose disc shows a hunter holding his horse's bridle in his left hand and a hare in his right while his hound prances at the horse's hooves.

28. See Robert Stevens, *Law School: Legal Education in America from the 1850s to the 1980s* (Chapel Hill, 1983), 51ff.; William P. LaPiana, *Logic and Experience: The Origin of Modern American Legal Education* (New York, 1994), 22ff.

29. I should not be understood as claiming that cases should not be studied—only that the present method of study is entirely unsatisfactory. If contemporary law review articles are so much ignored in teaching, as they are, in part because of the casebook approach, then that approach is to be applauded. If the present nature of law review articles is in part because of the casebook approach, then that approach is to be condemned.

30. "Extending the Grasp of the Dead Hand: Reflections on the Origins of the Rule Against Perpetuities," 126 *University of Pennsylvania Law Review* (1977), 19ff. at p. 20.

31. *The Rule Against Perpetuities*, 4th ed., ed. Roland Gray (Boston, 1942), 191.

32. Indeed there is a case that may be understood as meaning that it is not professional negligence for an attorney not to understand the Rule Against Perpetuities: *Lucas v. Hamm* 56 Cal. 2d 583, 364 P.2d 685, 15 Cal. Rptr. 821 (1961).

33. I tried the questions in a class on jurisprudence. I got no answers.

34. What we regard as feudal law results in fact from the breakdown of the feudal system. See Watson, *Roman Law and Comparative Law*, 141ff.

35. For Germany the *Bürgerliches Gesetzbuch* §2100 allows the possibility of a substitute heir after another had first been heir. Section 2101 declares that if a person unborn at the time of succession is named as heir, then in case of doubt that person is regarded as a substitute heir. Section 2109 prohibits, with exceptions, vesting in a substitute heir thirty years after the succession opened. The problems of the Rule Against Perpetuities are avoided. Cf. Otto Palandt, *Bürgerliches Gesetzbuch*, 14th ed. (Munich, 1995), on these articles.

36. For the absence of any equivalent in Scots law, see generally Robert Burgess, *Perpetuities in Scots Law* (Edinburgh, 1979).

37. The answer lies in the history of English land law, in tradition, and in the self-interest of practitioners.

38. See A. W. B. Simpson, *A History of the Land Law*, 2d ed. (New York, 1986), 81ff.

39. Y.B. 20 Edw. 3 (R.S.), pt. at 202 (ed. and trans. Luke Owen Pike); cf. Simpson, *Land Law*, 84.

40. Taltarum's Case (1472) Y.B. 12 Edw. 4, Mich., fo. 14, pl. 16, fo. 19, pl. 25; 13 Edw. 4, Mich., fo. 1, pl. 1; cf. Simpson, *Land Law,* 129ff.

41. See Simpson, *Land Law,* 215ff.

42. See Haskins, "Dead Hand," 20ff.; Simpson, *Land Law,* 208ff.

43. For arguments pointing to an answer in the positive, see Watson, *Roman Law and Comparative Law,* 97ff.

44. I am assuming that it is a reasonable desire of owners to want to exercise some control over their property after their death. This view would be generally acceptable in the United States today. But many societies, e.g., France for long before the Revolution and the *code civil,* have refused to recognize testate succession.

45. Except in a state where the wait-and-see doctrine applies.

46. For my argument, see Watson, *Roman Law and Comparative Law,* 221ff.; Alan Watson, *The State, Law, and Religion: Pagan Rome* (Athens, Ga., 1992), 63ff.

47. Pepper v. Hart [1993] A.C. 593.

48. For paragraphs 7, 8, and 9, see William Ewald, "Comparative Jurisprudence (II): The Logic of Legal Transplants," 43 *Am. J. Comp. L.* (1995), 489ff., and works cited therein.

49. Some may be less. But in general I do not exaggerate.

50. Such as the *American Journal of Comparative Law;* the *Journal of Law and Economics;* the *Journal of Legal Studies;* the *Law and History Review;* the *American Journal of International Law;* the *American Journal of Legal History;* and the *Supreme Court Review.*

51. I have asked various colleagues. They accept that law review articles are given this superiority, but they can give no reasons other than those I suggest.

52. Except by tenure and promotion committees.

53. The attitude toward other publications allows a degree of arbitrariness. It enables a professor if he wishes to discount a monograph by a female colleague while enthusiastically endorsing a book review by a male "buddy." When I have talked with colleagues this reason has been stressed. In one school that I am acquainted with, a disgruntled elderly professor claimed he deserved a chair because of his engagement with professional legal practice, which he regarded as the equivalent of scholarship. A colleague proposed him on that basis. He got his chair even though his practice went beyond the university's guidelines on outside work. The same school refused to regard a book on pension planning by a woman as relevant for tenure.

54. The relationship can be as corrupting as sex between professor and student.

55. Specific examples are needed, but they are invidious. One extreme—I hope—example known to me is of a professor at a prestigious law school who has many assistants. They study all the cases in her area, select those they regard as relevant, and make syntheses. The professor then works from the syntheses and never reads the cases.

56. The letter is on file with me. I have, of course, cut out words that would identify the professor.

57. See already, e.g., William Ewald, "Comparative Jurisprudence (1)," 1966ff., 1985.

58. For one illustration wide enough to demonstrate the practice, see Alan Watson, "Trade Secrets and Roman Law: The Myth Exploded," 11 *Tulane European and Civil Law Forum* (1996), 19ff.

CHAPTER SEVEN. SITZ IN LEBEN

1. See already Watson, *Roman Law and Comparative Law*, 97ff.

2. See, e.g., Watson, *Roman Law and Comparative Law*, 91ff., 221ff.

3. See, e.g., Watson, *Transplants;* "Aspects of Reception of Law," 335ff.

4. See, e.g., Watson, *Evolution*, 98ff.

5. See, e.g., Watson, "Aspects of Reception of Law," 345ff.; see also Watson, *Ancient Law.*

6. See, e.g., Watson, *Failures of the Legal Imagination*, 47ff.; 145ff.

7. For the same principle in a modern codified system, see the strongly worded article 4 of the French *code civil;* "The judge who refuses to judge under the pretext of the silence, obscurity or insufficiency of the law may be criminally prosecuted as guilty of the refusal of justice."

8. See, e.g., Watson, *Evolution*, 43ff.

9. See, e.g., Alan Watson, *Sources of Law, Legal Change, and Ambiguity*, 2d ed. (Philadelphia, 1998), 44ff.; *Evolution*, 50ff.; "The Evolution of Law: Continued," 5 *Law and History Review* (1987), 537ff. at 545ff.

10. For this and other examples, see, e.g., Watson, *Ancient Law.*

11. A judge could exercise his discretion, however, and this came to be common practice.

12. See T. B. Smith, *Scotland: The Development of Its Laws and Constitution* (London, 1962), 320.

13. See Alan Watson, "Artificiality, Reality, and Roman Contract Law," in *Essays on Law and Religion: The Berkeley and Oxford Symposia in Honour of David Daube*, ed. Calum Carmichael (Berkeley, 1993), 67ff. at 74f.

14. See Watson, "Artificiality," 73.

15. It is noteworthy that children, including Sarah, my ten-year-old daughter, draw a firm distinction between "trading" and "buying." In trading, namely barter, the expectation is of relative equality in the exchange. In buying, the store makes a gain. The children all know that if they try to sell unused to another merchant what they bought they will receive much less than they gave. In trading they expect a higher degree of equality or of good faith than in buying.

16. For the powerfully expressed view that the law of ancient Israel, especially as set out in Exodus and Leviticus, was not created directly in response to contemporary social problems but can be traced back to literary traditions preserved in the books of Genesis and Exodus, see Calum Carmichael, *The Origins of Biblical Law* (Ithaca, 1992); *The Spirit of Biblical Law* (Athens, Ga., 1996); *Law, Legend, and Incest in the Bible* (Ithaca, 1997).

17. 2d ed. (New York, 1985), 467.

18. *Tort Law and Alternatives: Cases and Materials*, 6th ed. (Westbury, N.Y., 1996), 22.

19. *History*, 300.

20. *History*, 18f.

21. Especially in *D*.9.2.

22. As exemplified by Voet *Ad Pandectas* 9.2.

23. For the development, see, e.g., Watson, *Failures*, 1ff.

24. The turning point was Painvin v. Deschamps, *Cour de Cassation, Chambre Civile*, 19 July 1870.

25. For subsequent case law and juristic discussion, see, e.g., the notes to article 1384 in the latest edition of the *code civil* published annually by Dalloz (Paris).

26. This approach results from the *code civil*, article 5.

27. I do not wish here to try to explain the underdeveloped torts law in early nineteenth-century England. But I make the following observations. (1) The law was not as underdeveloped as Friedman suggests; see, e.g., J. H. Baker, *Introduction to English Legal History*, 2d ed. (London, 1979), 336ff. (2) Tort was not the only area of law that could be considered "primitive" by continental standards. Contract was another; there is a startling contrast between "modern" contract law in late seventeenth-century economically backward Scotland, and "primitive" law in early nineteenth-century England. (3) Legal development in a rational fashion was much handicapped by the plurality of courts with differing jurisdictions and by the remnants of the writ system. (4) There was a lack of scholarly writings.

28. See above all Watson, *Society and Legal Change*.

29. My focus is also not on the traditional distinction between "law in action" and "law in books."

30. See, e.g., Paul Finkelman, *Slavery and the Founders* (Armonk, N.Y., 1996).

INDEX OF SOURCES

CASE LAW

Canada

Nova Mink Ltd. v. T.C.A. 1951 (2) D.L.R. 241   190n. 122

England

Armory v. Delamarie, 1 Strange 505, 93 Engl. Rep.
664 (K.B. 1722)   141ff.

Ashby v. White, 2 Ld Raymond 938   193n. 9

British Industrial Statistical Plastics Ltd. v.
Ferguson, 1938, 4 All E.R. 504   101

Hannah v. Peel, [1945] K.B. 509   142

Pepper v. Hart [1993] A.C. 593   195n. 47

Rust v. Cooper 98 Eng. Rep. 664 (KB 1722)   141f.

Rylands v. Fletcher (1866) L.R. 3 H.L. 330   121; 190n. 131

Taltarum's Case (1472) Y.B. 12 Edw. 4   195n. 40

Ware and de Freville v. Motor Trade Association
1921, 3K.B. 40 at 91   101

France

Painvin v. Deschamps, *Cour de Cassation, Chambre
Civile,* 19 July, 1870   197n. 24

Scotland

Reavis v. Clan Line Steamers 1925 S.C. 725   132

Stirling v. Bartlett, 1993 S.L.T. 763   193n. 17

South Africa

Abbott v. Bergmann 1922 A.D. 53   103; 189n. 103

Alliance Building Society v. Deretich 1941 T.P.D. 203   98; 100; 102; 136f.

Brandfort Munisipaliteit v. Esterhuizen 1957
(1) S.A. 229 (0)   137

Bredell v. Pienaar 1924 C.P.D. 203   97; 99; 102

Brink v. Choete Buch. 1869, 215   190n. 129

Brown v. Bloemfontein Municipality 1924 O.P.D. 226   187 n. 57; 189n. 87

Cambridge Municipality v. Millard 1916 C.P.D. 724   190n. 131

Cape of Good Hope Bank v. Fisher 4 Juta at 378   97

Cardoso and Another v. South African Railways and
Harbours 1950 (1) S.A. 773 (W)   191n. 170

Lucas v. Hamm 56 Cal. 2d 583, 364 P. 2d. 685,
   15 Cal. Rptr. 821 (1961)   194n. 32
McAvoy v. Medina 93 Mass. (11 Allen) 548 (1866)   192n. 6
Nebraska v. Iowa 143 U.S. 359 (1891)   193n. 17
Pierson v. Post 3 Cai. R. 175, 2 Am. Dec. 364
   (N.Y. Sup. Ct. 1805)   143ff.
Small v. Howard 35 Am. Rep. 363   127

MODERN STATUTES

England
   Divorce Reform Act of 1969   164

France
   code civil
   4   196n. 7
   1382ff.   167
   1384   167; 197n. 25

Germany
   Bürgerliches Gesetzbuch
   2100   194n. 35

South Africa
   Apportionment of Damages Act 1956
   S.2(6)   136
   S.2(7)   136

www.ingramcontent.com/pod-product-compliance
Lightning Source LLC
Chambersburg PA
CBHW011301210326
41599CB00037B/7108